Ohio
CURIOSITIES

Help Us Keep This Guide Up to Date

Every effort has been made by the author and editors to make this guide as accurate and useful as possible. However, many things can change after a guide is published—establishments close, phone numbers change, facilities come under new management, and so on.

We would appreciate hearing from you concerning your experiences with this guide and how you feel it could be improved and kept up to date. While we may not be able to respond to all comments and suggestions, we'll take them to heart, and we'll also make certain to share them with the author. Please send your comments and suggestions to the following address:

GPP
Reader Response/Editorial Department
P.O. Box 480
Guilford, CT 06437

Or you may e-mail us at:
editorial@globepequot.com

Curiosities Series

Ohio
CURIOSITIES

Quirky characters,
roadside oddities &
other offbeat stuff

SECOND EDITION

Sandra Gurvis

Guilford, Connecticut

917.0
GUR

The prices, rates, and hours listed in this guidebook were confirmed at press time. We recommend, however, that you call establishments to obtain current information before traveling.

To buy books in quantity for corporate use
or incentives, call **(800) 962–0973**
or e-mail **premiums@GlobePequot.com.**

All photos by the author unless otherwise noted.
Maps by M.A. Dubé © Morris Book Publishing, LLC
Text design: Bret Kerr
Layout artist: Casey Shain
Project editor: Meredith Dias

ISSN: 1934-5836

ISBN: 978-0-7627-6408-2

Printed in the United States of America

10 9 8 7 6 5 4 3 2 1

*To my children, Amy and Alex, who grew up in this
weird and wacky state. May your travels take you near and far,
but may you always come home to visit!*

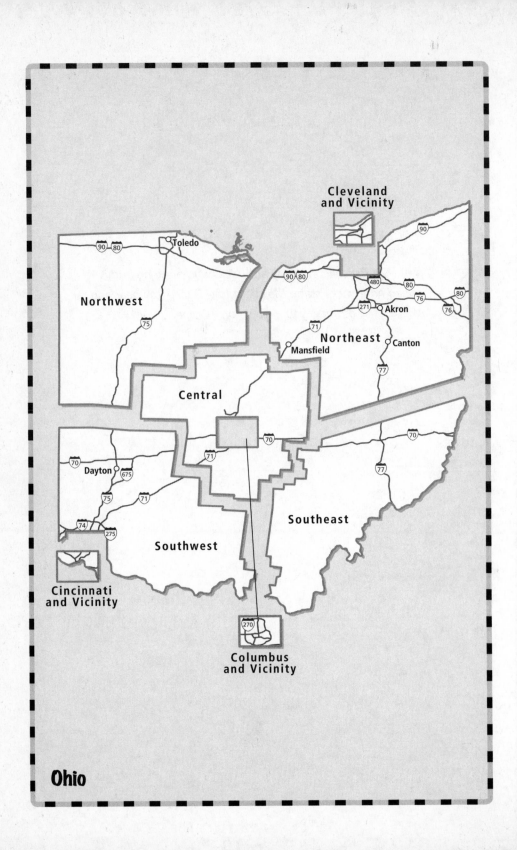

Cleveland
and Vicinity

Toledo

Northwest

90 80

90 80

480

80

271 Akron

76

80

80

71

Northeast

Canton

Mansfield

77

Central

70

75

71

70

Dayton 675

77

70

75 71

Southeast

74

275

Southwest

Cincinnati
and Vicinity

270

Columbus
and Vicinity

Ohio

contents

Looking for chili in Cincinnati? If you happen upon this giant air duct man outside of Jacobs Mechanical (1366 Hopple St.), then you're only about a block away from Camp Washington chili (3005 Colerain Ave. 45222).

JACKIE REAU

acknowledgments

When I was first asked to write this book, I thought, "What fun!" I have always loved strange and curious stuff, even as a child. Just ask my mother, rest her soul, who put up with my collections of miniatures, hair pieces, and all things John F. Kennedy. My friends, being my friends, said, "Oh, you can write about us. We're Ohio Curiosities!"

Ha! Ha! If only it was that easy.

In reality this book was a lot of work. Even this second edition required a lot of research and in-depth analysis, always a challenge, no matter how many years you've been writing. And it had to be funny–ha, ha, not funny–stupid. Hopefully I didn't cross that line too many times.

And I could never have done it without the help of friends, work colleagues, and fellow authors. For the first edition, that would be book packager, Michael Urban; my assistant, Kate Manecke; and Gia Manalio, my editor at Globe Pequot. Meredith Rufino, the Globe Pequot editor for the second edition, was equally supportive and encouraging.

Thanks also to the following folks (in no particular order), who helped out in various ways: Judy and Sam Roth, Bertha Ihnat, John Kiste, Sherry Paprocki, Marilyn McClellan, Karen Bernie Wolfe, Tom Cooper and Wally Higgins; and for the second edition, Vicki VanNatta, Jackie Reau, Ed McMasters, Linda Deitch, and John Faulkner, that mm-mm all-around good guy from Campbell's Soups! And last but not least my cats, Sasha and Savannah, for sleeping on the exact piece of paper needed for a particular entry and hawking up hairballs and/or demanding food at just the right moments.

I also owe a huge debt to the other books and websites about Ohio that provided rich mining for ideas: *Ohio Oddities and Strange Tales from Ohio* by Neil Zurcher; *Oddball Ohio* by Jerome Pohlen; *Weird Ohio* by Loren Coleman, Andy Henderson, James Willis, and Mark Moran; and *Ohio Off the Beaten Path* by George Zimmermann and Carol Zimmermann. Helpful websites included www.haunted-ohio.com, www.forgottenoh.com, and others too numerous to mention here. And if I overlooked someone—thanks to you as well.

These teenaged carolers at the annual holiday mannequin display at the Dickens Victorian Village in downtown Cambridge (43727) bear a suspicious resemblance to Beavis and Butthead. Heh-heh . . . no wonder the girls are pretending to ignore them!

introduction

★ ★

What can you say about a state whose plant, the buckeye, is poisonous and not particularly attractive and whose wood has been described by its own state extension service as "light, soft, weak, and decays rapidly when exposed?" Or whose four seasons consist of Winter, Still Winter, Almost Winter, and Construction? Or if you're on either coast and mention your home state, it usually evokes the reaction, "You're from Ohio?" Not only is Ohio in the middle of flyover country, but we personify it!

But if you've ever spent any time here you know that real buckeyes are these yummy peanut butter and chocolate concoctions and/or the champion Big Ten college football team. And that while we do keep road crews gainfully employed, Ohio has a ton of beautiful places and spaces that usually aren't too crowded, so everyone can enjoy them. And Ohio has weird stuff. Lots of weird stuff. So much so that several books have been written on the topic, especially in recent years when folks seem to be looking for cheap and relatively safe thrills. Many of the sites and attractions that are open to the public charge minimal admission or request a small donation.

So why this book? Well for one thing, there's always something new and different coming down the pike. For example, in Plain City, Select Sires, the world's largest artificial insemination service, just developed a "sexing technology" that determines with over 90 percent accuracy whether 'your baby will be a boy or a girl. If you're a bovine, that is.

In fact, the entire state seems to have a thing for cows. In 1926 Maudine Ormsby was elected Homecoming Queen at The Ohio State University (true Ohioans always preface any reference to OSU with "The"). One slight hitch, though; while Maudine was outstanding in her field and considered to be a star in her class, she also happened to be a Holstein. Then there was Texas Longhorn #215182, aka The Shadow. Born and bred at the Dickinson Cattle Ranch in Barnesville, weighing in at over a ton and with an amazing horn spread of 82 inches, his "shadow" was so large it might have been mistaken for a picnic shelter in daylight. Don't bring a red tablecloth, however. Even one of Ohio's premier cultural centers, the Dairy Barn in Athens, also pays homage to its milk-fed roots, although at one time it was also a mental institution.

Don't jump! It will get better . . . we promise! These goats on the roof of Herschberger's Farm and Bakery (5452 SR 557, Millersburg 44654) are part of the animal attractions that include a petting zoo and a super-size horse.

Which brings up the next point: Ohio is a veritable font of strange facts and history, unusual avenues that this book explores. Take the Neil Armstrong Space Museum in Wapakoneta. Where else can you learn how the first astronauts went to the bathroom in space? (Answer: very carefully). Or the fact that Circleville has a Hitler Road, named after the family of the same name (no relation), although there was a dentist named Gay Hitler who passed away shortly after World War II. Or in addition to its world-famous collection of swallowed objects, the Allen County Museum in Lima has the dead stuffed animal stylings of one J. E. Grosjean (1892–1920), a normal-looking Lima businessman who loved to arrange them in various tableaux and put them in glass cases. And they say California has fruits and nuts!

Ohioans are also great at manufacturing odd things, or items that we use every day but rarely think about. Many have quite a story behind

introduction

★ ★

**Arguably the world's only drive-through historical society
is located in Sabina (11 East Washington St. 45169).**

them: the washboard factory in Logan, a popcorn maker and museum in Marion, swords in New London, baskets in Newark (including the World's Largest Basket, which doubles as the company headquarters), shoelaces in Portsmouth, and doctors in Dayton. Doctors in Dayton? Made ya look: If you want to learn more, you'll just have to buy a copy!

In this updated and expanded second edition, not only has a specific section on Cincinnati been added, but even more odd stuff has been unearthed: the Midwest's own Stonehenge at the Temple of Tolerance in Wapakoneta, the self-explanatory World's Largest Horseshoe Crab in Blanchester, Ernest Angley's Cathedral Buffet in Cuyahoga Falls where you can eat 'n pray, and many more. Each entry now has a ZIP code, making it easy to find via GPS or other navigation system. And weird stuff continues to proliferate and entertain, regardless of the economic climate. Indeed, some of the best things in life are free—or close to it, anyway.

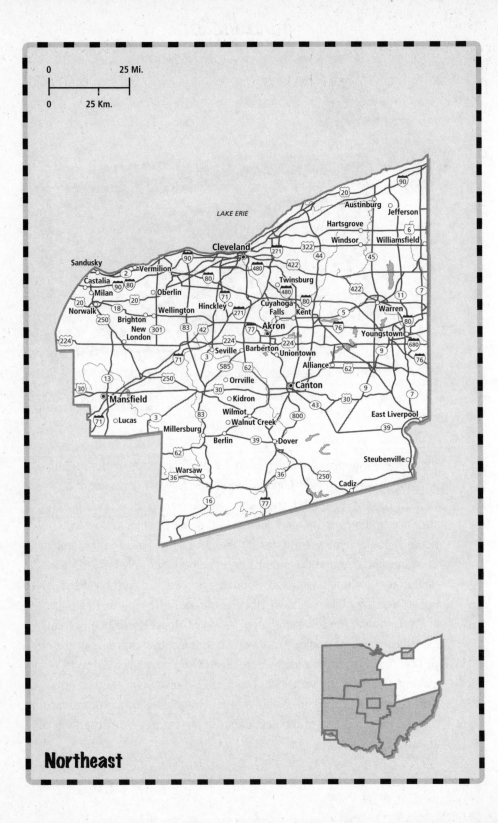

0   25 Mi.

0   25 Km.

LAKE ERIE

Austinburg
Jefferson
Hartsgrove
Windsor   Williamsfield

Cleveland

Sandusky
Vermilion
Castalia
Milan
Oberlin
Norwalk
Brighton
New London
Wellington
Hinckley

Twinsburg
Cuyahoga Falls
Kent
Akron
Warren
Youngstown

Seville
Barberton
Uniontown
Alliance

Orrville
Kidron
Canton

Mansfield
Lucas
Wilmot
Walnut Creek
Millersburg
Berlin
Dover
Steubenville

Warsaw
Cadiz
East Liverpool

Northeast

1

Northeast

The northeast corner *of the state is a veritable mother lode of curiosities and in fact has the largest number in this book. It's got quite an accumulation of Big Stuff, aka WLO (World's Largest Objects), a distinction that is often the subject of heated debate among various states and even countries. (Wars have been started over less—just look at the Middle East.) Nevertheless, they grow 'em big around these parts: a giant cockroach at TNT Exterminating in Akron, a super-size rocking chair in Austinburg, and an Amish buggy in Berlin—and also in Berlin is Behalt, a religious cyclorama so immense and detailed that it just might make your head spin (hopefully not a la Linda Blair in* The Exorcist*).*

Speaking of religious representations, you'll find a fifty-foot Madonna in Windsor and learn about the weeping one at a church in Barberton. At the opposite end—in so many senses of the word—is Hell Town, mostly a legend in its own mind, which has an "End of the World Road." Perhaps this balances out the "Center of the World" in Warren. At least that's what the Ohio Department of Transportation calls it, and how often has the government been wrong? (A question perhaps best left unanswered.)

It gets pretty cold up here, so people spend lots of time thinking up unusual things to do. How else can you explain the Buzzard Homecoming in Hinckley that occurs on the Ides of March? People descend on the pancake breakfast like vultures . . . at least we hope it's a pancake

★ ★

breakfast. Or the caterpillar races in Vermilion each autumn. Wow! It can't get any more exciting than that . . . can it? Yet folks line up to see what the fuzzy fellers have to say about the coming winter.

But if you're really looking to stimulate both body and mind, the McKinley National Memorial and Museum can't be beat. After climbing 108 steps to reach the massive dome-like structure, you can visit with the Prez and First Lady, both dead and alive (sort of). Not only are they buried there, but thanks to the miracle of animatronics, he and Ida will chat you up when you enter a ballroom-sized reproduction of their Victorian home. Of course it's a one-sided conversation and they're not at all interested in what you have to say, but still . . . The experience might even spawn a side trip to the Creegan Company in Steubenville. Since 1959 they've been supplying animated robots to Disney World, Sea World, and Hershey, Pennsylvania. They also perform Taximation—you guessed it—bringing taxidermy critters to "life."

And that's just for starters. So much to see! So much to do!

★ ★

What's Up, Dock?

Akron

It sits near the edge of an airfield at Lockheed Martin Tactical Defense Systems, a colossal gray-and-black behemoth bearing witness to an era when blimps were actually taken seriously and not eye candy bearing advertisements during nationally televised football games.

At twenty-two stories high and two Washington Monuments long, the Goodyear Airdock/Goodyear Tire & Rubber Company's Wingfoot Lake Airship Base (1210 Massillon Rd. 44315, 330-796-2800) is the world's largest building without interior supports and even has its own climate, occasionally creating a lightning system or fog. Once, after a heavy snow, a mini-avalanche from the rounded roof flattened a nearby security office. Goodyear built the hangar in 1929 to construct blimps—more than 239 airships from 1917 to 1995—and now it's used to manufacture aerospace products.

But the bummer is you need security clearance to get inside. So you'll be missing the cutting-edge stuff they're doing in there, such as developing a High Altitude Airship (HAA) military blimp and the related Integrated Security and Identification System (ISIS), which provides powerful surveillance, staying aloft at sixty-five thousand feet for up to a month. You are also denied access to the University of Akron's Lighter-Than-Air Society collection of documents and photographs, plus the corporate archives of the Goodyear Tire & Rubber Company.

If that doesn't float your dirigible, consider the fact that in May 2006 it was the site of a cool-looking explosion. Smoke and flames erupted from the hangar, and between fifteen and twenty Akron fire companies rushed to the scene. Fortunately, no one was hurt and most of the damage was to the exterior. But it makes you wonder what really goes on in there.

★ ★

Twelve Steps to Freedom

Akron

To paraphrase that other reformed sinner, Martha Stewart, "it's a good thing" that Dr. Bob Smith's home, the birthplace of Alcoholics Anonymous (855 Ardmore Ave. 44309, 330-864-1935,), is now in the hands of members of AA. Unlike the previous owners, who lined up whiskey bottles on the front porch to mock passersby who wanted to pay their respects, it is now treated with the loving care it deserves.

The story—which has taken on the patina of a legend—goes something like this: In 1935 stockbroker Bill Wilson went to Akron to engineer a takeover of a local company. The proxy fight failed, and Wilson was left with $10 in his pocket, unable to return to his home in Vermont (hey, during the Depression, everybody had lousy credit). Teetering toward a relapse, Wilson phoned local ministers to ask if they knew of any reformed alcoholics who could help him through his tough time. Meanwhile, an organization known as the Oxford Group had been praying for the recovery of Dr. Robert Smith from that very same disease. Wilson was introduced to Smith, and it was like the Reese's Cup all over again. Smith's last drink is said to have been June 10, 1935, the date of AA's founding.

Today AA's membership is estimated at one hundred thousand–plus groups, with more than two million members in 150 countries. Visitors to the humble abode will climb up twelve steps—an intentional change when the home was refurbished after its purchase in the mid-1980s—to the smell of strong coffee, a staple at all AA meetings. Many of the furnishings are original and authentically shabby, and along with photos of Bill W., Dr. Bob, and Bob's wife, Annie, you'll see the first copies of *The Big Book,* which is basically the AA bible. According to the tour guide, upon entering the bedroom of Dr. Bob, some visitors fall to the floor sobbing in gratitude. Along with serving as a halfway house, it was also the site of meetings where the principles of AA were pounded out.

It's no coincidence that there are twelve steps in front of Dr. Bob's.

Nonalcoholics may have difficulty grasping the need to hide empty bottles in various odd places, or the fact that Dr. Bob's family pretended they didn't know he was drinking when at one point his life was a nonstop bender. But anyone who's ever had a major hangover may find Dr. Bob's story testimony to the fact that the "hair of the dog" isn't the cure.

★ ★

True Grits
Akron

Ever wonder what it would be like to sleep in a Quaker Oatmeal box? Even if the thought never crossed your mind, you can experience the next best thing at the Quaker Square Inn at the University of Akron (135 South Broadway 44325, 330-253-5970, www.quakersquare. com). Constructed from a cluster of thirty-six silos originally built by Quaker Oats in 1932, the complex once housed 1.5 million bushels of grain. Each silo is 120 feet tall, and all the rooms are perfectly round, measuring twenty-four feet in diameter (unless you get a suite, which while also round, consists of one thousand square feet). Along with being almost soundproof, they're luxuriously appointed, as is the lobby with its striking combination of modern art and company memorabilia, including some original milling equipment.

What eventually became the Quaker Oats Company was the brain-child of one Ferdinand Schumacher (1822–1908). Since he used to grind oats and sell the meal as breakfast food in Germany, he figured he could do the same thing in Akron and the rest of America. By 1856 he bought an old wooden factory building along the canal, installed machinery, and was soon up to twenty barrels of oats a day. Despite fires, war, and economic setbacks, the company persevered, joining with other firms to form the American Cereal Company in the late 1800s. American Cereal went on to become the major component of Quaker Oats, which remained in what is now the hotel until 1970, when the company moved to Chicago.

The property has seen several incarnations and changes in man-agement. When it opened in 1975, it was privately owned, and later became a Hilton; presently it is under the aegis of the University of Akron, with floors four to nine being used as a residence for college students. The historic Trackside Grille, where you can dine in a circa 1880 Coleman railroad car, is usually only open when the college is in session.

So if you can get past the occasional partying students who get off at the wrong floor, wandering in circles looking for their room, there is a complimentary breakfast. And they do serve Quaker Oatmeal.

Rubber World
Akron

In 1898 thirty-eight-year-old Frank Seiberling borrowed money from his brother-in-law for a down payment on a factory, with plans to process raw materials like cotton and rubber into durable goods. Never mind that the raw materials had to be transferred halfway around the world to landlocked Akron, and the process of vulcanization (apologies, Mr. Spock)—the curing of rubber invented by the company's namesake, Charles Goodyear—had resulted in Goodyear dying penniless some thirty years earlier. (His heirs did quite well with royalties, however.)

Yet somehow, it worked. Bicycles and "horseless carriages" were all the rage during the turn of the last century. And in no time at all, it seemed, "Goodyear pedaled its way toward becoming the world's largest tire company, a title it earned in 1916 when it adopted the slogan 'More people ride on Goodyear tires than on any other kind,'" according to the corporate website, www.goodyear.com. Today, with more than 80,000 associates, Goodyear rolls out sales in excess of $18 billion and is still the world's largest tire company. Live long and prosper.

Bounce over to the Goodyear World of Rubber (1144 East Market St. 44316, 330-796-7117) and experience this history firsthand—well, almost. Located on the fourth floor of the company headquarters, this slightly outdated museum starts with a rubber "forest" and a detailed discussion on harvesting rubber, including flow charts showing how synthetic rubber is made, as well as radial tires. One might be surprised to learn that although tires do not grow on trees, rubber actually comes from them. Other displays revolve around topics such as the history of the interstate trucking industry and a discussion of the glory years of blimps, which peaked in the 1930s with elaborate and luxurious airships.

Looking for a spare? There's a moon tire left over from the Apollo mission, giant tires created for Admiral Byrd's 1940 Antarctic snowmobile, and—drum roll, please—the three hundred millionth tire made by the company, manufactured on August 9, 1939. Darned if it doesn't look like every other tire.

And if that's not enough, there are more self-guided tours, accompanied by faded videos with warbled soundtracks. Thus educated, you can turn on your heel and take a spin over to the Stan Hywet mansion in nearby Canton (see this chapter's "Life in the Big House" entry) and vicariously experience the real fruits of the Seiberling family tree. Who wouldn't love rubber, after that?

Roachzilla
Akron

If not for the giant, 15-foot cockroach on the side of its building, TNT Exterminating (92 North Main St. 44308, 866-535-6411, www.tnt exterminating.com) would be just another pest control company. It also expels any doubts about what a cockroach actually looks like. It's the thing that you've been telling yourself was a water bug that you found in the kitchen pantry the other day.

In business since 1936, this family-run enterprise is currently owned by Michael Grace, a third-generation pest control specialist. You might say extermination runs in their blood, a scary thought if there ever was one.

The oversize cockroach was his brainchild—sort of. "I was visiting a college roommate in Rhode Island, and I saw he had a giant termite on the roof of his company," Grace recalls. "I thought, well, we could do something, too."

So in 1996 the TNT roach made its (his?) debut, but today looks a bit worse for wear. "It definitely needs a paint job," remarked an employee who requested anonymity. "One year we dressed it up for

Better on the side of an exterminating company than in a hotel

Halloween, put a cape on it and everything." Who says people who kill bugs for a living aren't creative?

If you stop in during business hours, there's a wide selection of sprays and other deterrents to rid yourself of creepy crawlies common to northeastern Ohio—carpenter ants, bees, wasps, fleas, ticks, millipedes, spiders, earwigs, and, of course, roaches. Plus they offer large and small rat and mouse traps, and as a bonus have several tableaux depicting bugs and other pests so you can recognize them in their natural habitat. Fortunately most are fakes as well, though one certainly hopes that the giant cockroach is a gag, rather than a harbinger of possible mutations that might occur from spraying all this stuff into the ozone layer.

★ ★

Dead-End Downtown
Alliance

A lot of cities may need to revitalize their downtowns, but at least their streets allow you to head for brighter lights and bigger cities. Not Alliance. Its Main Street consists of two dead-ends, stopping at Sawburg Avenue on one side and Webb Avenue on the other. But people obviously have figured a way out, because Alliance has restaurants, shops, and attractions, just like any other small community.

But still . . . why? According to the website for the town historical society, www.alliancehistory.org, "Two major railroad lines intersected in Alliance. . . . The fact is that when Main Street was platted, it brought people to the train station which was the heart of the city's transportation hub." So they didn't really need to go anywhere, except to the railroad, right? Well, that's as good an explanation as any.

Once you circumvent the navigational confusion, there are a couple of things to do in the town, which was formed in 1850 in an alliance (get it?) of the villages of Williamsport, Liberty, and Freedom. There's the turn-of-the-last-century Glamorgan Castle (200 Glamorgan St. 44601, 330-821-2100), which is decorated in a mishmash of styles including Italian Renaissance, French Empire, Louis XV, Elizabethan, and Japanese and has bowling alleys, a billiard room, and a large swimming pool in the basement. You can also check out the Italianate architecture of the 1867 Mabel Hartzell Historical Home (840 North Park Ave. 44601, 330-823-1677). Considered a showplace in the late 1800s, it has an extremely long front porch and, according to Alliance's Rodman Library website (www.rodmanlibrary.com), contains "an unusual desk made in 1875, an old time parlor organ, an ember pot which was used to carry hot coals from one fireplace to start a fire in another, kitchen utensils, china, furniture, clothing, pictures, the red and brown hand crocheted coat and plaid dress Mabel wore the day she arrived to live in the house, and a letter written by Abraham Lincoln."

OK, so maybe Alliance isn't the most exciting place in the world. But at least leaving might be a challenge.

★ ★

Rock On!
Austinburg

This is one rocker that's too big for the britches of even Meat Loaf at his heftiest or the hip-hop group the Fat Boys. Built sometime during the 1960s or '70s—no one's exactly sure when—allegedly by a retired carpenter who's never home but whose answering machine implies that he and the wife are spending porch time with the grandkids, it now stands, immovable, next to its smaller brethren at the Country

Cheaper than shelling out hundreds of dollars to see "old rockers" like Mick Jagger.

★ ★

Cousins store (1933 Rte. 45, 44110, 440-275-1266), which sells mostly Amish-crafted wood products. At one time the twenty-five-foot rocking chair served as advertising for a local furniture company, and according to the manager of Country Cousins, was in Guinness World Records as—drum roll—the "World's Largest."

Or maybe not . . . Other places might say the folks in Austinburg are off their rockers, so to speak. The title of World's Largest Chair has been hotly contested, with several cities building bigger and better Duncan Phyfe, Mission, Ladderback, and Heywood-Wakefield styles, among others. A thirty-one-foot behemoth has been sighted in Anniston, Alabama, and there's yet another claim to the title in a seat of undefined height at Long's Consignment Furniture Store in Amity, Indiana (it's the one next to the chest of drawers that's several stories tall). A fifty-five-foot-high chair was completed on June 2, 2002, in Amboy, Illinois, with a reputed sixty-footer in Manzano, Italy, being catalogued in 2005.

Well, how about the World's Largest Boston Rocking Chair? Maybe. But does it really matter? It's huge, it's been around for decades, it's vastly entertaining, and unlike two-legged rockers, it doesn't charge an exorbitant admission. In fact, it's free!

The Bridges of Ashtabula County
Austinburg and Environs

Truss us: There's something very romantic about covered bridges. Just ask Robert James Waller. He's still out there somewhere, counting the money he made from his book and the movie *The Bridges of Madison County.*

Ohio has several covered bridges, in particular Ashtabula County, which boasts seventeen original, restored, and replicated from the nineteenth century. Every year during the second week in October, the county hosts a Covered Bridge Festival (440-576-3769, www.covered bridgefestival.org), with information on guided or self-driving tours available year-round.

★ ★

Bucolic, except for the biker bar across the street

Basically, the Ashtabula bridges consist of four types: Howe truss, Pratt truss, Town lattice truss, and inverted Haupt truss. According to the engineering textbook *Structural Analysis* (fourth edition), "A truss consists of a group of ties and struts so designed and connected that they form a structure which acts as a large beam. The members usually form one or more triangles in a single plane and are so arranged that the external loads are applied at the joints and theoretically cause only axial tension or axial compression in the members. The members are assumed to be connected at their joints with frictionless hinges or pins, which allow the members freedom to rotate slightly."

★ ★

OK, so you can truss them to hold up the bridges in different ways and make them look attractive, further enhanced by the fact that many are in picturesque rural places. And, to be perfectly honest, some of the bridges are kind of new, such as the one at Necher Road, a 100-footer funded by an Ohio Department of Transportation (ODOT) grant and opened in 1999. Still, there are plenty of oldies but still usable goodies, like the Mechanicsville Road Bridge, at 156 feet, the longest single-span in the county, built in 1867 and recently renovated and opened to traffic (including to the biker bar across the way), and, built a year later, the Harpersfield Bridge, a 228-foot two-spanner, the longest covered bridge in Ohio. It crosses the Grand River, adding the nail-biting tension of a possible collapse. (Not likely. Although it was partially washed away in 1913, it has since been reinforced and renovated).

And then there's the newest entry over the not-very-troubled waters of the Ashtabula River, the aptly named Smolen "Gulf" Bridge. Located on State Road, rising seventy-five feet above the scenic Indian Trails Park, this whopping 613-footer is the largest covered bridge in the USA. It opened in October 2008, just in time for the 25th anniversary of the festival. So there, Robert James Waller.

The Big Picture
Berlin

In 1944 seventeen-year-old Heinz Gaugel was drafted into Hitler's army. After only a few weeks of training, he was sent to the Western Front as part of a unit to be "sacrificed" in a fake attack to draw fire away from the main troops. Nearly all of his unit perished, and Heinz himself, in addition to being shot in the head and chest, spent time in a U.S. prison camp in France. Not surprisingly, he became a pacifist, and unlike der Führer, eventually gained renown as an artist.

Mennonite peoples from their Anabaptist beginnings in Switzerland in 1525 to pretty What Heinz Gaugel is known for in Amish country is *Behalt* (5798 County Rd. 77, 44610, 330-893-3192, www.behalt.com), a 10-by-265-foot cyclorama illustrating the heritage of the Amish and much the present day. Referred to as the "Sistine Chapel of the Amish and Mennonites," it is one of only four cycloramas in North America, and probably the only one of this size painted by a single individual.

But like many artists with a vision, Gaugel was thought to be kind of nuts at first. In 1972 he relocated to Holmes County from Canada, because he found kindred souls among the gentle people who spoke his native tongue of German. When they complained about the incessant picture-taking and questions from curiosity-seeking tourists, he decided to help in a unique way, and in 1978 began what became a fourteen-year project that was moved several times and held hostage in lieu of various expenses incurred during its creation. Eventually, in 1988, the partially completed painting found a home at what's now known as the Amish & Mennonite Heritage Center. Gaugel finished it there four years later.

It takes about forty-five minutes to make the circuit, which is broken by detailed storytelling by friendly guides. The renderings are far from sophisticated, as Gaugel was mostly self-taught. But no matter what your religious orientation, the story is compelling and hits close to its meaning of *behalt,* which is "to keep, hold, or remember." And it also rings true—in more ways than one—with the many Amish and Mennonites who take their youngsters there to learn about their history.

Along with a gift shop that has books on the religions and local crafts, the center has a pre–Civil War schoolhouse and a barn with a Conestoga wagon. You can even "round out" your Amish/Mennonite experience by viewing a display of Amish clothes and trying on a cap (women) or straw hat (men).

The Amish Hummer
Berlin

This is a great place to get hammered—or more accurately, to watch things being hammered, or to do your own hammering if you like.

For more than eighty years, Wendell August (7007 County Rd. 672, 44610, 866-354-5192, www.wendellaugust.com) has been

★ ★

The perfect vehicle for the Amish midlife crisis

hand-forging works of art—including commemorative plates, bowls, trays, and ornaments—out of pewter, aluminum, bronze, and silver.

Along with having a huge outlet for their stuff in Berlin, there's a hand-hammered-aluminum museum (try saying that three times really fast after a couple of margaritas), as well as actual craftsmen doing their thing the way it's been done for centuries, although some of the machinery uses electricity, so maybe it isn't quite the same. You can also "make your own" piece of metal art, but if you're looking for that perfect gift to help forge a good relationship with the boss or in-laws, you might want to check out what's for sale.

However, Wendell August's biggest attraction, both literally and figuratively, has nothing to do with metal, heavy or otherwise: it's the World's Largest Amish Buggy. Created by Amish carriage makers in nearby Winesburg, the massive ride is located toward the back of the huge building (you can't miss it). At 1,200 pounds, 10 feet ½ inch tall, 13 feet 9 inches long, and 7 feet 4 inches wide, it's a doozy. Even the wheels are five feet tall, which may give the somewhat vertically challenged a bit of a complex. But it's a favorite tourist attraction, and you can have your picture taken with it.

Even Amish country has its excesses, though they're pretty tame in comparison to the rest of society. And unlike its very distant cousin, the urban assault Hummer, this truly horseless carriage doesn't guzzle gas or look ridiculous in well-to-do suburbs.

Gussied Up Gun
Brighton

If you're ever at the intersection of Routes 511 and 18 in Brighton (44851), don't blink. You might miss the World War II cannon with whitewall tires, possibly the only one in the entire solar system (excluding Pluto).

OK, so it's not Magic Mountain or a Target superstore. But it's pretty exciting stuff for rural Ohio, especially since it's a mystery as to how the whitewall tires got there in the first place.

"No one knows," says Marilyn McClellan, the town's informal historian. "A bunch of surplus cannons were donated to places like Brighton and Rochester [another small town] right after the war, to honor the veterans." Like all the other cannons, this one had boring black rubber tires. Then one day, shortly after the cannon was installed in the town square, "they just appeared. No one ever fessed up."

★ ★

Whitewalls on a cannon . . . now let's talk rims.
CHERYL HINES

But hey, it's a good thing. "Lots of people call and ask questions about it, and it attracts attention when they drive through the town," McClellan says. Whitewalls were hot in the 1950s and gave the gun a fashion makeover, albeit a slightly dated one today. A one-gun salute, if you will.

Rhett's Rebirth
Cadiz

In 1983, some twenty-three years after his death, a call from a Quincy, Illinois, radio station came into the post office in Cadiz. The question posed by the DJ was simple: "Do you know whose birthday it is today?"

The postman, Pat Frazier, had no idea the DJ was referring to native son Clark Gable. Even worse, the town was doing nothing to commemorate it! And no one could remember the exact house Clark was born in. The approximate area had been razed in the early 1960s, anyway. Who knew that the Gable legend would live on after the man had shed his mortal coil?

But Cadiz had bigger problems. Not only was it facing a tremendous economic slump due to a downturn in demand for bituminous coal, its primary source of income, but unemployment was at an all-time high, resulting in loss of population and other social ills.

Not unlike his alter ego, Rhett Butler, Mr. Gable—or at least his celebrity persona—waited in the wings to rescue Cadiz, at least as a tourist attraction. A few months after that embarrassing phone call, three enterprising local burghers got together and decided to form the Clark Gable Foundation and erect a monument near the spot where he was born. The foundation held the first of many Clark Gable birthday celebrations on February 1, 1985, to help raise the tens of thousands of dollars needed to re-create the four-room, second-floor apartment where Clark spent the first few months of his life (138 Charleston St. 43907, 740-942-4989, www.clarkgablefoundation. com). They even got his son, John Clark Gable, to come all the way to tiny Cadiz and dedicate the new building in 1998.

Today visitors can tour the birthplace and check out memorabilia such as a sled, mug, pajamas, kitchen utensils, and his pipe. Stills and films, donated by Turner Entertainment, are on display, and there's even Gable's 1954 Cadillac. Then it's on to the gift shop to get your very own mementos and *Gone with the Wind* memorabilia.

But for the ultimate Rhett rush, stay at the adjacent bed-and-breakfast. It's decorated in the fashion of the Gable era, with unlimited books and movies featuring the "The King of Hollywood" himself. That way, you can say you slept with Clark Gable . . . sort of.

Hey, Jude

Who says good things don't come in small packages? The Shrine of St. Jude, aka St. Jude's Church of Barberton (594 Fifth St. Northeast 44203, 330-753-1155), can only accommodate a handful of people, but visitors have experienced a smorgasbord of miracles that would be pretty amazing even in the Vatican, although it's an Orthodox Catholic church, not a Roman one.

The story goes something like this: On March 10, 1992, one Anthony "Tony" Fernwalt was cleaning the twenty-four-seater, a former barbershop nestled between a railroad and a factory. At that time the church was only about a decade old and struggling to stay afloat financially.

Then Fernwalt came across a strange woman in the chapel. She was dressed in red, with stiff robes and an otherworldly glow, and she told him Jesus Christ was her son. Fernwalt, who had a police record and a history of mental illness, asked her in so many words to "hold that thought" while he got the priest, Father Roman Bernhard. By the time Father Roman arrived some twenty minutes later, the visitor had disappeared. What a surprise!

But what was verifiable were the tears rolling down a two-by three-foot portrait of the Virgin Mary that hung near the altar and several statues. Father Roman and his parishioners examined the painting carefully, checking for trickery that might lurk beneath the plywood mounting of the inexpensive oil canvas. They found none and contacted the news media. Soon thousands were stopping by to see for themselves what the *Akron Beacon Journal* described as "two very narrow glistening streaks . . . extending from the inner portion of each eye to the . . . [picture's] lower edge." They also made tracks in the paint, ruining the Blessed Virgin's makeup.

Accounts of other wonders began to trickle in. Some reported rosaries that changed from silver to gold. Others experienced an overwhelming smell of roses, a scent often equated with spiritual encounters. One morning a group of people in the parking lot who stared at the sky long enough even claimed to see the sun vibrate and pulsate over the church. Okaaay . . .

Another icon in the church wept during a procession, and there were claims of miracle cures, most notably from eighty-five-year-old Irma Sutton, whose gangrenous, ulcerated left leg was slated for amputation but miraculously cleared up after her niece took her to view the painting, even stumping (so to speak) her physicians.

Still, there were detractors and doubters, who cited reasons ranging from condensation to freak atmospheric conditions. And Father Roman and Tony Fernwalt parted ways, after the latter refused to abide by the rules of the sanctuary. At some point the sheriff was called, and Fernwalt left the area.

Although the icon has stopped weeping, visitors still stream in from time to time. And the shrine garnered enough donations to pave the parking lot and for other improvements, such as new carpeting. So if a leak was the cause, we'll never know—and Mary isn't talking.

* *

Drive-By Museum
Canton

This place is sure to rev the engine of any gearhead, and then some. There's the 1981 stainless-steel DeLorean driven by Johnny Carson, a gift from the namesake automaker, supposedly worth a cool half-mil. Carson was pulled over in it a few months later during his arrest for drunk driving and eventually sold the gull-winged beast. A flawlessly refurbished 1911 Ford Model S includes a "mother-in-law seat" behind the front bench (sorry, no ejection button). Canton's one and only 1937 Studebaker President police and riot-prevention car boasts bullet-resistant armor plating and one-plus-inch-thick window glass in addition to a closable tommy gun porthole.

Cool cars in an eclectic array

This is only a soupçon of the more than forty-five rare and antique vehicles interspersed with thousands of pieces of eclectic memorabilia at the Canton Classic Car Museum (555 South Market St. 44702, 330-455-3603, www.cantonclassiccar.org). Rows and rows of long, lean, and luxurious Packards, Cadillacs, Pierce-Arrows, and more conjure up mental pictures of gangsters, movie stars, and rumble seats (just because it was the Depression didn't mean they had to skimp on size, not unlike today). At the other end of the vehicular spectrum are the now-defunct Canton-manufactured King Midgets, one-passenger, single-cylinder gizmos that resemble early golf carts. In between you'll find gleaming 1950s, 1960s, and 1970s classics, blasts from the past, such as the 1956 V-8 Ford Thunderbird, similar to the one in *American Graffiti.*

Established in 1978 by Marshall Belden Sr. in one of the country's earliest Ford dealerships, it is maintained by his widow, Florence, and seemingly arranged in no particular chronological order, though certain models and years are grouped together. But don't be surprised if you're wandering through and are sidetracked by, say, an accumulation of vintage radios, millinery, or Burma Shave signs. Or historic photographs of Canton and business and manufacturing artifacts, along with an exhibit on Oriental culture. Or a funeral coach placed next to a headless black sylph topped by a lampshade.

It's whatever struck the Belden family fancy, and now by extension, yours.

Real-Life Wonka
Canton

You can tell yourself that you're taking the forty-five-minute tour of the Harry London chocolate factory (5353 Lauby Rd. 44720, 330-494-0833 or 800-321-0444, www.harrylondon.com) for educational purposes. But the truth is, you want to sample the goods.

And who wouldn't? The largest candy store in the Midwest has some five hundred varieties of freshly made treats, from peanut butter crispy joys to freshly "minted" edible $100 bills to chocolate-covered pretzels large and small. There are peanut butter buckeyes as well as all manner of bonbons, truffles, and caramels, and even a complete line of sugar-free candies, which are probably similar calorie-wise but won't raise your insulin level through the roof. Even thinking about the place is mouthwatering.

And they've been doing it for a while, at least since 1922 when steelworker Harry London decided to quit his job and turn full-time to chocolateering, a craft he learned from his father, Gilbert. Thus an enterprise traveled from the family kitchen to America's waistlines.

So much candy, so little room in the waistband!

Tours take place by appointment only (so you'll need to call first), and you'll experience the creating, molding, wrapping, packaging, and storing of various concoctions, depending upon what day it is. There's also a Chocolate Hall of Fame, consisting of plaques honoring various innovators. But who cares about that? Along with the aforementioned samples, those taking the tour get two bucks off any regularly priced order of $20. Sweet.

Girl Power
Canton

Behind every POTUS (President of the United States), popular or otherwise, is a First Lady. The National First Ladies' Library and Museum (331 South Market Ave. 44702, 330-452-0876, www.firstladies.org) is dedicated to celebrating this particular brand of spousal support. (That is, until such time when there is a First Man. Then they may have to change it to The National First Ladies—and One Man—Museum.) And it's a sight to see, a well-tended, impeccably manicured complex with two exquisitely refurbished buildings: a former City National Bank built in 1895 and the Saxton McKinley House, a Victorian gingerbread concoction constructed in 1840 by the family of Ida Saxon McKinley, wife of William and the twenty-fifth First Lady (see this chapter's "Dead President Talking" entry). It's mostly a girl thing, so guys might want to head for the Canton Classic Car Museum or Pro Football Hall of Fame instead.

Most tours start out in the library (known as the Education and Research Center), which consists of more than 12,500 books, photos, and slides of First Ladies. Also on display are their outfits—a partially restored frock worn by Martha Washington, as well as those belonging to Dolley Madison and lesser-knowns like Jane Pierce (wife of Franklin, fourteenth POTUS). Rotating exhibits of original, reproduction, and miniature inaugural gowns and other dresses testify that these women were petite (though sometimes the fabric has to be bunched to avoid fraying seams). Hey, they didn't have a whole lot of time to sit around, eat chocolates, and watch reality TV. Another highlight is the intimate rococo Victorian theater, where special programs are held.

★ ★

**The power behind the Oval Office at the
National First Ladies' Museum**

Then it's on to the McKinley house, with its gleaming wood and flowery "First Lady" wallpaper and its parlor, office, and sitting room mostly restored with furnishings from Ida's heyday, circa 1880–1900. You'll find more pictures of the Ladies at work and play in the third-floor ballroom. Many of the photos are so candid, you might not initially recognize who they're depicting. Or you may glimpse a side of them that you've never seen before, such as the formidable and usually intimidating Barbara Bush biking along the beach accompanied by her dog. Displays change frequently, so there's always something new.

The gift shop offers First Lady–themed china, ornaments, books, and chocolates wrapped in everyone from Louisa Adams to Jackie O. No matter what you think of their husbands, the candy tastes the same.

King (or Queen) for a Night
Canton

Ahh, the good life. Not everyone can afford it, and not everyone wants to. But if you're looking for a brief foray into the upper crust, try an overnight stay at the Glenmoor Country Club (4191 Glenmoor Rd. Northwest 44718, 330-966-3600, www.glenmoorcc.com). It's all the privileges of membership and none of the Groucho Marx issues that come with belonging to a club that would actually invite you to join.

Formerly the Brunnerdale Seminary, for decades an austere training ground for Catholic priests, the 167,000-square-foot Gothic-style clubhouse is now a year-round social, business, and activity center, with luxuriously appointed guest rooms and a 7,018-yard, par 72,

A "fore"-star place to stay and play

championship Jack Nicklaus signature golf course. Also located on the verdant property, which is surrounded by an equally ritzy housing development, are three dining facilities, a spa, tennis courts, and an Olympic-style swimming pool. Talk about doing a 360 . . .

The building is so large that those staying in the hotel must walk down several hallways to reach the clubhouse. Restaurant choices include the Black Heath Grille—an exclusive setting with correspondingly pricey steaks, chops, and seafood, among other gourmet offerings—and the more informal Scot's Grille (but still with an *e*), which overlooks the golf course. Or mingle with the old, nouveaux, and wannabe riches at the Loch Bar, with its eighty-inch flat-screen TV. No one will know, or care, what your credit score is as long as you look the part—and can pay the bill.

Filling a Vacuum
Canton

The tour guides at the Hoover Historical Center in North Canton (1875 East Maple St. 44720, 330-499-0287) are probably tired of hearing about how their museum sucks. And Roomba jokes aren't appreciated either, especially since Hoover doesn't manufacture them.

Still, the hundred-plus vacuum cleaners found in various rooms throughout the small house make for an impressive lineup and illustrate the, um, sweeping changes that have occurred throughout the last century or so. In one corner is the very first Hoover, the 1907 Model "O" invented by Murray Spangler, a janitor who drummed up support for his contraption by enlisting the help of his cousin's husband, William "Boss" Hoover, the prosperous owner of a horse collar, saddle, and leather-goods factory. Spangler died a few years later, but did manage to pull in some royalties.

Before Spangler came along, the quest for the perfect, practical vacuum cleaner created a virtual whirlwind of activity. Between 1850 and 1900 some 250 different types of sweepers were made, none

(Continued on Page 30)

Main Street, USA

Before interstates, the only way you could get from the East Coast to the West was through a series of gravel roads, mud paths and then perhaps . . . nothing. There were no signs and no maps to follow. So it was the train or else, because by the time the automobile came around, pioneer wagons were pretty much passé.

Enter Carl Fisher, an Indiana entrepreneur who helped organize the Indianapolis Motor Speedway and was one of the driving forces behind the development of Miami Beach. In 1913 Fisher teamed up with Frank Seiberling, president of Goodyear Rubber in Akron, and Henry Joy, head of Packard Motor Cars in Warren. Fisher envisioned a coast-to-coast hard-surfaced road that would stretch almost 3,400 miles, the shortest practical route from New York to San Francisco, cutting a swath from Times Square to Lincoln Park, and snaking its way through some fourteen states.

The men created the Lincoln Highway Association, with Joy as president. Not only did they obtain cooperation from various governmental and civic bodies, they also persuaded private and corporate sources to cough up the needed funds. Within a few years, you could snake your way coast-to-coast on two-lane roads and twisty turns via U.S. Highways 1, 30, 40, and 50 and even less exciting state highway numbers as long as you followed the signs. The "Main Street Across America" also brought prosperity to hundreds of cities, towns, and villages.

By 1925, the U.S. Bureau of Public Roads had taken over the nation's highways—leave it to the government to step in when most of the hard work is done. Although much of the original thoroughfare may be gone, it's not forgotten. Today there's still a Lincoln Highway Association (www.lincolnhighwayassoc.org) with state chapters. According to the Ohio chapter, the state has some of the best sites in the country, including several brick-paved sections. The Lincoln Highway enters Ohio from the east on US 30, and although much of it has been rebuilt as a four-laner, it mostly follows or parallels the original route. You can see markers on US 30 in East Canton if you're not too busy whizzing by on I-77.

(Continued from Page 28)
of which worked very well, though an early Bissell manual sweeper
on display is basically unchanged from what's available today. After
Spangler and Hoover teamed up, the latter placed a small ad in the
Saturday Evening Post offering a free ten-day home trial of the cleaner
and was swept off his feet with requests. By 1920 Hoover's company
had shut down its leather business and was producing 275,000 cleaners annually.

If these vacuums could talk, what stories they would tell! Lifted by
its own exhaust, the 1956 Walk-on-Air canister floated behind the

A sweeping display cleans up.

★ ★

user. The portable 1962 Model 2100 traveled to Paris in a light-green plastic suitcase—what museum folk jokingly refer to as the "Hoover in the Louvre." There's also lots of other memorabilia from the Age of June Cleaver, including miniature toy vacs from the '50s and '60s, portable hairdryers, and other assorted pastel-colored household devices. A 1910 Kotten weighed more than a hundred pounds and consisted of a platform over two horizontal bellows, oddly resembling a skateboard sans wheels. The woman—and it was always a woman—stood on the platform and rocked it back and forth. Today it's a favorite with kids, and that sucker still picks up dirt!

The museum is part of the larger Hoover Historical Park, which is affiliated with nearby Walsh University. You can also visit Boss's boyhood home, with all sorts of farm and pioneer memorabilia, and maybe watch the baseball team, the cleverly named Hoover Sweepers, clean up from May through September.

But most people are pulled in by the cleaners, anxious to hear the dirt behind the Hoover success story.

Dead President Talking

Canton

The McKinley National Memorial and Museum (800 McKinley Monument Dr. 44708, 330-455-7043, www.mckinleymuseum.org) is a true American original. Not only are William and wife Ida entombed in a humongous, domelike structure reachable by 108 steps—a challenge for any would-be Rocky with excellent knees—but the museum itself has the world's largest collection of all things McKinley, including campaign memorabilia, furnishings, personal effects, textiles, souvenirs, photographs, papers, correspondence, and books. It also houses Discover World, a hands-on science center for kids of all ages, with fossils, rocks, and the inevitable reproduction dinosaur, among many other things. Visitors can also explore the Street of Shops and Historical Hall, with their Victorian-era parlor, pioneer kitchen, antique toys, and more.

★ ★

But the real *pièce de résistance* is the second floor. Here you'll find a huge fish-eye photo of an 1896 McKinley "front porch" campaign speech, and as the friendly guard tells visitors, his (McKinley's) eyes as well as that of the audience follow you from one side of the wall to the next as you stride across the room. Oooh, spooky . . . Then step into a ballroom-size reproduction of the president's Victorian home, complete with statues of him and Ida. All of a sudden, they start talking—one minute you're there by yourself, and then these two strike up a conversation about the White House and the upcoming Pan American Exposition in Buffalo (where, alas, the president would be shot by Leon Czolgosz on September 6, 1901). Pretty inane stuff, not unlike many married couple conversations. The animatronic figures are activated electronically, so they shut up when you leave—supposedly.

So who was William McKinley, anyway? The twenty-fifth president (1897–1901) was born in Niles, Ohio, in 1843. Yet another Republican—Ohio seems to produce them like Texas does beauty queens and cheerleaders—McKinley's administration was noted for its high tariffs. During his presidency the United States fought and won the Spanish–American War and annexed the Philippines, Puerto Rico, Guam, and Hawaii.

OK, so he was no Lincoln or JFK, nor nearly as memorable as his successor, Teddy Roosevelt. But he was assassinated by an anarchist, and he's the only POTUS whose pre-presidency residences were destroyed. So try to be nice when you run into him and Ida.

Life in the Big House
Canton

Let's say you were an industrial baron around the turn of the twentieth century. And despite pots of money, you still hungered for what British nobility had enjoyed for centuries—great estates, a name honored and passed down for generations, and fear from underlings.

Well, as the song goes, two out of three ain't bad, and since most robber barons already had the latter, like his peers, Frank A. Seiberling, founder of the Goodyear Tire & Rubber Company, had great architectural expectations. Vanderbilt built his Biltmore, Rockefeller erected Kykuit, and Hearst had San Simeon. So between 1912 and 1915, in the true spirit of "Jonesing" (as in "keeping up with"), Frank and wife Gertrude constructed their country estate, Stan Hywet (714 North Portage Path 44303, 330-836-5533, www.stanhywet.org).

Rather than being an ancient Scottish clan with its own kilt pattern and family crest, the meaning of the name Stan Hywet is actually a bit of a buzz kill: It's Old English for "stone quarry," mostly what the property consisted of anyway. Still, the Seiberlings had a, uh, blast putting together the Tudor Revival manor house, grounds, and surrounding buildings. It gave them a good excuse to visit England several times for furnishings and decorating ideas, and to engage the services of exclusive architect Charles S. Schneider. The manor house alone had three thousand separate blueprints, and a railroad spur was even constructed to deliver supplies to the property.

No detail was overlooked. In addition to dozens of stained-glass windows, twenty-three fireplaces each with a uniquely designed chimney, and hand-carved wood paneling, the opulent manor house boasted hidden telephones, radiators, and closets; custom hand-woven Persian rugs; and various "theme" (e.g., Chinese, music) rooms furnished with authentic period pieces.

"Every room tells its own story of the Seiberling lifestyle—from the Billiard Room where Mr. Seiberling entertained his business associates and sealed deals over a brandy and good cigar to the ornate Music Room where famous celebrities like Will Rogers and Shirley Temple entertained the Seiberlings and their friends," states the website.

Visitors might also have encountered Frank's eldest daughter, Irene Seiberling Harrison, who still resided on the grounds and would reminisce about her childhood in the "Big House" until her death in 1999 at the astounding age of 108.

Like many of the great American homes, however, Stan Hywet almost met the wrecking ball around 1960, after Frank died and the

★ ★

family formed a foundation. They wanted to donate it to the city of Akron, who deemed the operating expenses out the roof. But a group of dedicated preservationists banded together to ensure Stan Hywet's status as a national landmark and a successful nonprofit enterprise. And like the product that paid for it in the first place, they've done a pretty decent patch job so visitors can still enjoy it today.

Bottomless Refills
Castalia

Perhaps only in Ohio would people actually pay money to see a hole in the ground filled with blue-green water. But that's exactly what they did for nearly six decades, drawn far and wide to the seemingly bottomless, glassy, crystal-clear pond, which at one point in time was believed to reach all the way down through the earth. (Could there have been an equally mysterious pool at the other end, in China?) Fed from an under-water stream, it lacked oxygen and thus was unable to sustain plant or fish life, although a strange-looking, slimy stuff grew on the bottom and sides. Plus the dang thing never froze, remaining about 48 degrees Fahr-enheit year-round. Back then, cheap thrills were hard to come by.

Truth was, there were about twenty other "blue holes" in the area, because for eons, underground streams and rivers continuously pumped out hundreds of thousands of gallons of water per hour, cre-ating Erie County's eeriest phenomenon. Though the Wyandot tribe had used the spring for its curative powers and, in fact, made it the site of a medicine camp, it took the palefaces to turn it into a money-making venture. Major Robert Rogers of the colonial rangers "discov-ered" it in 1761, calling it "a remarkable fine spring," and in 1836 the village was named for the Fons Castalius Fountain near Delphi, Greece. And so word of the blue hole spread far and wide, culminating in the 1930s when the owners put up a gate and charged admission to help defray the cost of the mess left behind by the curious.

But modern times and technology caught up with the blue hole. For one thing, it was measured and found to be only about seventy feet

★ ☆ ★ ☆ ★ ☆ ★ ☆ ★ ☆ ★ ☆ ★ ☆ ★ ☆ ★ ☆ ★ ☆ ★ ☆ ★ ☆ ★ ☆ ★ ☆ ★ ☆ ★ ☆ ★ ☆ ★ ☆ ★ ★

deep. The "endless" thing was just a trick of light, the same phenomenon that happens when you put a large convex magnifying glass over
water and deflect light rays, creating the illusion of depth. So it closed in
the early 1990s, trumped by video arcades and the fact that it needed
to be revamped to comply with the Americans with Disabilities Act.

However, there was a light at the end of the funnel, so to speak.
The State of Ohio purchased a fish hatchery next to the former attraction; the area was ideal for raising trout and other finned critters. And
guess what? They found another blue hole, approximately the same
size as the first! So they made it safe for everyone, and it's open regular hours, which may vary with the season (7018 Homegardner Rd.
44824, 419-684-7499). But it doesn't quite fill the gap of the original.

Eat, Pray, Watch TV
Cuyahoga Falls

It's a TV station! It's a cathedral! It's a restaurant! The combo Ernest
Angley Cathedral Buffet and Banquet Center (2690 State Rd. 44223,
330-922-0467, www.cathedralbuffet.com) is a feast for belly, eyes,
and, if you're so inclined, spirit. The intellect, however may be a different story, since it's also the location of WBNX-TV, the Cleveland affiliate for the CW, home of such fare as *The Tyra Show, Gossip Girl,* and
even more paradoxically, *Hellcats,* a drama about college cheerleaders.

However, most people go there to pray, eat, and check out the
Jesus art, not necessarily in that (or any) order. The sprawling campus, which architecturally resembles its 1954 outdoor revival origins,
consists of a ginormous, circus-tent–shaped cathedral, with a thirty-
two-ton indoor cross illuminated with 4,700 lights. Led by intrepid TV
evangelist Ernest Angley—he of the very bad rug and/or hair dye job—
it has remained close to its Pentecostal roots of "salvation, healing,
and the Holy Spirit Baptism," according to church press materials.

Other types of carpets—tacky red ones—also abound in the huge
cafeteria/museum, which is open every day of the week except Monday, when, in a nod to their Creator—hopefully the one Upstairs and

★ ★

WWJD . . . at the salad bar?

not Angley—employees are given a rest. It's separated by an outdoor walkway so along with churchgoers, families, and those lured by the relatively low prices, plentiful food, and the fact that no one's trying to overtly convert them, can dine in relative anonymity.

But a real bargain is on the lower level, home of the *Life of Christ* display (minimum donation: $1). The self-taught artist, Paul Cunningham, learned his craft from Gutzon Borglum, sculptor for Mount Rushmore, although on a much, much smaller scale.

Along with black velvet paintings (shades of a different King!), thirteen miniature dioramas present various highlights of Jesus's life, including the Sermon on the Mount, the Last Supper, and so forth.

In addition to titles like "Bear that cross!" ("Go, Hellcats!"), each display provides descriptions, such as, "He could condense a mile of space into five feet of depth" (that would be Cunningham, not Jesus), "Human fingernails were used on many of the figures," (eeew) and "startling details—even… a tiny bumblebee on an Easter lily—give depth to . . . these inspiring scenes." That's a lot of buzz for only a few bucks.

A Secular Ernest Carves a Different Niche
Dover

Most everyone loves a rags-to-riches story—as "witnessed" by the previous entry—although in this case, it's more rags to economic security. But what a tale . . .

Ernest "Mooney" Warther's (1885–1973) parents were poor Swiss immigrants; his father died when he was a toddler, leaving the family of five with "an old cow and about 20 cents," according to a museum guide. But everyone pitched in, including little Ernest, who began herding cows for pennies, earning the nickname "Mooney" (from the Swiss slang *moonay,* which means "bull of the herd").

And it stuck for a reason: Mooney's interest in carving began shortly thereafter when he found a rusty pocketknife in the road. He whittled anything he could get his hands on—using wood from the ground, fighting the dog for soup bones—making teeny working pliers that he passed out to everyone. Mooney eventually created the "Pliers Tree," a thirteen-inch-long piece of black walnut with 511 of the little suckers, which was featured in *Ripley's Believe It or Not!* It's now in his museum, after being on loan to the Ohio State Historical Society. But we're getting ahead of ourselves here.

Mooney was one busy beaver. He married and had five kids, and worked in a steel mill for twenty years. But during the times he was laid off, he carved several dozen locomotives with actual working parts, a miniature version of the mill where he was employed, and Abraham Lincoln's funeral procession in ebony and ivory (before the latter was banned), among other things. He also created his own utensils for carving, which eventually became a knife business that still exists today.

Mooney refused to sell any of his pieces, even though he was offered large sums of money. "Our roof don't leak, we ain't hungry, and we don't owe anybody," he was fond of saying. With his wild hair and booming voice, he always attracted an audience and became a public relations spokesperson for the New York Central Railroad, traveling the country with his models. This led to financial independence and the eventual establishment of the Warther Museum (331 Karl Ave. 44622, 330-343-7513, www.warthers.com).

Along with the aforementioned pieces, you can see the ornate canes Mooney created for presidents and other dignitaries; the History of Steam exhibit, some sixty-four models that reflect forty years of effort; and the train de résistance, the 8-foot-long Empire State Express, carved from an elephant tusk.

The second, third, and fourth generations of the family continue to run the enterprise, which also includes a knife-making shop, gardens, arrowheads, and wife Freida's button collection, some 73,282 different ones on the walls and ceilings of a small house on the grounds. Well, she had to do something while Ernest was out sticking his knife into every available piece of wood.

Not So Pretty
East Liverpool

Who would have thought that the death mask of "Pretty Boy" Floyd would end up in the laundry room of the Sturgis House bed-and-breakfast (122 West Fifth St. 43920, 330-382-0194, www.sturgis-house.com)? That's almost as much of an insult as being called "Pretty Boy," a nickname Charles Arthur Floyd hated, and corrected even as he lay dying.

A few days before his demise on October 22, 1934, he and his gang blew into town to rob the Tiltonsville Peoples Bank. Police and FBI were put on high alert throughout Ohio, and Floyd was gunned down at the farm of Ellen Conkle, after she gave him a nice meal of spareribs, potatoes, and rice pudding. Were the locals trusting or what?

Not really . . . On the one hand were the feds and especially super–crime fighter Melvin Purvis (who'd knocked off John Dillinger in Chicago and also helped nab "Baby Face" Nelson), who were convinced that Floyd and his gang were responsible for just about every bank robbery and related crime known to humankind. This included but was hardly limited to the Kansas City Massacre, the shootout and murder of four law enforcement officers and a criminal fugitive at the Union Railway Station a year before, which Floyd denied involvement in. On the other hand were the farmers and the formerly working but now unemployed stiffs, many of whom were pissed at the banks for foreclosing on their mortgages. So this bad boy and his gang held a certain romantic appeal, and as a result Floyd got some sympathetic press.

Still, his death was pretty grisly, with the bloody, muddy corpse being hauled in the back of a local police car to the Sturgis Funeral Home, now the B&B. The $120 and change found in Floyd's pockets was used to defray the cost of embalming, while swatches of his suit were passed out as souvenirs. Some ten thousand people filed past the corpse to get a last glimpse before he was shipped off to be buried in Salisaw, Oklahoma.

Along with the aforementioned death mask, the B&B has a display of embalming equipment and the little metal sling used to prop up the Boy's pretty head, along with photos and papers, including a graduation shot of Frank Dawson, the mortician who did the honors. The rest of the "death trail" includes a marker along Sprucevale Road between East Liverpool and Rogers at the location of the Conkle farm, where the former Public Enemy No. 1 with the girly-man moniker drew his final breath.

★ ★

Roadkill Convention
Hinckley

Every dog has its day, so why shouldn't buzzards, aka turkey vultures? The folks in Hinckley, a few miles south of Cleveland, certainly think so. Since 1957 they've been hosting an annual Buzzard Homecoming (corner of State Road and West Drive in Hinckley Reservation in Hinckley Township 44233, www.clemetparks.com/events/buzzards_sun. asp), which although it doesn't directly involve buzzards, other than the ones found in a cage in the back of the park ranger's pickup, does attract thousands of two-legged scavengers who partake of an "early bird" breakfast of pancakes, sausages, and more. Roadkill never tasted so good.

There's a crunchy granola version and a gross version as to how this came about. The latter is that in December 1818 the people of Hinckley Township had a big hunting party and killed some six hundred deer, wolves, and bears, oh my! They left the carcasses out all winter, which was cool—literally—until spring, when the snow began to melt and the yucky, stinky mess attracted gangs o' buzzards, who marked March 15 on their calendars and decided to make it an annual thing. Or so that story goes.

The other version resulted from the discovery of an old manuscript by William Coggswell, "who as a youth with his uncle, Gibson Gates, were the first white men to set foot in the township in 1810," according to the now-defunct Hinckley website (Cleveland Metroparks now oversees the proceedings). Along with describing their explorations, the manuscript detailed "finding the 'vultures of the air' at the gallows at Big Bend of Rocky River around the foot of the ledges where the Wyandots had hanged a squaw for witchcraft two years before. This indicated that these turkey vultures had made their home on Hinckley Ridge long before the white men settled west of the Cuyahoga River, and it moved their occupancy back into the midst of the Indians' legend." That would be the natives, not the Cleveland baseball team.

★ ★

Anyway, "in 1957 a reporter from the *Cleveland Press* became interested in a claim by Metroparks Ranger Walter Nawalaniec," continues the site. "He told the reporter that he had personally observed the buzzards arrival in Hinckley each March 15 for the past six years and that his predecessor, the late Charlie Willard, had kept a personal log of their arrival for the past twenty-three years."

Of course, if you put it in the paper, it has to be true. And soon "naturalists, ornithologists and reporters repeated and embellished the original story and suspense mounted. March 15 arrived and so did the buzzards—who arrived right on schedule at 2 p.m. that day." Prompt little suckers.

Soon thousands were attending every Ides of March, peering anxiously into the sky at the Buzzard Roost at the Hinckley Reservation. In recent years, however, the event has been held on the Saturday closest to the 15th, with hikes and tours, exhibits and programs, and buzzard-themed treats thrown in for good measure. Hopefully without actual buzzards as the ingredients.

Carriage Trade-Off
Jefferson

Located in a far corner of northeastern Ohio—aka the middle of nowhere—the Victorian Perambulator Museum (26 East Cedar St. 44047, 440-576-9588, www.perambulatormuseum.com) is a Gilded Age treasure trove, with more than 200 ornate baby and doll carriages. Many are handmade from natural fibers such as wicker and fashioned into intricate designs, with styles like the Swan, Peacock, Butterfly, Seahorse, Tulip, and Gondola. Topped with parasols or other protective covers, they shelter stuffed animals and dolls trussed up with ribbons, lace, and curls. It's enough to make you swoon from aesthetic overload. And they probably don't have smelling salts.

But that's only part of this one-of-a-kind collection. The rest—a throng of circa 1900 toys, carousel horses, miniatures, and games,

★ ★

That's OK, Mom, I'll drive.

along with things known as velocipedes, pre-twentieth-century bicycles with pedals attached to the front wheel—is located in what formerly was a private residence. "Our family had a baby buggy, and that got us interested," explains Judith Kaminski, who along with her twin sister, Janet Pallo, opened the nine-room museum in 1988. Soon they were rolling in perambulators and other stuff from all over the world.

Highlights—and you really do need a guided tour for this—include a Model T commemorative carriage with porthole windows and fake "headlights," an 1885 F. A. Whitney perambulator made with original materials, and a miniature red carriage from the 1920s used by Queen Elizabeth when she was a child. You'll also find the "Guignol," a rare Punch and Judy stage from France, as well as a German mini–merry-go-round from the 1890s that still operates. Many of the perambulator styles are reproduced in their natural habitat via colorful Victorian scenes through the paintings of Art Fronckowiak, with proofs and prints available for sale in the tiny gift shop.

If the museum hasn't moved by the time you visit, make sure to go to the restroom beforehand, as the one in the current building may not be available. And in addition to answering the call of nature, call to make sure they're open as well, as hours of operation may vary.

Fashion History 101
Kent

The Kent State University Museum (515 Hilltop Dr. 44242, 330-672-3450, www.kent.edu/museum) has a baker's dozen worth of royal underwear, including Queen Victoria's knickers. But really, who would want to see someone's previously worn bloomers, anyway?

Well, actually lots of people, if it's presented in the right manner and is, it goes without saying, clean. A good portion of this classy museum's nearly twenty thousand objects consists of costumes and accessories, in addition to American glass, fine furniture, textiles, paintings, and other decorative items. Most garments are from the twentieth century, though there are several excellently preserved eighteenth- and nineteenth-century pieces as well. The Beaux Arts building in which the museum is housed was constructed in 1927, when such items as marble, handmade woodwork, and glittering chandeliers came standard.

This pantheon to good taste would never have happened if not for Shannon Rodgers and Jerry Silverman, manufacturers of better dresses on Seventh Avenue in New York City, who donated some four thousand costumes and accessories, nearly one thousand pieces of art, and a five

★ ★

thousand–volume reference library to the university in 1982. Along with other local collectors, many major American and European designers, including such trendsetters as Calvin Klein, have also donated artifacts, records, and samples.

Highlights include an aluminum Naugahyde suit, "energy dome" (crazy red hat), and 3-D glasses from DEVO band member Mark Mothersbaugh, who was a student at Kent State during the May 4, 1970, shootings there; an original bright red, sparkly evening gown designed by Bob Mackie; one of Princess Diana's dresses; and a frock worn by Vivien Leigh (aka Scarlett O'Hara) in *Gone with the Wind*. And yes, there's an impressive selection of lingerie and corsets (ouch!), including one that uses whalebone insets and another made from metal (double ouch!). A Chinese collection consists of banners that hung behind the throne in the Forbidden City, summer and fur-lined winter court robes, lotus slippers for bound feet (triple ouch!), feather hair ornaments, and Imperial Guard uniforms.

Exhibits change regularly, so you might get a glimpse of The Age of Nudity—but no actual skin; it's the period between 1780 and 1825 when society was scandalized by the use of fewer and lighter-weight fabrics. Or you might learn about modern designers such as Yves St. Laurent, or discover a seeming oxymoron: fashion on the Ohio frontier. No matter what's up for consideration, it's usually pretty to look at.

More Exciting Than It Sounds
Kent

In 1966, during an interview with the *National Hearing Aid Journal* (now *Hearing Journal*), the words "hearing aid display" and "museum" came up in conjunction with Professor Kenneth Berger's stated desire to establish such a collection at the Speech and Hearing Clinic at Kent State. Before you could say, "What's that again?" hearing aids began flooding in from all over the United States and abroad; one individual who'd been in the business since the 1930s sent in five hundred different models. Today the Kenneth W. Berger Hearing Aid

✦ ✦

Museum and Archives (Music and Speech Building, Kent State University 44242, 330-672-2672, www.kent.edu/ehhs/spa/museum) has more than three thousand models and is the largest of its kind in the world, giving the department something to shout about.

It's everything you always wanted to know about hearing aids but might have been afraid to vocalize. Displayed in various cases throughout the hallways, you can trace their ear-as, starting with pre-electric horns, collectors, domes, trumpets, and resonators (1850s–1960s), including the museum's oldest model, a 160-year-old silver ear trumpet from the United Kingdom; electric (or carbon-based) hearing aids based on the principles of the telephone (1902–1940s); and the rather self-explanatory vacuum tube types (1921–1940s). There are 1950s transistor numbers popularized when Eleanor Roosevelt was photographed with an eyeglass version (geekiness squared?), behind-the-ear/in-the-ear jobs still used today, and finally, twenty-first-century digital versions, many of which are currently being developed.

Listen to a couple more really unusual examples: a 1923 Vibraphone, known as the "Radium Ear" due to a radium coating that may or may not have had a glow-in-the-dark effect, and an ear candle, a hollow tube made of fabric and wax. According to the museum website, "the smaller end . . . is placed into the outer ear canal and the opposite tip of the candle is lit. The flame is thought to create a vacuum and along with the heat, soften the [impacted ear] wax." That is, if you didn't set your hair on fire first. There are hearing aids made with a tuning fork, as well as those found in a wristwatch, fan, or pen. Hey, spies go deaf, too.

Visitors can also blast through an accumulation of audiometers used to test hearing loss, from a pre-electric 1910 Struycken Monochord up to 1960s models. Technical data sheets, advertising, photographs, patent information, house organs (so to speak), and trade journals are also available for those who might be interested in sounding out their own version of a better mouth trap.

★ ★

Eat, Drink, and Be Insulted
Kent

Toughen up your skin and haul your butt over to Mike's Place (1700
Water St. 44242, 330-673-6501, www.mikesplacerestaurant.com)
for an unparalleled dining experience that begins the moment you
pull into the parking lot. Along with an X-Wing fighter ("Sorry, display model only," states the website. "Mike uses the working model
to get to work everyday [*sic*]."), the building is annexed by a full-size
tour bus, complete with tables and chairs inside, and a faux castle that
looks like painted-over brick . . . or maybe papier-mâché. Whatever.

Mike's Place was unleashed on September 5, 1987. The world—or
at least the immediate surrounding area—hasn't been the same since,
according to the website, resulting in the addition of a mall ("built in
honor of Mike's Place") and a nearby Bob Evans, failed takeovers by
Burger King and McDonald's (in which the clown and other minions
reportedly left dejected), and a fire where "Ace Cooks Jeff and Wally
(a.k.a. Wally & the Beav) . . . Accidentally calls [*sic*] the Fire Dept.
instead of the Marshmallow Patrol, Spoils Kent's biggest Cookout
ever." Well, OK.

And then there are the rules of the house set forth by owner Mike
Kotensky, with the first one being "Mike is always right. (Just don't
ask his wife)." They basically boil down to shutting up and ordering
what's on the menu and making sure your kids behave "or we will
provide duct tape to help in the control process." This equal opportunity insult universe also refers to servers as wenches or trolls, depending upon their sex. There also seems to be an obsession with Hooters
(the restaurant chain), but let's not go there.

So why would anyone want to eat here in the first place? For one
thing, there's all manner of cool stuff on the walls, from neon signs to
license plates to pictures of visiting celebrities, as well as video games
galore and an impressive beer list. So just about every demographic
base is covered. And the menu itself is worth a guffaw or two: sandwich groaners include the 12-inch Dirk Diggler, the Reformed Yuppie

★ ★

with "chicken bosom," the Julius Cheezer, and a Bucket O' Balls—sauerkraut rounds which, if burned, are taken out back and swatted with a nine iron, or so they say.

All that "fore" play should intrigue diners, but it's the food that keeps 'em coming back. But make sure to tip the server, "or else you'll find out why the catapult is aimed at Bob Evans."

Low-Tech Superstore
Kidron

You know you've arrived in Amish country when you see minivans parked across the way from horse-and-buggy combos (the latter being the ones next to the piles of poop). And there's no better place to get acquainted with the "Plain" people than Lehman's Hardware (4779

Be careful of the horse poop on your way back to the minivan.

★ ★

Kidron Rd. 44618, 877-438-5346, www.lehmans.com), although many of the customers are English (non-Amish) retirees and schoolkids on field trips.

Nevertheless, Lehman's is a pantheon to good old-fashioned American ingenuity, the kind that thrived before the turn of the twentieth century. Founded by Jay Lehman in 1955 to serve the local Amish and others without all the modern conveniences, he took a tiny, one-room hardware enterprise and turned it into a big-box Valhalla of historical technology. It's a reminder that much of the world does without what most Americans consider to be the basic necessities of electricity and microchips. Even Hollywood has cranked up Lehman's products for such movies as *Cold Mountain, Pirates of the Caribbean,* and *Open Range* (gas or coal?).

The main entrance is the original store, which is fronted by several random antiques: a hundred-year-old Oil Pull farm tractor that supposedly occasionally still runs; a Civil War–era barn, rebuilt piece-by-piece; and that ultimate shoplifting deterrent, a jail cell, which is also a big hit with the youngsters. The ancient building is an almost dizzying miasma of new old stuff—unlike modern stores, every nook and cranny is filled with various gewgaws and gadgets. You definitely need to know what you're looking for and like hardware. A lot.

Still, it's an organized chaos, with housewares, stoves (including wood-burning) and accessories, gas appliances, and more in various rooms. It's fascinating in its own way—who knew that there were so many different varieties of oil lamps and water pumps? And it's easy to get turned around, so you might feel lost among legions of garden tools and weathervanes. But the employees are friendly and must have great memories because they know the location of just about every piece and part.

The Amish love it. The tourists love it. And, with a great website and an old-fashioned catalogue, it has a foot in both worlds. Who says there's no future in the past?

Here's Lookin' at You, Kids

Lucas

Back in the 1930s, when Hollywood glamour reigned supreme and stars and starlets had no worries about Internet sex tapes or stalking paparazzi, there was Malabar Farm (4050 Bromfield Rd. 44843, 419-892-2784, www.malabarfarm.org). It was the vision of Pulitzer Prize–winning author Louis Bromfield and his family, who moved back to his native Richland County from France. Bromfield used pioneering conservation methods to restore the land to its original fertility and worked to preserve the beauty of the surrounding forest.

The original mid-nineteenth-century "Big House," where the Bromfields lived, was remodeled extensively in 1939, resulting in thirty-two rooms of elegance and charm. In his book *Pleasant Valley*, Bromfield wrote, "Every inch of it [the house] has been in hard use since it was built and will, I hope, go on being used in the same fashion so long as it stands." Aw, c'mon, Louis, what was the real reason you left France for the middle of Ohio?

He's not talking—he's been dead since 1956—but he did the region a big favor on many levels. For one thing, like Mohammed, the world came to him in the form of famous personalities, most notably Humphrey Bogart and Lauren Bacall, who got hitched there in 1945. And it doesn't matter how old you are or even if you plan on never getting married (or married again), there's something special about going down the famous staircase where they walked to the tune of the "Wedding March," which emanates from the player piano. Many mementos, pictures, and books remain unchanged from the Bromfield era, along with antiques dating from the 1700s.

In addition to being an internationally acclaimed man of letters, Bromfield's ideas about conserving soil and sustainable agriculture are still in use today and are at work on the 914-acre estate, which includes the 2,500-plus-document Bromfield Resource Center, an agricultural library. Along with touring the smokehouse, dairy barn, and petting farm with its horses, pigs, goats, sheep, and more, you

★ ★

can also camp and fish on the grounds, though those age sixteen and older will need an Ohio fishing license. Or purchase organic produce at the Malabar Farm Gardens, some of which also shows up on the home-cooked menu at the Malabar Farm Restaurant, a restored stagecoach inn built in 1820.

It was Bromfield's goal to have the state take over the management of Malabar Farm, and indeed it did. Initially operated jointly by Ohio's Department of Natural Resources and Department of Agriculture, it became an Ohio state park in 1976. In death, as in life, what Louis Bromfield wants, he gets. Good thing he came back to Ohio.

Bible Studies
Mansfield

Everyone knows how boring Sunday school can get, sitting there for hours on end, amen, listening to someone drone on and on about parables and prophecies. Well, it doesn't have to be that way: Just take the kiddies to the Living Bible Museum (Diamond Hill Cathedral 44902, 500 Tingley Ave., 419-524-0139 or 800-222-0139, www.livingbiblemuseum.org) and they—and you—may never view the Old and New Testaments the same way again. There's also a collection of rare Bibles, woodcarvings, American folk art, and a Christian art gallery.

With more than seventy scenes and three hundred figures, it has the dubious honor of being Ohio's only life-size wax museum that depicts stories from the Bible. Never mind that some of the likenesses bear a suspicious resemblance to celebrities recycled from now-defunct collections. So even though Elizabeth Taylor, Donna Summer, and the Sweathogs from *Welcome Back, Kotter* have been spotted in various tableaux, keep in mind that this is the history of humankind we're talking about. Well, the Diamond Hill Cathedral congregation's version of that history, anyway.

Like so many journeys of its ilk, this began with a single step, thanks to pastor Richard Diamond and his late wife, Alwilda, who passed away in 2008. Back during the Vietnam War era, the Diamonds

Bringing religion to life—so to speak

had started Faith Revivals, an in-the-rough version of the current church, which was also known to some locals as the "congregation of those damn hippies." In the early 1970s the couple attended a crusade in Atlanta and happened upon a wax museum. "After viewing scenes of past presidents, generals, and war heroes to their surprise the last scene was the Ascension of Jesus Christ," recounts the Living Bible website. "As they both stood looking they were both brought to tears

★ ★

and brought to their knees. As they were feeling God's great holy presence, Rev. Diamond knew what one day he was to accomplish for the Lord."

The Diamonds' mining efforts have resulted in gems of scenes depicting the life of Christ, including the prophecy, his birth, his ministry, and the Passion, which begins with the Last Supper and ends with something called "The Great White Throne Judgment," which hopefully won't involve a trip to the bathroom. Then it's on to the Miracles of the Old Testament, which is chock-full of those familiar stories about violence, destruction, and mayhem, or rather "faith, courage, and hope," according to the brochure. Finish your sojourn with the Sowers of Faith, a mini-version of the Old Testament, as well as displays about Christian martyrs and the Reformation.

By now you may have worked up quite an appetite—so much suffering, so little time—so if it happens to be open, a quick stop at Solomon's Snack Bar might be in order'. There's also usually a Christian dinner theater on Saturday nights as well. Chow down on an apple-free Eve's Fruit Salad or a Samson Burger—or maybe not. No one really knows what happened to his hair after Delilah got through with him.

Well-Preserved
Mansfield

Fans of the mice-scenario taxidermy of Barry (Steve Carell) in the recent movie *Dinner for Schmucks* will find the Mansfield Memorial Museum (34 Park Ave. West 44902, 419-524-9924, www.the mansfieldmuseum.com) to be the cat's meow. Along with a band of rats playing a symphony are a variety of critters frozen in the motions of Victorian-era life: getting married, going to work, having tea, sawing wood. Created by the museum's founder, Civil War veteran Edward Wilkinson, their authenticity is enhanced by the fact that they appear to not have been touched since being placed in the display case sometime around the turn of the twentieth century.

Elektro contemplates his return to Hollywood.

In fact, the entire hodgepodge collection—tucked rather anonymously in a somewhat creaky late 1880s building in not-so-bustling downtown Mansfield—has something for everyone. There's Elektro the robot, star of the 1939-1940 New York World's Fair. You'll also find the world's largest collection of ¹⁄₇₂ scale airplanes, built by the (obviously bored) Mansfield Ohio Air National Guard in the late 1970s, after the war in Vietnam War had ended and the students had stopped rioting, as well as the usual stuff found in museums—a collection of Native American artifacts dating from prehistoric times, remnants of the Zulu Wars of 1879, masks and more dead animals from Africa, Civil War memorabilia, and so on.

★ ★

But most people come to see Elektro. He has held up pretty well, considering the fact that he was in pieces for decades, his head given to his creator, Westinghouse executive Harold Gorsuch, as a retirement present, and the rest of his body stuck in a storage locker until he was resurrected in the mid-2000s for a display at the museum about early robots. The first "true" robot who could walk by voice command, Elektro and his faithful dog Sparko were assembled at the Mansfield Westinghouse appliance division plant in the late 1930s.

While the science behind Elektro's amazing (for the times) feats seems somewhat quaint and involves vacuum tubes, photoelectric cells, telephone relays, and a 78-rpm record player, the seven-foot-tall, three hundred–pounder got around, in more ways than one. Along with answering audience questions and even telling dirty jokes—he had a limitless vocabulary, as long as he was supplied with fresh records—he could "smoke" a cigarette, count, play the piano, and order Sparko to do tricks. In the '40s and '50s, he traveled the country in the Elektromobile, promoting the company's line of household products and eventually ended up as a display at an amusement park in Oceanside, California.

Thanks to YouTube and the Internet, Elektro's film career also lives on. While his screen debut was in the 1939 movie *The Middleton Family* at the New York's World Fair, his most memorable role was two decades later as "Thinko" the college's supercomputer in *Sex Kittens Go to College*. In one scene, shared with chimp Voltaire, he ogles strippers, making suggestive noises and flashing his eyes. Definitely worth checking out when things get slow at work or home.

Along with Elektro, the museum also features memorabilia and artifacts of other early robots including predecessor Televox, built in 1927. Sparko seems to have wandered off permanently, although maybe someday the mechanical tail-wagger will resurface in another Steve Carell movie.

Big Fun House
Mansfield

When you drive up to the Mansfield Reformatory (100 Reformatory Rd. 44902, 419-522-2644, www.mrps.org), make sure to turn onto Reformatory Road, and not the parking lot of the adjacent Richland Correctional Institution. Otherwise, you may find your stay will last more than just a couple of hours. But at least you'll have an actual "prison guard encounter." While although the guards are polite to the accidental visitor, they will make sure you see their billy clubs and big guns.

And you really can't miss it—the Dracula-esque colossus, with its seemingly endless stretch of stone Gothic spires, stands out in twenty-first-century mid-Ohio like a Circuit City in 1880s Transylvania. It's

A two-fer: prison and Halloween attraction

almost as if a clever promoter thought, "What a great idea for a Halloween attraction!" Which it is, among other things.

But back in 1896, when it was first opened as the Ohio State Reformatory (OSR), Cleveland architect Levi T. Scofield designed it to encourage the inmates—mostly juvenile and first-time offenders—to experience a "rebirth" of their spiritual lives. Nice thought, but that didn't stop it from being the site of the murder of two corrections officers in 1926 and 1932; the genesis of the 1948 spree of the "Mad Dog Killers," who murdered OSR farm superintendent John Niebel, his wife, and their twenty-year-old daughter, among others; and the suspicious 1950 suicide of a prison superintendent's wife and his subsequent death from a heart attack nine years later. It's a prison, for crying out loud (and the inmates undoubtedly did a lot of that as well).

By the early 1930s the reformatory had already become overcrowded and outdated, and in subsequent decades was deemed to have passed its cell-by date. So it was decreed unfit to serve as a prison, and was closed in that capacity in December 1990. Nevertheless, the building is extremely cool-looking and was considered one of the top institutions of its time. And though it's mostly crumbling, chilly, and rather spooky inside, it still houses the world's largest freestanding cell block, which is six tiers high.

But there's life in the old castle yet. A Hollywood favorite, it's been the site of such movies as *Air Force One, The Shawshank Redemption,* and *Harry and Walter Go to New York;* travel documentaries; and even a video for the heavy-metal band Godsmack (who?). The Mansfield Reformatory Preservation Society (MRPS) was formed in 1992; they now hold the deed and are in the process of renovating certain sections. Along with Sunday tours (daily during warm weather), they also do a land-office business as a Halloween haunt and have overnight ghost hunts.

In 2003 the MRPS added an electric-chair replica display, although no one was officially put to death while it was a prison, and it never housed such an actual device. As if the building itself doesn't have enough shock value.

Loose Caboose

Milan

Sorry, would-be lovers. Rather than being a dating service or a honeymoon spot, the Coupling Reserve is twenty acres of somewhat rugged, sloping land near a river bottom that includes paved trails for easy hiking and get-togethers for all ages, as well as a more challenging lower level accessed only by a gravel road for canoeing, picnicking, and climbing. Since it's near water, the trails can get slippery when wet, so wear practical shoes and bring a walking stick if necessary.

Although the Coupling refers to train and not human hookups, you can attempt the latter in the little red caboose near the entrance of

A place to "couple" . . . or not

the park (11618 Rte. 13, 44846, 419-625-7783, www.milanarea.com/couplingreserve.htm). That is, if you don't mind the bunkhouse setup (it sleeps eight), the fact that showers are located in the nearby station depot, or the occasional mouse or other uninvited critter. There's also a less aesthetically pleasing boxcar next door that can accommodate up to another eighteen people, so you may have lots of two-legged neighbors as well. Still, it's a deal: The whole shebang can be rented year-round for a nominal fee for family gatherings and "other approved activities," according to the park brochure, which probably doesn't include parties involving racy underwear and other accoutrements meant to spice up one's love life.

But romance? You might have better luck in a private cabin or an overnight lodge at another state park.

Bright Idea Man
Milan

Little-known facts about Thomas Edison and his birthplace (9 North Edison Dr. 44846, 419-499-2135, www.tomedison.org):

In 1847, the year he was born, his hometown of Milan was the second-largest wheat-shipping port in the world (after the Ukrainian city of Odessa). A shipbuilding center, it also produced seventy-five lake schooners that year.

Young Tom was considered "addled." His father beat him regularly, and he also got into trouble at school. Of course, Dad became impressed with his son's brilliance after Tom invented the phonograph and incandescent light.

Edison was granted 1,093 U.S. patents, more than any inventor before or since. He was also working on a device that would communicate with the dead, but he passed away before he could test it out.

Edison only lived in the abode—which was rather luxe by the standards of those days—until he was seven, when the family moved to Michigan. Because much of their original furniture was lost in moves and in a fire at their Port Huron home, the kindness of strangers,

Faded photographs and phonographs from the Edison Museum

relatives, and friends had to be relied upon to refurnish the birthplace as authentically as possible when it was turned into a museum. But you can see the room—and bed—where Tom was born and a rare collection of Edisonia, such as faded photographs advertising his "moving pictures," phonographs, a talking doll that sounds like a bunch of men yelling (they were), a mimeograph machine, and a stock ticker, among many other things. And the guides—especially the ones who have been around for decades—are full of amusing stories and anecdotes about the Edison family's idiosyncrasies.

Although Edison didn't die until 1931 at the age of ninety, his family was devoted to preserving his legacy early on. In 1894 his sister, Marion Edison Page, purchased the house, adding a bathroom and other modern conveniences. Edison became the owner in 1906, and was shocked on his last visit in 1923 to find it was still lit with lamps and candles. After his death his second wife, Mina Miller Edison, and their daughter, Mrs. John Eyre Sloane, made it their personal mission to memorialize the home, and it opened on the centennial of the inventor's birth in 1947.

It's one of the few structures that didn't end up at old pal Henry Ford's Greenfield Village in Dearborn, Michigan, or at Glenmont, Edison's mansion that's now part of the National Park Service site in West Orange, New Jersey. Tom would have been proud of this iconoclastic outpost that preserves his memories and spirit of originality.

Plowshares into Swords
New London

Let's face it: When it comes to combat, a bowie knife such as those manufactured by the Ames Sword Company (South Railroad Street 44851, 800-345-3682, www.amessword.com) is no match for the standard USMC Shoulder Mounted Assault Weapon, which with a single wave of thermobaric power, can take out an entire building. Or even stun guns and Tasers, which incapacitate rather than kill. Beam me up, Scotty.

Nevertheless, practically since the Revolutionary War—since 1791 in Chelmsford, Massachusetts, to be exact—Ames has been hacking away at the ever-dwindling sword market. Part of the reason for its longevity is that it's only had a couple of changes in ownership: The M. C. Lilley Company of Columbus purchased it from the Ames family in the mid-1930s, and the C. E. Ward Company bought it in 1951, which is how it ended up in rural New London, in the middle of plowshare country.

Along with being the oldest, it also has an edge as the foremost supplier, having provided swords for Uncle Sam since 1832, through the Civil War and beyond, for everyone from field soldiers to generals

★ ★

to U.S. presidents, producing the first presentation swords ever commissioned by Congress to honor heroes of the Mexican War. In fact,
it's probably safe to say that until recent times, when the government decided it was cheaper to contract our weapons out to the very
Third World countries who might want to see North Korea become a
dominant nuclear power, an Ames sword has been in just about every
battle the United States has ever fought.

Each of the armed services has its own ceremonial and regulation
swords and sabers (you never know when you'll need a backup, even
if it is low-tech). And societies and fraternal organizations, such as the
Knights of Columbus and the Masons, still use them for their secret
macho-guy rituals. Even mohels might employ them for Jewish circumci-
sions . . . well, maybe not. Still, they're ornate and handcrafted, and if
you want to stop in and buy one, you won't need a weapons permit.

The production process has remained relatively unchanged, and
Ames has one of the largest brass, bronze, and iron foundries in the
country. They used to give informal tours, but due to a sharp rise in visitors chopped that off because they're too busy making swords. Still, the
website offers a virtual tour, along with a complete lineup and (groan!)
sword tips. Oh, and their president is named Russel L. Sword. Really.

Mother of All Flags
Norwalk

Back in the 1960s, during the height of the Vietnam War protests,
you could get arrested for wearing an American flag on your person.
Today not only can you purchase clothes that look like Old Glory, but
they've made a flag so big it takes fifteen to twenty people and a tractor to raise and lower it. How times have changed.

This mother of all flags came about in 1976, during the American
bicentennial, when the Norwalk Veterans of Foreign Wars (140 Milan
Ave. 44857, 419-668-2335) purchased the largest flag to ever fly
from a mast. At 46 feet wide and 70 feet long, it weighs 120 pounds
and requires a specially built 150-foot tower. The stars are two feet

across, and the stripes are forever—actually, they're four feet wide. It can only be flown when the weather is calm; otherwise, whoever is raising or lowering it may become airborne, which happened at least once. The monster flag is usually only displayed on special occasions like the Fourth of July and Veterans Day, though a phone call to the VFW yielded the response, "When is Veterans Day, anyway?" (Answer: November 11, even if it doesn't fall on a Monday.)

In 2003 disaster struck: A strong gust of wind blew through the flag, and it became entangled in the pole, taking it out, along with a baseball backstop. Even worse, it ripped right down one of the red stripes and was seriously damaged. You might say it flagged itself down. The manufacturer, Norwalk Furniture Company, kindly offered to repair the flag.

The VFW is taking no chances with the replacement pole, which consists of seven tons of fabricated metal. Not only does it have an electric pulley, but its four-foot-wide concrete base reaches twenty-two feet into the ground. So these colors won't run, no matter what.

Stairway to Heaven
Oberlin

It resembles a locomotive version of the old Led Zeppelin song, but the railroad tracks rising out of nowhere in the middle of the Oberlin College campus (South Professor Street near the intersection of West College Street 44074) are actually a tribute to the town's abolitionist routes, er, roots. In 1977 the college celebrated the community's ties—railroad and otherwise—through this rather odd-looking seventeen-by-eighteen-foot metal and iron sculpture.

Although to the uninformed eye it may seem more college prank than serious art, the temporary exhibit by student Cameron Armstrong, which was so well received it became a permanent installation, honors the "conductors" and others in the small town who, prior to the Civil War, helped scores of slaves escape to freedom. Not only was Oberlin Stop 99 on the Underground Railroad—with Stop 100 being Canada and freedom—but town and gown united in the Oberlin-Wellington Rescue of 1858, in which citizens intervened in the apprehension of fugitive slave John Price, storming the hotel where Price was being held by federal marshals and ensuring his safe passage to Canada.

Members of the community also participated in abolitionist John Brown's historic October 16, 1859, raid on the federal arsenal in Harpers Ferry, Virginia, with the plan of using the weapons to arm slaves for a revolt. Within thirty-six hours of the attack, most of the twenty-one men had been killed or captured, and Brown himself was hanged on December 2 of that year, folks back then not being much for delaying trials or filing appeals.

A group of citizens, the Friends of the Oberlin Underground Railroad Center (www.oberlinundergroundrailroad.bravehost.com, 440-774-1731), is trying to pump steam into a larger memorial: an Oberlin Underground Railroad Center in the historic Gasholder Building south of town. They also conduct tours of local historic sites, including Freedom Walks to raise awareness about John Price and the Oberlin-Wellington Rescue.

Although such places are hardly "curiosities," the notion of one human being owning another is stranger than any bizarre exhibit, intentional or otherwise.

Smucker's Mother Ship
Orrville

It stands like a beacon in the middle of Ohio farm country, a tall white timber-frame barn with giant kissing strawberries. Your mouth starts watering the minute you hit the parking lot: You've arrived at Simply Smucker's (333 Wadsworth Rd. 44667, 330-684-1500, www.smuckers.com/simplysmuckers), the Orrville flagship store with its all-inclusive array of all things Smucker—some 350 different jellies, jams, toppings, and more. It just has to be good.

There's lots of other cool stuff as well: kitchen gewgaws, magnets and clothing adorned with the trademark gingham, a twenty-nine-foot handcrafted apple press, a Pillsbury Doughboy cookie jar that just begs

★ ★

to be stomped on because when you open it, it makes that annoying trademark giggle (the J. M. Smucker Company purchased Pillsbury in 2004). But at around $50, it would hardly be a cheap thrill.

Pretty amazing, considering that Orrville resident J. M. Smucker's pressed cider allegedly originated from plantings from none other than the Big Appleseed himself, Johnny. Smucker opened his first mill in 1897, later expanding his offerings to apple butter, which he sold from the back of a horse-drawn wagon. He signed the lid of every crock, and four subsequent generations spread out (so to speak) to fruit and ice-cream toppings, peanut butter (they also acquired Jif), and Crisco. If it goes on with a knife, it's fair game. Today the J. M. Smucker Company has more than 3,500 employees worldwide and distributes products in forty-five-plus countries.

Simply Smucker's has a basic game plan: You walk in, grab a basket, and start sampling. Expect to spend a lot of time deciding whether you want fruit butter, jam, jelly, low-sugar or sugar-free preserves, simply fruit, or a squeeze bottle. It's a dizzying array of choices, and to their credit, the Smucker folks have included a lot of items for folks with special dietary needs. There's also a peanut butter and jelly activity corner for the littlest customers; they start 'em young and keep 'em hooked on the gingham jar. Ice cream and other treats can be found at an old-time soda shop.

OK, so it's pretty kitschy, but you can always rationalize the visit by purchasing a gift basket for Aunt Esmeralda.

Living Large
Seville

The biggest thing to hit the hamlet of Seville (population: approx 2,100) came after the end of the Civil War in the form of human giants Captain Martin Van Buren Bates and his wife Anna Swan Bates. Together they wielded almost a half-ton of influence: A native of Kentucky, the captain stood 7'9" and weighed 470 pounds. Anna, who was born in Nova Scotia, was 7'11" tall and weighed 413 pounds.

Unlike these somewhat to scale reproductions,
the married giants did have facial features.

Intimates of royalty, friends of celebrities, and renowned in international medical circles, they received more feet of newspaper coverage than any other couple in the county's history.

Born in Kentucky and trained as a schoolteacher, Martin rose to captain in the Confederacy, freaking out the other side with his size and ferocity. He returned there at the end of the war but, tired of the ongoing feud between the still-clashing sides, ran away to join the circus in Cincinnati because he, unlike most people, actually could. The circus toured Canada, where he met his future wife Anna. Big love ensued, and they wed in 1871 at St. Martin-in-the-Fields in London. It was huge in more ways than one: Thousands tried to attend and Queen Victoria herself, who was a personal friend, gave them ginormous diamond-studded gold watches as wedding presents.

Just why they picked Seville after leaving the circus is not quite clear, but their super-size home on 130 acres boasted fourteen-foot ceilings and customized furniture built to scale. Anna gave birth twice, to an eighteen-pound stillborn girl in 1872, and then again seven years later to a twenty-two-pound son who died shortly thereafter. She herself passed away in 1888, and Martin married a normal-sized woman two years later, living in as much anonymity as someone of that magnitude could until his death in 1919.

You can experience their life and times in several ways. The Seville County Historical Society (70 West Main St. 44273, 330-441-2115) features papier-mâché reproductions of the couple and artifacts from their original farmhouse, including a huge crib constructed for their second child. A few blocks away on East Main Street at the Mound Hill Cemetery is their grave with a life-size (read: extremely large) statue of Anna commissioned by Martin from Europe after she passed away; Martin and their son are buried there as well. And each September brings the Giantfest (www.giantfest.com) to town, with its oversized veggie display, pie-eating competition (for big appetites), Bates family tent featuring Martin's descendants, and tallest man and woman contest. The latter should be easy to spot; they'll be head and shoulders above the rest.

★ ★

It's Alive! (Sort Of)

Steubenville

Remember Beary Bear, Plentiful Penguin, Strawberry Bunny, and the Gamuffins? Hmm, maybe not . . . Well, how about those animated characters for SeaWorld, Hershey's Chocolate World, and Disney World? Or those displays in the Vegas casinos at the Excalibur and Venetian hotels? Now we're talking!

As are some of the products of the Creegan Company (508 Washington St. 43952, 740-283-3708, www.creegans.com), the nation's largest manufacturer of animated and costumed characters, which according to their motto has been "making things move since 1959." They also have brought to life—at least as close as humankind can get, short of actual cloning—such notables as Albert Einstein, Alexander Graham Bell, King Tut, and G.I. Joe. Plus they have enlivened various tableaux for Christmas, Halloween, Easter, and other seasonal events as well as for amusement parks, shopping malls, and retail stores.

And you, the lucky consumer, can take a tour of the place and according to the website, watch "artists and crafts people design, sculpt, decorate, and mechanize" the critters on "the three-floor factory [where] your guide leads you into a virtual craft heaven containing what must be thousands of spools of ribbon of every color, pattern, and texture. Puppet heads, scenery, and props lurk behind silk flowers and craft paraphernalia." Ooh, scary . . . not!

Like most successful enterprises, they've worked out a system. A sculptor creates the basic design, which is sent to a huge vacuum machine that makes faces—of the mold, that is. Elves, er, workers then paint on expressions and put together costumes. The shelving area is a bloodless morgue of plaster heads, feet, and hands. A trip to the mechanics/electronics department reveals "workbenches laden with toolboxes, hand tools, lathes, vises and drill presses. Peek inside some headless mechanized bodies to discover some figures' detailed electronic insides and to see how the parts unite to produce a character's body movements." All the excitement of *CSI* and *House* without the gore.

★ ★

The folks at Creegan also specialize in a process called Taximation, bringing dead critters such as squirrels, bobcats, and coyotes back to robotic life. Fortunately, they haven't extended it to include human corpses. Now that would be creepy.

Don't Go There
Summit County

Some people have way too much free time on their hands. Such may be the case with the Internet-fueled horror of Hell Town, a Bermuda quadrangle of mostly deserted land located in northern Summit County (44223), including Boston and Boston Township and parts of Peninsula, Sagamore Hills, and Northfield Center Township.

The setup: First settled in 1806, Boston, the oldest village in Summit County, was home to a prosperous paper mill. Everything was fine until the late 1960s, when preservationists (aka "tree huggers") kicked up some dust about the destruction of natural resources to make—you guessed it—paper. So in 1974 President Gerald Ford stumbled onto some legislation enabling the National Park Service to preserve hundreds of acres in the area as Cuyahoga Valley National Park, thus saving the forests for the trees.

The sting: You can't fight City Hall, and especially not Uncle Sam if he wants your house. So people evacuated in droves, emptying entire towns, leaving vacant, boarded-up residences fronted by scary-looking, formidable U.S. Government NO TRESPASSING signs. Some were burned down as exercises for local fire departments, while others stood next to them deserted, giving the impression that entire populations had been whisked away by unfriendly aliens (which, in a sense, they had).

The legend: Now the rumor mill began to grind, undoubtedly fueled by the region's rolling, spooky fogs. "When darkness falls and black fingers of horror claw through this mist-shrouded valley, spirits of the dead rise from their graves," speculated an article in the Cleveland *Plain Dealer.* "Satan worshippers celebrate midnight candlelight masses in country churches marked by inverted crosses. The screaming ghosts of murdered children ride for eternity in a spectral school bus. Abandoned houses are haunted by mutant humans deformed by toxic chemical spills that forced them from their homes. Motorists lost on lonely wooded lanes are dragged from their cars and slain by an ax-wielding madman."

The reality: Of course, the article went on to disprove 99 percent of this, citing ghostbusters such as James Willis, head of a nonprofit group dedicated to researching alleged hauntings in the state. Willis debunked sixteen Hell Town legends on his website (www.ghostsof ohio.org), exposing, for example, the haunted school bus as a vehicle converted into a temporary residence by a remodeling homeowner, and the upside-down crosses as a common element found in the architecture of Gothic Revival churches. And the stupid questions ("Are you a local Satan worshiper?"), midnight graveyard visits, and related pranks by curiosity-seekers were beginning to piss off the remaining villagers, who were very much alive.

Sure, you can try to go to Hell Town, but do you really need to? Yeah, there's the cemetery and the Mother of Sorrows Church and such purported landmarks as the End of the World Road, Cry Baby Ridge, and the Crazy House in the Woods. But there might be more thrills in a Stephen King novel or *Friday the 13th* horror movie. And if you run into the descendants of the giant python that reportedly escaped from a traveling circus several decades ago, then you really might have a problem.

Amish Disneyland
Trail/Walnut Creek

Getting to Yoder's Amish Home (6050 Rte. 515, between Trail and Walnut Creek 44654, 330-893-2541, www.yodersamishhome.com) can be a real challenge. It's actually fairly close to Behalt, not several miles away in Millersburg as the address indicates. And getting lost in Amish country—even if it's only for a short distance—can be a real time suck, especially if you're behind a parade of buggies on a winding

★ ★

Home is where the plain stuff is—at least for the Amish.

country road in a no-pass lane (though many buggy drivers are courte-
ous and will pull aside to let you pass). And you can basically forget
about GPS and MapQuest. They're usually not very accurate out here,

so you may find yourself pulling up to an actual Amish person's home, with hanging laundry and the whole nineteenth-century schmear, and doing the old-school thing of asking for directions. Or you could just call Yoder's (recommended).

But once you get there, it's Amish Disneyland without the lines or giant animated characters. You can have your very own black buggy ride around the 116-acre farm with its friendly animals, although petting the ducks, pigs, and chickens is probably not a good idea. More critters can be found inside the 1885 barn, which in the spring is full of baby bunnies, lambs, puppies, and colts (awww . . .).

Also on the property are two authentic homes. The first contains furnishings typical of an Amish farmhouse in the late 1800s. Built in 1866 its wood floors, simple furniture, and hand-powered appliances provide a glimpse of what it's like to be a Plain person, straight pins and all, which they still wear in their clothing today. The larger residence, constructed in 1885, had been lived in for a hundred years and was the site, like many Amish homes, of church services, which lasted for three hours. But the kitchen is redolent of freshly baked breads, cinnamon rolls, and lots of different kinds of cookies. Yum! It almost makes you yearn for the simpler lifestyle, until you think of sitting there for half a day on that hard wooden bench, hoping that the pins in your clothes won't stick you if you get restless and wiggle too much. Never mind.

A tour of the farm works toward demystifying the Amish. Their young people do have an opportunity to experience the "English" way of life and drive cars and wear trendy clothes (with buttons and zippers!), though most of them return to the church. And contrary to popular belief, the Amish do pay taxes and utilize modern medicine. Nevertheless, they're likely not going to get rich, because also unlike Disneyland, you can visit the craft shop—with its quilts, pottery, and other handmade goods—and come away with change in your pocket. Just like McDonald's . . . actually, more like Old MacDonald's.

★ ★

Double Your Fun
Twinsburg

Seeing double? Perhaps not, if it's the first full weekend in August in Twinsburg during Twins Days (44087, 330-425-3652, www.twinsdays.org).

And it's no cutesy marketing ploy that the town is named Twinsburg, either. In 1819, according to www.twinsburg.com/homemain.

Good News

According to some sources, Holmes County has the largest Amish community in the United States, if not the world. So it should come as no surprise that *The Budget* (330-852-4634, www.thebudgetnewspaper.com), the big-time newspaper serving the Amish and Mennonite communities around the globe, should be located near the epicenter—big-time, of course, being a relative term.

The local edition is similar to most papers: It has a front page with news, a sports section, and feature articles. There are also fat advertising circulars that fall out when you pick it up. However, the national edition is an entirely different animal, with a format basically unchanged since the paper's inception in 1890. It cannot be found on the websiteand must be purchased manually (of course, subscriptions are always available). Information is supplied by Amish and Mennonite "scribes" in the form of colorful missives describing events in their communities.

For example, this just in from Osceola, Missouri: "Noah Stutzman had a frolic 2 days in a row last week to work [on a roof for] their house . . . A lot of nails were bent trying to drive them into dried ash

asp, Aaron and Moses Wilcox, identical twins from Killingworth, Connecticut, "purchased some 4,000 acres of land and began selling small parcels at low prices to attract other settlers."

It was definitely a twofer: They "offered six acres of land for a public square and $20 toward starting the first school if the residents would change the settlement's name from Millsville to Twinsburg." Additionally "they were lifelong business partners; held all their

2 x 4s. Dan M. Gingerrich carried a little plastic cap of axle grease to lubricate his nails so . . . working close to him was a plus." The ones on his fingers or the ones being used for the roof? (Answer: the latter.)

Or this, from a Loganville, Wisconsin, scribe: "Recently we were eating lunch, when we heard a thudding on the ramp . . . We looked toward the door, expecting someone . . . the racket kept on and on and we went to look . . . and whom [sic] should it be but a horse! Our son Ferman's horse Buddy." And he didn't even knock!

And then there are cooking tips (from Shipshewana, Indiana): "Today I went to visit Paige Creek School and am planning to treat them with cheater donuts. They are very simple; use rolls of refrigerator biscuits, make a hole with a thimble, drop in hot oil, fry til golden, roll in sugar and pop them in your mouth." You might want to let the little posers cool first.

The secret of *The Budget*'s success is simple, according to the website: "[It] has earned a faithful following by providing its readers with a unique newspaper; a newspaper in which the good news reported in its pages routinely outweighs the bad." Not to mention the unintentionally hilarious.

★ ★

property in common; married sisters; had the same number of children; contracted the same fatal ailment; died within hours of each other and are buried in the same grave in Twinsburg's Locust Grove Cemetery." Wow, talk about imitation of life!

Twins Days came about in 1976, as a way to honor the dynamic duo. Only thirty-seven sets of twins, mostly from northern Ohio, showed up and spent the day dedicating a monument to the Wilcoxes and doing the usual festival things. But most importantly, they had twice as much fun and decided to duplicate the event every year! It's grown into a two-day (but of course) international gathering that attracts some three thousand pairs of twins, including assorted triplets, quadruplets, and quintuplets, who even though there are even more of them, are charged the same per head as twins (whose festival is it, anyway?). The festival has earned a place in *Guinness World Records* as the World's Largest Annual Gathering of Twins (well, duh!).

They come from as far away as Asia and Africa and usually dress alike, especially for the highlight Double-Take Parade. There are contests for Most Alike and Least Alike, a fireworks display, a golf tournament (double bogies?), a talent show, and the Royal Court, "with a pair of Kings, Queens, Princes and Princesses," according to the Twins Day website. "They ride in a special vehicle near the front of the parade, and sit at the review stand at the end of the parade. All royalty get sashes. Kings get crowns, queens and princesses get tiaras, princes get scepters. There is no bias given to identicals; many fraternal sets have been chosen as royalty." Twin PC, as it were.

But everyone, even the lone twin whose sidekick failed to make it to the event, gets to participate in the group photo. Still, you'd better be able to prove your double (or more) identity.

★ ★

Brothers of Invention
Uniontown

Wow. Menches Brothers Original Hamburgers (3700 Massillon Rd.,
Suite 130, Shops of Green 44685; 330-896-2288; www.menchesbros.
com) claims a triple crown in terms of inventing convenience food: the
hamburger, the ice-cream cone, and—last but not least—what eventually became Cracker Jack. What a prize!

Weight watchers, before you take a contract out on these folks,
please understand there are lots of contenders for the title of alpha
burger-meister. They include "Hamburger Charlie" Nagreen, who
cooked up a flattened meatball sandwich in 1885 in Seymour, Wisconsin; Louis Lassen of New Haven, Connecticut, who concocted a
burgerlike sandwich in 1890 for a customer in a hurry; and Fletcher
"Old Dave" Davis of Athens, Texas, whose creation was widely recognized as popularizing the burger at the 1904 St. Louis World's Fair. Or
maybe it was just a meat-ing of like minds.

Regardless, the Menches' story goes like this: In 1885 brothers
Charles and Frank traveled to the Erie County Fair in New York as part
of a concessionaire operation. At the time, the Menches specialized
in sausage sandwiches, but ran out of pork at that particular festival.
So they asked "Where's the beef?" and found some, which they fried
up on a gasoline stove. It tasted rather bland, so they added coffee,
brown sugar, and a "secret ingredient," creating a recipe still used
today. The thing needed a name, and since they were in the town of
Hamburg . . . get it? So there, posers.

But as the TV ad says: Wait, there's more. The brothers peddled
caramel-coated peanuts and popcorn with a prize inside at the 1893
World's Fair in Chicago, calling their product Gee Whiz. But über–food
producer Frito-Lay, which alleges to have sold enough Cracker Jack to
circle the globe nearly seventy times, gives credit to F. W. Ruckheim
and his brother for rustling up that particular snack at the same time
and place.

★ ★

The origin of many of today's major food groups

The competition heats up even more with the ice-cream cone. Here, some sixty people claim to have invented it at the 1904 World's Fair. The Menches' version involves Frank and Charles making waffles with Parisian irons, and wrapping said waffles around a fid, a cone-shaped tool used to splice ropes. Voila, an edible, hand-held ice-cream-eating device.

Whatever . . . The bottom line is that it tastes good, and you can still get the original flavors of burger and ice-cream cone, among other comfort foods like pasta, prime rib, and mac and cheese. And the critics also say "bite me"; Menches has won "Best Cheeseburger," "Most Creative Hamburger," and "Best Overall Burger" from the Akron-based National Hamburger Festival (www.hamburgerfestival.com) for several years running.

Much to Do about Very Little

Vermilion

Ohioans and others in nearby states must really love a parade. Otherwise, why would tens of thousands of 'em gather each fall in the charming resort town of Vermilion to celebrate . . . caterpillar races?

OK, so we're not talking about just any old crawler—it's the "woolly bear" caterpillar of the Isabella tiger moth, kind of a cute critter (for a larva) that got its name from its fluffy appearance. This particular species has black at both ends and a coppery red racing stripe down the middle. They're especially prominent in the fall, and legend (or urban myth) has it that the amount of black fuzz on the bug will predict the length of winter. The more black, the more snow. If the middle stripe is wide, winter will be mild. If the front end is dark, winter will start out severe. If the rear is dark, the end of winter will be cold. You could base an entire Woolly Bear Weather Channel on it or maybe a reality show.

For now, devotees will have to settle for a one-day family festival, the largest of its kind in the state (44089, 440-967-4477, http://vermilionohionews.homestead.com/Woollybear.html). There's a two-hour parade with woolly bear–clad kids and pets (dogs, cats, ferrets, etc.) in hay wagons, twenty marching bands with nearly two thousand musicians, vintage automobiles, queens (the kind you crown), floats, clowns, and more. There are costume contests, two-legged races, and appearances by TV personalities from Cleveland's Fox affiliate, Channel 8. But the worm really turns at 5:00 p.m. during the woolly bear races and the final predictions. Actually, it's probably more entertaining to watch the crowd at that point.

The festival began in the early 1970s when the PTA of the nearby tiny community of Birmingham was fishing for a way to raise funds. They'd heard about Dick Goddard, a veteran weatherman at Fox 8, who'd been talking up an idea about a celebration based on the woolly bear's forecast. The PTA baited the hook by offering to stage the festival, with Goddard as host. They snagged so many participants that they had to cast a wider net and moved it to the larger town of Vermilion.

So if you enjoy fast-paced events such as watching paint dry and caterpillars race and like seeing people and animals dressed up in weird costumes, you've come to the right place.

Wild Thing Kingdom
Walnut Creek

Have you ever wanted to be so close to a zebra or giraffe that you might get pooped on? Offer food to a llama only to have it spit on you? Be slobbered on (or maybe accidentally nipped) by a half dozen exotic species of hungry goats, sheep, cattle, or deer? Get a whopping case of poison ivy, because you forgot to put on close-toed shoes and instead wore sandals?

If the answer to any of these is "yes," then the Amish owned and operated Farm at Walnut Creek (4147 County Rd. 114, 44681, 330-893-4200, www.thefarmatwalnutcreek.com) may be for you. Even if it's "no" you might want to check it out, if only to view and feed some of the over five hundred animals from six different continents. They include buffalo, watusi (the cow, not the dance), red kangaroos, Nilgai antelope, dromedary camels, Vietnamese pot-bellied pigs, and many more critters not normally seen around these here parts.

There are a couple of options for touring. You can take the weenie route and drive your own car through the 120-acre compound into the enclosed wildlife area. At best you will get some great photos (animals only, no Amish since their religion forbids it) and can linger as long as you wish. At worst, your car may get head-butted by rambunctious longhorn cattle or the buffalo—you're not supposed to feed them, for obvious reasons.

Or climb aboard the jostling wagon and rub shoulders with Amish and English alike, while the friendly driver discusses the various species, with the animals in hot pursuit of their next meal. (Not you, but rather the buckets of grain feed given to visitors.) Take care to keep purses and sunglasses under the seat lest they fall out—those emus are slaves

✦ ✦

to fashion—and anything with a beak should be fed directly from the pail, unless getting pecked is on your bucket list. Afterwards, you can explore the grounds, with its blacksmith shop, produce stand, gift shop, and authentic farm houses, and reminisce about your wildlife encounter.

Down (or is it up?) on The Farm

* *

It Takes a Village . . .
Warren

Did you know the center of the world is located on Route 5 in Warren (44481), near the intersection where it diverges from Route 82? Most people don't, but there's an Ohio Department of Transportation (ODOT) sign saying so. And it's the government, so we have to believe them, right? Anyway, back to this teeny-weeny sign in Warren. Well, it's not that small, but it's not exactly easy to locate either when you're navigating traffic and people are passing you giving you another, more universal sign because you're driving a tad below the speed limit.

The whole "Center of the World" thing got its start in the 1840s, when Pennsylvanian Randell Wilmot moved to Warren and opened a store, stagecoach stop, and tavern with the same name—which it probably was, for road-weary stagecoach and other travelers. Then the Cleveland and Mahoning Railroad started taking away Wilmot's business, so he relocated to nearby Cortland, where he opened another enterprise and called it—ta dum!—"The End of the World," which, sadly, it was for Wilmot, because he died there.

This inflated sense of importance is not just limited to Ohio, or the planet Earth for that matter. The suburb of Fremont near Seattle, Washington, claims to be the "Center of the Universe," something to do with a Native American legend and the artistic community's official motto, *Delibertus Quirkus,* which supposedly means "Freedom to be Peculiar." Okaay . . . And then there's the "Hub of the Universe" in Boston, a title coined by none other than Oliver Wendell Holmes, who actually referred to the statehouse there as the hub of the solar system. Today it's commemorated by a plaque in the sidewalk in front of Filene's department store—which it is, for bargain hunters.

Praise the Lord and Pass the Pasties
Warsaw

In August 2010, a gaggle of strippers turned the other cheek—literally—when they started showing up for Sunday services in bikinis

at the fundamentalist New Beginnings Ministries church, waving protest signs with biblical quotations. But, as the Bible itself says, an eye
for an eye—for the past four years, churchgoers, led by pastor Bill
Dunfee, had regularly picketed the strippers' place of worship, club Fox
Hole. Brandishing signs, bullhorns, and video cameras, congregants
photographed and posted patrons' license plates on the Internet,
harassing everyone who passed through its portals in an attempt to
save their souls.

Since Dunfee had invited owner Tommy George and his strippers
to the church on numerous occasions, they decided to take him up on
it, although not in the way the congregants were praying for. Armed
with lawn chairs, Super Soakers, and snacks, they settled in for the
duration, grilling hamburgers, munching on Cheetos, and waving at
passersby who honked vigorously, whether or not they loved Jesus.

At first, Dunfee piped his sermon outside in hopes he might rein in
some rebellious sheep. But according to an account in the *Columbus
Dispatch,* that "agitated" the strippers, and made them dance in the
streets.

In their defense, the girls stated that they were just making a living
and the church, located 9 miles away from the club, had no right to
try to take an axe to their poles. Dunfee held his ground, telling the
Dispatch that "The word of Jesus Christ says you cannot share territory
with the devil."

"When these morons go away, we'll go away," club owner George
countered, and after a few weeks of tit-for-tat, Sheri Brown, who
preaches to strippers in California, and Anny Donewald, a former strip-
per who now bares only her soul, sashayed into town and negotiated
a come-to-Jesus between Dunfee and George. It basically ended in a
standoff, although both strippers and churchgoers reconciled somewhat, exchanging kind words, hugs, and tears. Well perhaps there
may be a divine intervention compromise after all, a "nude beginning"
so to speak.

★ ★

Horse-Drawn Banking Machine
Wellington

Since it's located near Amish country, it might make you think it was one of the locals doing some banking at the LorMet Community Federal Credit Union (216 Main St. 44094, 440-647-1999). But on closer inspection, this horse-and-buggy combo doesn't appear to be moving. And there's nobody inside except for—oh my goodness!—an automatic teller machine. So it's either a quantum physics screwup in time travel or the world's only ATM located inside a horse-drawn carriage.

Albert Einstein and H. G. Wells died before the invention and installation of one of the first ATMs in 1970, more than a few miles down

Giddyup! To the ATM.

the road at the City National Bank in Columbus, so we can't pin it on them. Credit (so to speak) goes to LorMet CEO Dan Cwalina, who wanted the technological convenience to blend in with the quaint Victorian look of the town. And putting the thing together was no mean feat: Although the fiberglass horse was fairly easy to obtain, the carriage had to be specially constructed to fit over the ATM vault.

The important thing is, people actually use ye old automatic teller. So when an SUV or minivan pulls up alongside it to make a transaction, the sound you hear is of worlds colliding.

Take Me to Your Leader
Williamsfield

Who's this nation's daddy? Not George Washington, according to Nick Pahys Jr., DDG, CH, AdVS, A.G.E., LDA, FIBA, author of *What Every American Should Know,* and founder of a museum honoring the first president of the United States of America—John Hanson.

Huh? According to the self-appointed Ambassador of Grand Emminence (his spelling), Hanson was the first official POTUS elected under the 1781 Articles of Confederation. That Washington guy was the first president elected under our current Constitution eight years later, in 1789. In addition to Hanson, there were seven others before Washington: Elias Boudinot, Thomas Mifflin, Richard Henry Lee, John Hancock, Nathaniel Gorham, Arthur St. Clair, and Cyrus Griffin.

All this and more is celebrated at the One and Only Presidential Museum (6585 Howard Rd. 44093, 440-344-0523, www.oneandonly-presidentialmuseum.com). Recently moved to a new location, the basic focus remains the same: a cluttered confusion of photos, books, and assorted items about the various presidents, including a room dedicated to those born in Ohio. Though every POTUS is represented, the star exhibit and largest picture is . . . Nick Pahys himself.

Pahys, who claims to be descended from Czechoslovakian royalty, also maintains he was nominated for a Nobel Peace Prize, among many other honors. He's anxious to spread the truth to anyone who will listen and is still waiting for the government to recognize No. 44, Barack Obama, as POTUS No. 52.

But, to put a fine point on it, two other men, Samuel Huntington and Thomas McKean, held the title President of the United States in Congress Assembled before Hanson became the first man to serve a full term as President of the Continental Congress under the Articles of Confederation. Before that, there were presidents of the First and Second Continental Congresses. So in a sense, Peyton Randolph, who took office in 1774, was the first President of the United States. So it stands to reason that Washington, D.C., could have been called Peyton Place.

Since its move, the museum has regular hours, although you should probably call first. Or maybe you should just keep driving; Do you really want to know what all those initials after his name stand for?

Get Thee to a Winery
Wilmot

It's been a long day in Amish country. Between dodging piles of poop left over from the horse-and-buggy combos and sidestepping other tourists, who, although smiling the whole time, think nothing of elbowing you to hone in on whatever piece of kitsch they've set their sights on, you're ready for a break, even if it's more of the same home-cooked, calorie-laden fare that's the signature of most restaurants around here.

You're coming over the hill to the Amish Door Restaurant & Village (1210 Winesburg St. 44689, 888-264-7436, www.amishdoor.com), grateful that it's a hotel and not a bed-and-breakfast where you'll have to listen to Grandma and Grandpa chatter endlessly about their RV travels and offspring, when you see the sign on the barn—AWARD WINNING WINES OF OHIO! It's enough to make you slam on the brakes and turn around to see if it actually is a wine store in the middle of Wholesome Heaven (or Hell, depending upon your perspective).

Indeed it is. Gateway Place (14875 US 62, 44689, 330-359-5535, www.gatewayplacewine.com) features over two dozen Ohio vintages

An oasis in a desert of kitsch

and, along with nearly every other store in Holmes County, wooden Amish toys and antiques. "But people come here for the wine," notes proprietor John Switzer, who runs it with the help of his wife, Nancy. "I can't tell you how many people tell us they almost had an accident when they saw the sign. They can't believe we're actually here." Well, duh.

The 1890 home (is there any other kind around here?) has been lovingly restored and retrofitted, with dozens of bottles housed on wooden shelves. And samples of the various vintages are available for a nominal fee. Plus you get to learn about Ohio wines, discovering that there are many surprisingly good ones, which taste even better after mini-cupfuls.

According to the Switzers, even the Amish stop by occasionally. Who can blame them?

Super-Amish

In recent years, and in spite of (or perhaps because of) the declining economy and increase in technology, Amish Country has become big business. In some cases, enterprises started off as family undertakings only to hit it big as the tourists started flocking while in others the Amish themselves banded together to create a booming enterprise. Regardless, the plain folks got nothin' on Harvard Business School. To wit:

- **Der Dutchman/Carlisle Gifts** (several locations, www.dhgroup. com). In 1969, three Holmes County business owners opened a small, seventy-five-seat family eatery in a renovated hardware store in Walnut Creek. From little acorns do mighty enterprises grow: Cashing in on their and the area's Amish and Mennonite heritage, they developed a winning formula of calorie-laden but tasty homemade food, cleanliness, and courtesy. Today the Dutchman Hospitality Group now includes five restaurants, two inns, four bakeries, seven shops, and a wholesale food supplier sprinkled throughout Amish Country and small towns in Ohio and even Indiana. So visitors to Walnut Creek, Sugarcreek, Plain City, and Waynesville can eat, sleep, and shop without ever leaving the property!

- **Charm Harness and Boot** (4441 County Rd. 70, Charm 44617, 330-893-0402). Featuring Crocs, UGG boots, Birkenstocks and other trendy footwear as well as work, western, and hunting boots, cowboy hats and shoe repair, the place is more "boot" than "harness." If you're looking for the latter for two-legged friends, well, that's a different store entirely.

- **Keim Lumber** (4465 State Rte. 557, Charm 44617, 330-893-2251, www.keimlumber.com). They've been around since 1911, but recently opened a 120,000-square-foot superstore that makes Home Depot look like an armpit. Their two-story showroom has everything from scoops to nuts (the kind that go with bolts) as well as dozens of types of gleaming hardwood for every part of the home; patio and garden supplies; building material; paints; wallpapers; kitchen and bathroom fixtures; and a heck of a lot more. It feels more like 90210 than horse-and-buggy.

- **Yoder's Drieds and Gifts** (7062 County Rd. 77, Millersburg 44654, 330-674-5603). The first question might be "Dried what?" but it's answered the second you walk in. Dried flowers . . . lots and lots of dried flowers . . . hanging everywhere: upside-down on the ceiling, on the walls, by the cash register . . . Good thing they stopped at flowers! But there's plenty of other stuff at what's locally known as the Amish Wal-Mart: Plain people nightgowns that for most non-Amish would ensure that the only thing going on in the bedroom would be sleeping; kids' clothes; and elixirs such as Worms Be-Gone, Kidney Flush, and Bone/Flesh/Cartilage Balance. Toy space guns and bazookas share shelf space with handmade doilies and tablecloths. Yikes! What if this place does become as successful as Wal-Mart? Scary thought indeed!
- **Berlin Grande Hotel** (4787 Township Rd. 366, Berlin 44610, 877-652-4997, berlingrandehotel.com). Why is it no surprise to learn that a group of Amish burghers banded together to create a luxury boutique hotel, with an "e" after "Grand" for good measure? And there it is, in all its flat-screen, leather couch, triple-sheeted glory, with bath products from Gilchrist & Soames thrown in for good measure. The "Grande Entrance" (their words) boasts a wall fountain and there's also an indoor salt-water pool and fitness center. Kind of makes you long for the days when the only choice for lodging was a local B&B or small hotel with one three-channel TV in the lobby.

And don't forget to check out the cheese, chocolate, and wine stores/wineries that seem to be proliferating on every corner. Using neither gas nor electricity, the Amish were green before it became fashionable. And now they seem to be rolling in it.

★ ★

Mega-Mary
Windsor

Tucked away in a far corner of the Servants of Mary Center for Peace
(6569 Ireland Rd. 44099, 440-272-5380, http://guadalupeohio.com/
servantsofmary), fifty acres of wooded farmland owned by Ed and Pat
Heinz, is a giant statue of the Virgin Mary. This thirty-three-foot representation of Our Lady of Guadalupe stands atop an angel who appears
to be holding her up. He's assisted by a mosaic cloud consisting of
450,000 colored tiles that comprise the base, making the height of the
entire shebang a whopping 50 feet. Not bad, considering the largest
effort to date of the sculptor, Texas art professor Richard Hyslin, had
reportedly been a 15-foot King Kong for a miniature golf course.

This was truly a labor of love for the Heinzes, devout Catholics who
had nine young children when they obtained the property in 1987.
The original thought was that it be used as a Catholic youth camp,
but Ed, a nuclear engineer, fell victim to an economic meltdown and
ended up declaring bankruptcy. The entire family moved to England for a couple of years for his new job and prayed that somehow
they could return. At one point Pat even briefly visited the property
and built a statue of St. Joseph and a medal of St. Benedict on the
grounds. And through a series of fortunate coincidences (some might
call them miracles), no one bought the farm, so to speak, and the
Heinzes were able to reclaim it, retiring the debt, thanks to Ed's successful UK venture.

By August 1992 the Center for Peace began to host programs and
devotions, and through even more coincidences/miracles, the idea
was born to build a shrine to Our Lady near the large pond in back.
The statue was completed in 1995, after sculptor Hyslin and his crew
raised and finished the concrete substrate and allowed it to cure over
the winter. After that she was ready to do some "curing" of her own.

The statue can only be accessed through a partially finished walkway, so expect quite a hike if you want to see her up close and personal. On the way you'll pass a large quartz crucifix and an enclosed

That's a big load you're carrying, young man!

★ ★

wooden pavilion that serves as a chapel. Also on the grounds is a shrine to Padre Pio, a recently sainted mystic, confessor, and priest.

Optimal viewing is at night, when Mary is lit up from behind and the lights surrounding the lake form a rosary. It's pretty cool, even for nonbelievers. Otherwise, you'll see the coils looping behind her, giving the odd impression of the world's largest upright hot plate, with Our Lady as a main dish. And if the sun is setting, you'll have to squint to even see the statue.

But it's a lovely, peaceful setting, and no one will bother to try to convert you, though it would be wise to call to make sure they're open. Given the potential for electrical conductivity (projecting wires, the lake), you might want to stay away during a thunderstorm. Unless, of course, you're seeking an entirely different form of illumination.

My Mother the Museum
Youngstown

What better way to honor your mother than naming a museum after her? That's exactly what the late Youngstown radiologist John C. Melnick, MD, did in 2001 when he opened this collection inspired by his mother, who inspired him to join the medical profession. According to the museum's website, "it was [his] dream to create a museum that would cultivate an interest in medicine and promote medical history among the students, physicians, and general public of Youngstown and the Mahoning Valley." Thus the caduceus is passed. Although to be perfectly accurate—this is a museum after all—the symbol of medicine is actually the single-snake, wingless rod of Asclepius, named after the Greek god of healing.

Located at Youngstown State University, the Rose Melnick Medical Museum (655 Wick Ave. 44455, 330-941-4661, http://melnick-museum.ysu.edu/visit.html) warehouses thousands of medical instruments, equipment, and research materials covering 200+ years of local doctoring in all specialties. Must-sees include a pre-polio vaccine iron lung that resembles a reverse human cannonball; a cancer-producing wooden X-ray machine; and the pre–Industrial Era *pièce de résistance,* a Civil War–era amputation kit with multiple size saws and evil-looking picks. Obamacare or not, you don't want to be on the receiving end of that bad boy.

Along with a detailed display about the scourges of polio, the development of the Sabin oral vaccine, and mass local immunizations of same, the museum operates under the premise that if it's about the region, it's worth saving. And indeed it provides a microcosm of medical history through photographs and artifacts on early dentists and physicians and various health care facilities and nursing schools as well as tracing the evolution of doctors' offices from the late nineteenth century to the mid-1930s, when more standard practices began to be used. Along with a revealing exhibition on X-rays, an array of quack devices features odd ducks ranging from blood-letting instruments to magnetic cures to electrotherapeutic devices and more. There's also a display of, in the words of the website, "attempts by the government, the medical profession, and others" to regulate what they deemed as questionable treatments. Hmm, seems some things never change. Nevertheless, there's lots here to make Mom proud.

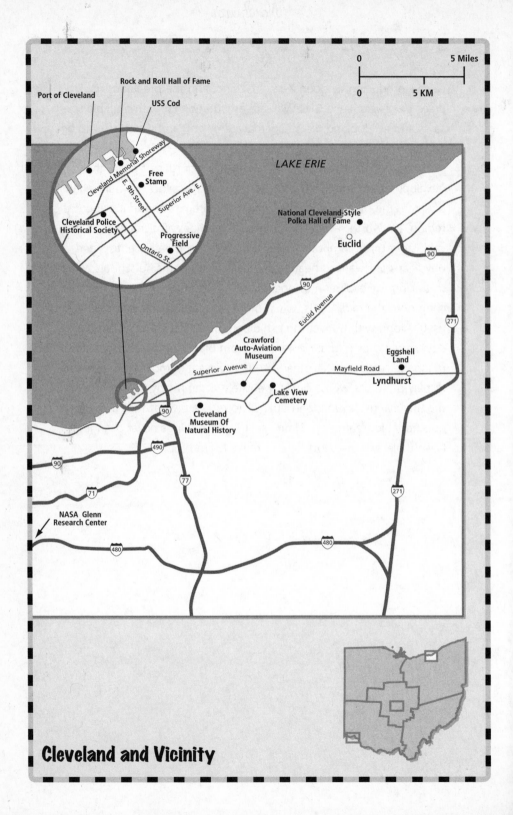

Cleveland and Vicinity

2

Cleveland and Vicinity

Cleveland has ramped up its image considerably since the 1970s, when "the mistake on the lake" was the butt of many jokes. Along with revitalizing its downtown, it began to promote its colorful, ethnic neighborhoods, and added attractions, like the Rock and Roll Hall of Fame. So why is that a curiosity? Well, it's in Cleveland for starters and not New York or L.A. And rightfully so, because Cleveland is where music pioneer and DJ Alan Freed coined the phrase "rock & roll" in the early 1950s. Lawrence Welk fans and aficionados of that genre can take an entirely different (but perhaps equally long and strange) trip to the National Cleveland-Style Polka Hall of Fame.

Many attractions have been around for decades: the Cleveland Police Historical Society, with its wealth of information about the infamous 1930s Torso Killer; Eggshell Land, in nearby Lyndhurst, where since 1957, the Manolio family has been shelling out displays of Easter cheer in the form of colorful arrangements of eggs; and NASA Glenn Research Center, the closest thing to Houston or the Kennedy Space Center without leaving state borders.

Plus, there's loads of shopping—Tower City, Legacy Village, Crocker Park, Beachwood Place, and many more, not to mention all the great restaurants in the various neighborhoods. What better way to unwind after visiting the famous and infamous residents of Lake View Cemetery?

★ ★

To Preserve and Protect

Cleveland

Want to experience law enforcement without going to the Big House? Parents of potential juvenile delinquents and others might want to check out the Cleveland Police Historical Society. It's actually located at the Cleveland Police Headquarters on the first floor of the Justice Center (1300 Ontario St. 44113, 216-623-5055, www.clevelandpolice museum.org). On your way there, you might get to see some bona fide members of the criminal element, along with mostly bored-looking cops and security guards.

As if that's not exciting enough, there's the museum itself, with its death masks of four victims of the Torso Killer, a 1930s sicko who hacked up various fringe members of society and left their body parts around town. Even Eliot Ness himself, who was Cleveland's safety director at the time and had already bagged Al Capone, couldn't (excuse the pun) finger the guy, who was believed to be a butcher or doctor, due to his skill in dismembering someone's mama (as well as male victims). This was well before the advent of DNA technology, so the case is still cold.

Other highlights include a circa 1880s *Descriptive Book of Thieves,* a turn-of-the-twentieth-century call box, and a display of uniforms that basically covers the entire fashion evolution of the Cleveland Police Department since its inception in 1866. An exhibit of departmental and confiscated firearms provides visitors with information as to exactly how much damage they can inflict, and will hopefully serve as a deterrent to anyone who thinks that carrying a gun is "cool." There are other nifty law enforcement accoutrements: a couple of motorcycles, several radio transmitters, a life-size replica of a police horse, and a 1970 remote-control device used to disarm bombs that looks uncannily like the Johnny Five robot from the movie *Short Circuit.*

And finally, the ultimate disincentive: a gen-u-ine jail cell with actual graffiti and a fingerprinting table. Even though the door is permanently welded open and you can't possibly get locked in, it's a creepy

Victims of the Torso Killer, who still remains unmasked

experience when you step inside. You can buy souvenirs from the smallish but cleverly titled Cop Shop and get a copy of their newsletter, the *Hot Sheet*. (Hey, these folks are good.)

Visitors wanting to see the rest of the museum, with its display honoring fallen officers and other memorabilia, will have to go through electronic screening, similar to an airport. But you may want to pass . . . it's a little too reminiscent of the other unpleasant experience that's rapidly becoming the equivalent of being pulled over by an officer of the law: flying on a plane.

★ ★

What a Gas
Cleveland

When you try to pin down the "first" of anything, you often get con-
flicting signals. This is especially true of the first traffic light. Nonetheless, a very early version was installed at the corner of Euclid Avenue
and 105th Street in Cleveland on August 5, 1914 (not to be confused
with the longest-running traffic light in Ashville; see Central chapter).

Some sources (such as www33.brinkster.com/iiiii/trfclt) claim that
it was based on the design of James Hoge, while others, such as the
Crawford Auto-Aviation Museum (Western Reserve Historical Society,
10825 East Boulevard 44106, University Circle; 216-721-5722; www
.wrhs.org) give the green light to Garrett Morgan, an African-American
inventor. Additionally, they credit him with the creation of the gas
mask (also hotly contested on www33.brinkster.com/iiiii/gasmask/page
.html) and the zigzag stitch attachments for sewing machines.

Regardless, you can see Morgan's take on the light, an unusual-
looking T-shaped pole with three positions: stop, go, and an all-
directional stop position that allowed all pedestrians to cross the street
safely. Morgan received the patent for it in 1923, and supposedly sold
it to General Electric for the then-princely sum of $40,000. The precur-
sor of the modern traffic light as we know it today was developed by
Detroit policeman William Potts and is on display at the Henry Ford
Museum in Dearborn, Michigan.

Still, Morgan's light makes for an interesting detour at the recently
remodeled and refurbished Crawford museum, a bumper crop of some
150 antique, vintage, and classic automobiles, motorcycles, bicycles,
and aircraft. "Offerings range from an 1897 Panhard et Levassor (the
first enclosed automobile) to Bobby Rahal's 1982 March Indy Car (the
first winner of the Cleveland 500). Huh? Yes, there was actually such
a race in Cleveland, more recently known as 'the Grand Prix of Cleveland, but cancelled in 2009 on account of the recession. Who knew?

Visitors will also find that Cleveland contributed a lot to the auto-
motive industry, with more than eighty models originating in the area

between 1889 and 1931, including such off-brand classics as the 1905 Stanley Model "E" Gentlemen's Speedy Roadster, the 1908 Firestone-Columbus Model 209 Motor Buggy, the 1909 Simplex Model 90 Double Roadster, and the 1911 Hupmobile Model 20, which according to the museum, was the first to go around the world (Hup! Hup!). Bonus: a circa 1912–1914 Curtiss Hydroaeroplane flown by Cleveland's most prominent aviator, Al Engel.

At the very least, it's a humbling reminder that, although we may think we're original and clever, few of us achieve recognition for our work beyond our lifetimes.

The Biggest Things in Life Are Free
Cleveland

Ohio has its share of larger than life (LTL) stuff, some of which is chronicled in this book. But Cleveland's LTL offering was not only created by well-known artists Claes Oldenburg and Coosje van Bruggen—who also unleashed giant plugs, binoculars, safety pins, and more upon an unsuspecting public—but it was free. Really free. As in a 28-by-48-foot rubber stamp—the kind an office worker might use—with the word *free* on top (Willard Park 44178, Lakeside Ave. East). And it actually was free—it didn't cost the city a cent.

Ironically, the aluminum and steel stamp with a red handle was commissioned by an oil company, the last place you'd expect to find anything gratis. But that was back in 1982, before Standard Oil was purchased by British Petroleum (BP) and Ronald Reagan was too busy with Star Wars to concern himself with the Middle East. It was originally supposed to sit in front of Standard Oil's soon-to-be-constructed headquarters building on Public Square with the free facing downward and hidden from view. Well, that makes sense.

Anyway, before the stamp was delivered, BP took over and management from across the pond didn't particularly care for the piece of art (as in rubber stamping the fact that we're no longer the Colonies, perhaps?). So it sat in a warehouse in Indiana for seven years, where

★ ★

it was not free because BP had to pay the storage fee every month. Finally, they offered it to the city of Cleveland as a piece of public art. The city politely refused, noting that it wasn't free for them either, since they had to pony up the funds to set it up and maintain it.

But then BP offered to install it . . . for free! So in 1991 the artists modified the stamp so it would sit on its side, revealing the *free* lettering, symbolizing the "flinging" of the stamp across downtown from the BP Building to Willard Park, a heavy thought indeed. It now sits across from City Hall, reminding all the downtown office workers what they are not—at least until they retire or quit.

Icons on Ice
Cleveland

For years, she greeted visitors with open arms at Healthspace Cleveland (formerly known as the Health Museum of Cleveland) a favorite of the anatomically curious of all ages. Currently in storage at the Cleveland Museum of Natural History (1 Wade Oval Dr. 44106, 216-231-4600, www.cmnh.org), Juno, the Transparent Talking Woman may also be invisible, at least for a while. 'But back in the day, during the 1939 New York World's Fair, this clear-headed—and bodied— female was quite the phenomenon in terms of seeing what made a person tick. Her organs lit up one by one as she described how they all worked together.

Backed by a group of doctors and other medical professionals, the original Health Museum opened in 1936 with a sometimes-controversial tradition of providing health education and information. Juno and some other exhibits were brought in in 1940, and according to the Cleveland *Plain Dealer,* "Those reared in Northeast Ohio were most likely introduced to the museum on a grade-school field trip, the images of test-tube fetuses and Juno . . . burned into their memory." However, the CMNH, as it is known, has lots of other icons to explore, along with permanent and changing exhibits, classes, and programs. The former

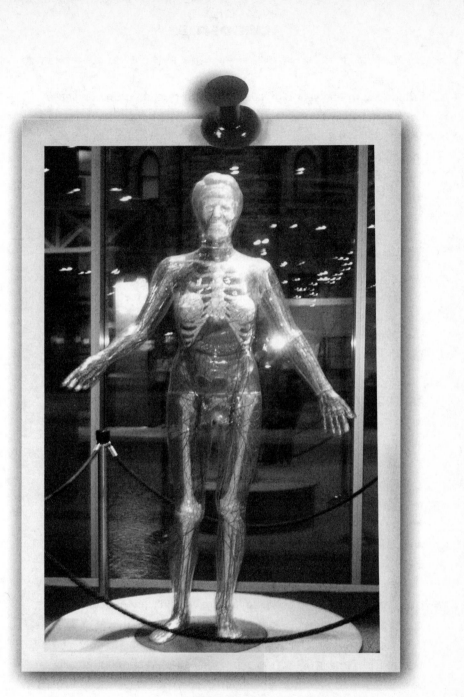

Clothing-optional Juno is now in the
closet—at least for the time being.

★ ★

include 3.2 million-year-old "Lucy," a reconstruction of the original skeletal materials of one of the oldest species of human ancestors. There's Balto, the heroic Siberian Husky sled dog (and inspiration for the annual Alaskan Iditarod sled dog race), who led his team during a 1925 serum run to Nome, Alaska, transporting the diphtheria antitoxin to combat an outbreak of the disease. Brought to Cleveland by a businessman, his (Balto's) comfortable retirement was augmented by good taxidermy upon his demise eight years later. With nearly 50 percent of his bones being actual fossil material, "Happy" aka *Haplocanthosaurus delfsi,* is half the Late Jurassic sauropod he used to be. Nevertheless, at a complete-looking seventy feet long and fourteen feet high, he still still cuts quite a figure and boasts a six-foot-four-inch femur (thighbone) that's the oldest displayed anywhere in the world. Bring Juno back into the mix, and there will be even more to smile about.

Serving Both the Living and the Dead
Cleveland

What a fun place: Not only do they have a speaker's bureau, a library, a newsletter, and special events, such as a holiday program of music and lights, but they sell their own root beer for $1. You can also get married in the Wade Chapel there, which according to the website, "provides a lovely location for an intimate wedding." We're talking about . . . Lake View Cemetery (12316 Euclid Ave. 44106, 216-421-2665, www.lakeviewcemetery.com).

Well, for one thing, they don't have to worry about the residents complaining about the noise. And there certainly are enough distinguished ones: former U.S. president James A. Garfield over in Section 15; John D. "Moneybags" Rockefeller in Section 10; über–crime fighter Eliot Ness in Section 7; and perhaps less known but equally valiant, Raymond Johnson Chapman (Section 42), a Cleveland Indians shortstop and the only major-league baseball player to die due to an injury during a game, in 1920 after he was hit in the head by New York Yankee pitcher Carl Mays. ("Dedicating the season in memory of

'Chappie,' the Indians won the league and world championship for the first time," according to the website.) Wow, what a lineup!

Before you go thinking this is the K-Mart of burial grounds ("Attention, shoppers! There's been a sighting of the ghost of actress Gloria Hershey Pressman in Section 43, Lot 678! You may remember her from the Little Rascals short films and *The Virginian.* She's ten rows back, near her headstone behind a tree . . . "), the place was founded in 1869. Modeled after the great garden cemeteries of Victorian England and France, according to the website, it sits on some 285 acres and has more than 102,000 permanent inhabitants with another 700 new additions to the neighborhood annually. And it's equal opportunity: "Anyone can be buried at Lake View, without regard to race, creed, religion or walk of life." At that point, who cares? Still, it's a good way to get comfortable with the inevitable.

Not Dead Yet
Cleveland

Only in Cleveland would you find both the Rock and Roll Hall of Fame and the National Cleveland-Style Polka Hall of Fame (605 East 222nd St. 44123, 216-261-3263, www.clevelandstyle.com). OK, so the structure is a former school and not a soaring steel-and-glass vision by architect I. M. Pei, but they both have inductees and lots of rocker relics—though much of the polka fan base might be considered relics sitting in them, rather than trying to emulate their lifestyle.

In spite of the fact that polka's considered uncool by many, it looks like it's here to stay, like pocket protectors and sweatshirts emblazoned with flowers, baby rabbits, and the words "Somebunny loves you!" And the museum has its induction ceremony on Thanksgiving weekend, giving people something to do. It's usually attended by a couple thousand enthusiasts and industry folks, who either have no family or are looking to get away from them.

Cleveland's museum focuses on "Slovenian style," whose popularity reached its zenith during the polka heyday of the 1940s and 1950s.

★ ★

Many Clevelanders have Eastern European origins, so it's no surprise that it became wildly popular here. And today's head-scratching names—Frank Yankovic (no relation to Weird Al); Cleveland's own "Polka King" Johnny Vadnal (along with brothers Frankie, Richie, and Tony—how ethnic is that?); Kenny Bass; and more—were celebrities back then, appearing on film and TV and even in Las Vegas (back when it was mostly run by Wayne Newton and the Mob).

By the 1960s rock 'n' roll sealed polka's doom as a mainstream form of music, and Lawrence Welk drove the nails of squaredom into the coffin. Polka had a public-relations image similar to Cleveland's during that period—the butt of jokes, if mentioned at all. Today polka lives on, in church and summer festivals, at square dances (the style, not the participants), and at fiftieth wedding-anniversary parties. And in the museum, where you can see the accordions and fancy-shmancy stage outfits worn by polka's superstars (an oxymoron?); captioned photos of the complete history of Cleveland-style polka, from the mid-1880s on; and pictures and biographies of the Hall of Fame inductees. And don't forget to stop at the gift shop, the largest outlet with the most complete selection of Cleveland-style and other polka music in the world, for your musical memento of this pantheon to good, clean fun.

Spaced Out: Part I
Cleveland

Few people realize that NASA has been around in some form or another since before World War II. Established in 1941, the Glenn Research Center (Cleveland Hopkins Airport, 21000 Brookpark Rd. 44135; 216-433-2000; www.nasa.gov/centers/glenn) is one of the program's granddaddies, back when it was the National Advisory Committee for Aeronautics (NACA) and space and air travel were just a twinkle in John Glenn's eye. Far out!

But this venerable laboratory has soldiered on into the twenty-first century and remains one of the premier centers of its kind in the

The origins of rocket science

United States, conducting cutting-edge research on such technologies as "intelligent" stealth engines, aerospace propulsion systems, power use in space, and astronaut endurance, to mention a few. In other words, you probably should be a rocket scientist to work there.

However, since 9/11 stricter security measures require that most visitors be U.S. citizens and go through various checkpoints. So while getting in can be somewhat of a hassle, once you're there, it's a treat. Not only is there a Skylab 3 Apollo command module that was really launched as part of an actual mission (as opposed to the model at that "other" space center in Wapakoneta, in the Northwest chapter), but there's an entire display on John Glenn himself with the space suits that he wore and everything. You can even ask him questions via a

★ ★

prerecorded voice-recognition program. (Now that he's retired, he has better things to do than hang around his namesake center and give the same answers over and over.')

The tour is mostly self-guided, so you could spend hours learning about the various facets of space travel, from wind tunnels to microgravity to the effects of weightlessness. Everything's tastefully done, and there's lots of reading, so young children and people with short attention spans might get somewhat bored. Still, you can test your ability with a flight simulator, choosing from aircraft starting with a Sopwith camel (aka the "Snoopy plane") to a Lear jet, and check out the Lucite-embedded moon rocks, which are illegal for citizens to own because they're considered "priceless" by the government. According to museum personnel, a NASA employee in another part of the country got thrown in a federal prison for trying to sell moon rocks on eBay. Well, maybe not everyone there is a rocket scientist . . .

It Never Dies
Cleveland

This is one act that's hard to follow. With cantilevered architecture and a glass "tent" designed by architect I. M. Pei, a rock star in his own field, the 150,000-square-foot Rock and Roll Hall of Fame (One Key Plaza, East Ninth St. 44114; 888-764-7625; www.rockhall.com) provides candy for both eyes and ears. It's the only place on Earth where you can see Pete Townshend's handwritten notes on *Tommy* (Who??), a complete history of Ohio's official state rock song, and Jim Morrison's Cub Scout uniform. And that's just the tip of the Ice Cube.

Where to begin? Step inside and it's an almost overwhelming world of color, sound, and motion, with a very prominently displayed gift shop that, under other circumstances, might tempt you to skip the museum entirely. Floor after floor contains interactive exhibits, films, videos, and artifacts, as well as several temporary displays that change throughout the year. Information on one-hit wonders and legendary inductees share space with photos, recordings, and more on rock's roots in gospel, country, and blues as well as big-city music scenes.

Other exhibits document the political protests against rock 'n' roll and the interplay between fashion and rock. There are also concerts, lectures, panel discussions, film series, and other events.

This is not a place to be visited in a couple of hours, or even only once. Because when there's this much stuff, you're sure to miss something (or, more realistically, several hundred things). So if you don't see David Bowie's "Ziggy Stardust" jumpsuit, Prince's "Purple Rain" coat, or Madonna's bustier from "Like a Virgin" on this go-round, you might catch handwritten lyrics for the Beatles' "In My Life" and "Lucy in the Sky With Diamonds," ZZ Top's "Eliminator" car, and Janis Joplin's psychedelic Porsche. And as a bonus, you might run into someone famous: Godsmack, Squirrel Nut Zippers, and Vertical Horizon have all stopped by when they're in town. Don't know who they are? Oh well, as the song goes, "It's only rock 'n' roll . . . "

Cod Peace

Cleveland

Just a block away from the Rock and Roll Hall of Fame is the USS *Cod* (1089 East Ninth St. 44114, www.usscod.org, open seasonally). The only remaining relatively intact, almost fully functioning World War II submarine, the 1,525-ton 312-footer was launched in 1943, making its underwater bones during the final years of World War II when it sank twelve enemy vessels with steam-powered torpedoes. No yellow submarine this.

In 1945 the *Cod* was also part of the first and only international submarine-to-submarine rescue, saving the crew of a Dutch O-19 when it ran aground in the South China Sea. After rescuing fifty-six Dutch sailors, it destroyed the O-19 so the enemy couldn't get to it. A few weeks later, during a thank-you party with the two crews, they received word of the Japanese surrender. Today the *Cod*'s battle flag and conning tower both carry a cocktail glass above the name O-19 to commemorate the rescue and the party. Cheers!

Decommissioned in 1954, the *Cod* ended up a naval reserve training vessel in Cleveland, also finding new life as a favorite spot with kids on field trips. But by 1971 she was stricken from the register of U.S. Navy ships.

Enter the Cleveland Coordinating Committee to Save *Cod,* a group of war vets and others determined to rescue her from the scrap heap, petitioning the Navy to give up the ship so she could become a World War II memorial. At one point they even used labor and food donated by a committee member's local restaurant to promote their cause. Whether or not sub sandwiches were served is lost to history.

In 1976 the USS *Cod* opened to the public, and ten years later became a National Historic Landmark. Lovingly restored and cared for, she is the only U.S. submarine with intact stairways and doors, so twenty-first-century peacetime visitors can climb up the same vertical ladders and hatches used by her undoubtedly more fit and trim crew. The interior also serves as a reminder of how much equipment, furnishings, and people can be crammed into a small space. And even though they had an ice-cream machine on board—standard issue on all U.S. Navy World War II submarines—war was still hell.

Hard-Boiled
Lyndhurst

If it's Easter in Lyndhurst, it must be time for . . . Eggshell Land (1031 Linden Lane 44124, 440-442-6061, http://eggshellandeaster.tripod .com)! Since 1957 Ron and Betty Manolio have been shelling out colorful tableaux, always with a fifty-foot cross and their mascot, the Easter Bunny. The 2010 display consisted of 32,740 real eggshells, with the theme of "We Can Fly," highlighting various species of birds as well as the logo for the Cleveland Cavaliers basketball team with the possible connection being that Larry Bird of the Indiana Pacers would take the coaching helm. (He refused the Cavs' offer. Alas, poor LeBron, we knew thee well.) Exhibits, which change from year to year, usually only last ten days, starting on the morning of Palm Sunday and running through the Tuesday after Easter.

According to their website, everything is done by hand: "Ron makes a hole the size of a dime in the egg and Betty shakes out the contents. The shells are then washed and the edges of the hole trimmed. After painting, the shells are stored by color in boxes, with 250 in each box. They are used over and over again each year, and repainted, if necessary, in the proper colors." Local children and other helpers (the Easter equivalent of Santa's elves) put in the pegs that anchor the eggs and help set them out, resulting in . . . an eggs-travaganza!

Some might wonder why the Manolios do this and if they spend all their spare time boiling, counting, and painting eggs. No one knows what goes on behind closed doors, but they do seem to enjoy the attention. And the tradition was started on a much smaller scale by Ron's mother, who used to place dyed eggshells on bushes in front of her home. "My husband said nobody decorates for Easter," Betty told WKYC-TV in Cleveland. The first year "we had 750 eggshells, and it got in the newspaper and that inspired us. So the next year we had to make it bigger." Since then they've been the subject of a documentary (titled "Eggshelland"—how original!) and featured on national TV and in numerous magazines and newspapers.

But perhaps most importantly, they enjoy seeing how their creations light up the faces of youngsters. "That's the whole reason for doing it," Ron told the TV station. "We always do things that they'll recognize."

Of course, if you're going to make an "omelet" of such proportions, you can expect some breakage, through both human error and Mother Nature, such as a 1998 hail storm that shattered 10,238 shells, a 2002 snow-and-ice combo that smashed 11,941, and another big snowfall in 2005 that cracked 5,633. How they can calculate exactly how many shells were destroyed in the messes will forever remain a mystery.

Still, the Manolios have been married since 1955 and still own the car they had their first date in, a beautifully maintained 1950 DeSoto sedan. So they must be doing something right and obviously don't need to walk on eggshells around each other.

State Roundup: Foodfest!

Ohio may have more festivals than any other state. Subjects of adulation range from popcorn to tomatoes to pumpkins, with melons, walleye, and bratwurst thrown in for good measure. You'll also find festivals that celebrate different cultures, the arts, even autos. But, no matter what the occasion, it provides a great excuse to stuff your face, with diet-sabotaging and/or unusual fare. So the few described here provide "ample" opportunities to add to your bottom line, so to speak.

For more information and to obtain a list of festivals in your area(s) of interest, contact the Ohio Department of Development, Division of Travel and Tourism, 77 South High St., Columbus 43216, (800) 282-5393, www.ohiotourism.com. Additionally, local Convention and Visitor Bureaus and Chambers of Commerce publish detailed information on area festivals, and there's an online resource, Ohio Events and Festivals Association (OFEA), www.ofea.org.

- **Geauga County Maple Festival, April** (Chardon 44024, 440-286-3007, www.maplefestival.com). Tap into something sweet at what bills itself as "the first festival of the year in Ohio," always held the weekend after Easter. Along with celebrating the production of maple syrup, according to the site, "the leading agricultural industry in Northern Ohio" there are parades, bathtub races (Huh?), a bucket coloring contest, a queen pageant, a syrup and candy competition, and a sap run, which involves people, not syrup. They also have something called a celebrity bricklaying— no doubt once Paris Hilton and Kim Kardashian get wind of this, they will most certainly be the first to sign up.
- **Melon Festival, September** (Milan 44870, 419-621-5770, www.milanmelonfestival.org). Here you can actually compliment someone on their melons without getting slapped in the face or

with a sexual harassment suit. The well-rounded event includes an elaborate car display, a tractor pull, muskmelon ice cream and watermelon sherbet, as well as plenty of the fresh stuff.

- **Mantua Potato Festival, September** (Portage County 44255, 330-274-0770). This spud's for the farming community that really dug potatoes and made them a viable slice of the economy. Candy, doughnuts, pancakes, bread, and cookies are made from tubers along with more conventional favorites like soup and chips. Included among the usual mish-mash of kid's games, rides, live entertainment, and craft tents are a 15K Potato Stomp, potato bake-off, raffle, presentation of visiting queens, and crowning of the festival queen on Sunday. Eat your heart out, Atkins followers.

- **Geneva Area Grape JAMboree, September** (Geneva 44041, 440-466-5262, www.grapejamboree.com). The first three letters of this event are capitalized in case jellyheads don't get the whole schmear, so to speak. Along with celebrating the nearby wine industry and harvesting of grapes, you can taste them in their various permutations: au naturel, in grape juice, in vino, and other products. Squeeze more fun into the "JAM-packed weekend for the entire family" with an art show, craft fair, street dancing, sports competition, raffle, and two parades. There's a Miss Grapette pageant, which this author is not even going to comment on. All grandstand entertainment, including a "grape stomping," is free, toe jam (eeew) optional.

- **Reynoldsburg Tomato Festival, September** (Reynoldsburg 43068, www.reynoldsburgtomatofestival.org). Along with live music, a beauty pageant, a fitness challenge, and a free screening of *The Attack of the Killer Tomatoes,* there is—really!—a blood drive. That should have you seeing red.

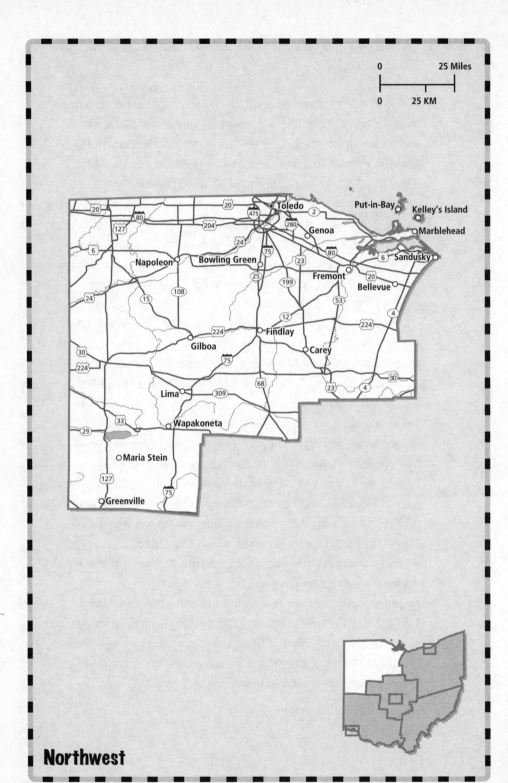

0   25 Miles

0   25 KM

Toledo
Put-in-Bay
Kelley's Island
Genoa
Marblehead
Sandusky
Napoleon
Bowling Green
Fremont
Bellevue
Findlay
Gilboa
Carey
Lima
Wapakoneta
Maria Stein
Greenville

Northwest

3

Northwest

Other than Toledo, *northwest Ohio lacks big-city action, and folks from Columbus might have issues with the fact that it's really close to Michigan, home to that "other" archrival football team. But Toledo does have tasty hot dogs and celebrity autographed buns at Tony Packo's, a restaurant made famous by native Jamie Farr. So what if the buns are Styrofoam? Chewing gum also gets the wretched excess treatment at the Maid-Rite Sandwich Shop in Greenville. For decades customers have stuck their gum wads on the outside wall there while ordering or waiting for food.*

And you truly will find things seen nowhere else, in this corner of the state: the USS Maine's *bathtub at the Hancock Historical Museum in Findlay and a twelve-hole privy in Genoa, the only outhouse listed on the National Register of Historic Places. Hmm, perhaps that's not a totally bad thing . . .*

And there's Put-in-Bay/the Lake Erie Islands, a veritable font of cheesy weirdness. Mystery Hill and the Prehistoric Forest in Marblehead have been family favorites for decades, although both have been untouched by time since they opened in the 1950s, even down to the smiling green dinosaurs that look suspiciously like now-defunct Sinclair Oil giveaways. Check out the Beer Barrel Saloon at Put-in-Bay. It's "Girls Gone Wild" for baby boomers, not always a pretty picture. For tamer entertainments, try Crystal Cave and the Perry Statue and Monument and, nearby at Kelley's Island, the Glacial Grooves.

★ ★

Going Postal
Bellevue

Got some extra time on your hands, say about five years? That's how long it would take to view the million-plus acquisitions at the Margie Pfund Memorial Post Mark Museum and Research Library during their business hours. That's an average of 600 postmarks an hour. And by the time you're done, there might be several hundred thousand more new donations—so you've got your work stamped out for you.

And who the heck was Margie Pfund, anyway? A charter member of the Post Mark Collectors Club (PMCC), she began collecting guess-whats and related items in a small upstairs room in her home in the 1940s. With the encouragement of Reverend Walter Smith of Bath, Maine, the museum was dedicated at the first PMCC national convention in 1962. Other PMCC members mailed in the results of their own assemblages, so soon the museum outgrew its location and was forced to move several times. Presently it can be found in two buildings in Historic Lyme Village (5001 Rte. 4, 44811, www.postmarks .org), one of which was the original Lyme post office, which served the community for fifty years until its closing in 1894.

Along with the largest single postmark collection in the world, the museum contains reference material on postmark collecting from each state in the United States, Canada, and around the world. The research library has more than 1,500 publications relating to postal history and procedures. You'll also find vintage post-office boxes and cancelling stamps as well as postmark slogans like the "Pray for Peace" series.

Still not overly thrilled? Well, if postmark collecting is your (mail) bag, you might be impressed by the Willet-Thompson collection, the combined efforts of two veteran PMCC members, Mr. Lawrence Willet and Dr. Howard K. Thompson. According to the PMCC website, Dr. Thompson "raised the quality of his personal collection by remounting his postmarks on special acid free paper. Each page is covered in museum- quality mylar sheet protectors and held in over 300 large binders."

Completed and still maintained by volunteers from the club, the entire Willett-Thompson collection was placed on microfilm and makes up nearly half of the museum's postmark holdings.

OK, so it's not exactly Cedar Point. But at least you won't have to stand in line, even if it is a post office.

Pheasant (and Fingers) Under Glass

Bowling Green

People may say they go to the Wood County Historical Center (13660 County Home Rd. 43402, 419-352-0967, www.woodcountyhistory .org) to see the general store, the Victorian parlor, and the government room, but what they really come for is Clark Gable's stuffed pheasant (in the parlor) and especially the three fingers of Mary Bach (in the government room).

So let's cut to the chase, so to speak. In 1881 Bowling Green resident Mary Bach was murdered by her husband, Carl, a nasty SOB who went into the barn, retrieved a large machete, and hacked her into little pieces. But in the end, he got his: a public hanging, held during the local county fair to a ticket-only, sold-out crowd. Plus, the noose, the murder weapon, and other related documents were on display for years at the Wood County Courthouse as a deterrent to crime, along with Mary's fingers, which were pickled and preserved in a jar and used for evidence during the trial. The bird met an un-pheasant, er, unpleasant ending as well, as Mr. Gable shot him while hunting in the area in the 1930s.

It seems fitting that this museum was originally a poor farm during the Civil War, and then expanded a few years later to include a lunatic asylum, transferring residents from the nearby County Insane Farm. For decades it sheltered the mentally ill, the orphaned, and the homeless, but by the 1950s it was primarily a nursing home for the elderly. It had also begun to show its age and failed to meet modern building codes. So the residents were moved elsewhere, and it was refurbished, opening its doors as a historical center in 1975.

★ ★

Many of the exhibits center around the complex's original function, focusing on the development of mental health practices and medical implements used during the 1900s. Others are less closely related: a collection of early oil well–drilling rigs; a homemaker's guide to kitchen and laundry (could arguments over cooking and cleaning have caused additional tensions in the Bach marriage?); and a "hands-on" guide to technology for kids. There's even a Ku Klux Klan exhibit. "History isn't always pleasant," notes the museum's website. Yeah, we got that.

Conspicuous Communion
Carey

The next time someone complains about using religion as a crutch, point them toward Our Lady of Consolation (315 Clay St. 43316, 419-396-7107, www.olcshrine.com). Along with free holy water—you supply the container—you'll find a virtual orthopedic bicycle rack of hundreds of spontaneously discarded braces, wheelchairs, corrective shoes, and crutches, along with notes from satisfied customers who've experienced a miracle cure. Here's P. J. Columbus from Lima: "I walked home and to this day I can see perfectly and am enjoying full health. Thanks to the Almighty God and the Virgin Mary." The note was penned in 1916, but the shrine's website also has more recent testimonials.

Our Lady of Consolation has its origins in the second century, when St. Ignatius of Antioch bestowed the title "Mary, the Consoler of the Afflicted" upon the Blessed Virgin. In the 1600s, when the bubonic plague ravaged Luxembourg and Germany, a group of the faithful got together to pray to Mary the Consoler, building and enshrining her image. Legend has it that many believers were cured, and the area became a magnet for those seeking Mary's special favors.

Fast-forward to 1875, when some of her followers immigrated to Frenchtown, Ohio, taking a reliquary (small portion) of the statue with them in addition to an icon from the Luxembourg basilica. As the procession to install the statue in its new home in nearby Carey

★ ★

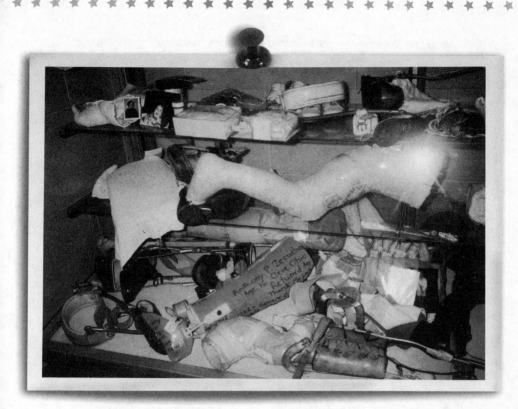

Kiss those prosthetics goodbye.

commenced, a thunderstorm began to rage, yet the sun continued to shine on those in the presence of the statue. Whether it was a miracle or yet another example of weird Ohio weather, we'll never know. But one thing is certain: Our Lady of Consolation is one-stop shopping for the faithful as well as those on the cusp.

To begin with, the main basilica/shrine is an Italianate stunner, despite its rather plain brick exterior. Murals, sculptures, and marble saturate the first floor in a mélange of Byzantine and Romanesque designs. The arched ceiling and dome above the main altar boast gold-etched, jewel-encrusted paintings, and the altar is decorated with tile and bronze inserts, among other things.

And the statue—oy! Surrounded by various marbles, mosaics, and vigil lights, it's elevated to avoid fingers of the curious and sticky kind. And there's security, lots of it, since a 1991 theft of the icon's ornament and crown.

The lower church, as it's known, has less palatial chapels. But in addition to the chapels, there's the exhibition of cures whose beer cans, cigarette packs, and pill containers attest to renunciation of vices as well, and Our Lady's wardrobe, a collection of some two hundred frocks for every season, to rival the Miss America evening gown competition. But hey, She's worth it.

In addition to a miraculously well-stocked Christian gift shop, you'll find a wooded area with picnic benches, a Shrine Cafeteria, and plenty of parking for cars and those huge blue-hair-laden tour buses that visit regularly. It's open 24/7, so you can always call on this house of God.

A Tub to Remember
Findlay

Why would anyone go to a museum to see a rusted-out, scuzzy-looking bathtub? Well, not just any old tub: It belonged to Captain Charles Dwight Sigsbee from another, much bigger and more famous tub, the USS *Maine.* Remember that one? The ship that exploded and sank in Cuba's Havana harbor, starting the Spanish–American War in 1898 because the United States thought the Spanish were using weapons of mass destruction? Oops, wrong conflict. Or is that the sound of history repeating itself? Today, historians believe the explosion may have occurred because of a structural failure.

Regardless, you can see this relic in all its nonglory at the Hancock Historical Museum (422 West Sandusky St. 45840, 419-423-4433, www.hancockhistoricalmuseum.org). And if it could talk, it would have quite a tale to tell.

1911. Raised from the Havana harbor, all available parts and pieces of the *Maine* were salvaged, including the enamel and steel tub, which was acquired through the efforts of a local congressman. After much wrangling and infighting, Findlay snagged the prize when Urbana turned it down in favor of a 10-inch piece of mortar shell.

1913. The tub arrives, and everyone's disappointed because it looks like crap. Hey, who wouldn't after being underwater for fourteen years? So it was stored in a municipal building, falling into even greater disgrace as a city hall coal bin.

1914. Somehow the town of Lima got wind of the tub's sorry fate and raised a ruckus, so veterans of the Spanish–American War promised to bronze it and put it in a park (perhaps as a birdbath?). But it never happened, and the tub ended up in the Findlay courthouse, where a janitor taped on a sign (USS *MAINE* BATHTUB) in case anyone asked (and they did, often).

1960. Due to a courthouse renovation, the tub and its case were moved to the Findlay College Museum. Recognizing a prize when they saw one, the museum immediately put the case to use for another display. The tub ended up in an old cigar factory, a nice karmic touch if you consider that the best cigars come from Havana.

1974. The tub reached its final destination (so far), the Hancock Historical Museum, where it was promptly relegated to the basement.

1998. Not allowed to rust in peace, the tub was dragged upstairs to commemorate the one hundredth anniversary of the sinking of the USS *Maine*, and also to mark the release of a commemorative stamp (about the ship, not the tub). It has been at the museum ever since.

So the next time you think you're all washed up, remember the *Maine* bathtub!

Presidential "Firsts"
Fremont

It's the first presidential library in the United States, and the president's horse, Old Whitey, who served with him in the army, is buried near him and his wife. His son, who also saw honorable military service, campaigned Congress for six years so he could install the White House gates used during the president's administration—which had been replaced with larger ones—at the entrance of the estate, which also includes the library, museum, and the home where he died.

Obviously we're not talking about Washington, Lincoln, or FDR. Instead, it's Rutherford B. Hayes, the nineteenth POTUS (President of the United States). His Presidential Center (Spiegel Grove 43420, 419-332-2081, www.rbhayes.org), which opened in 1916, is doing well, thank you very much. What happened during the Hayes administration, anyway?

Well, for one thing, there was a disputed election involving Florida, and Hayes gave lip service to many causes, though not much seemed to get done. Sound familiar? Still, Hayes was wounded four times during the Civil War, and his administration (1877–1881) was home to several "firsts": Wife Lucy was the first to be called "First Lady" (see sidebar), and the man himself was first to travel to the West Coast during his term. Hayes was the first president to install a telephone and a typewriter in the White House, among other things. In 1878 he also instituted the Easter Egg Roll for children on the White House lawn, a tradition that still continues. He also steered clear of invading foreign countries, always a nice touch.

Although his administration may not have been the most exciting, there's lots to do in his neighborhood. The holiday season alone could fill a calendar: Along with sleigh and carriage rides through Spiegel Grove and other festive happenings, there's a layout with four operating model trains weaving among late-nineteenth-century wintertime scenes. Other special events are on tap throughout the year as well.

Even without an occasion, you can visit the thirty-three-room mansion filled with the family's original furnishings and the carriage and guest houses, the latter being decorated in ornate Victorian style. The museum itself consists of more than ten thousand objects and items on loan. With a million-plus manuscripts, the library also has all of R. B.'s diaries and letters in addition to first-source Civil War information.

A hike on the wooded estate will lead to the tombs of Hayes and his wife. And while you're there, you might want to give a nod to that other old war horse, Whitey.

RB Hayes Roundup

Sometimes you have to wonder if Ohioans have too much time on their hands. Case in point: Located about 150 miles south of Fremont, the Lucy Hayes Heritage Center (90 West Sixth St., Chillicothe 45601, 740-775-5820, www.lucyhayes.org), celebrates the life and times of Lucy Webb Hayes at her birthplace through an annual spring tea, a cake and ice cream social in August (her birthday), and a New Year's gathering commemorating the anniversary of the Presidential couple. The circa 1825 house, restored and moved to its present location several decades ago, consists of four rooms furnished with antiques and five showcases of Hayes memorabilia, including

A "doll" moment at the birthplace of Lucy Webb Hayes

a miniature reproduction of the interior when she resided there. And you'll learn why they loved Lucy, from her childhood experiences and education (along with being the first female to attend Ohio Wesleyan College, she was the first President's wife to earn a college degree) to the fates of her eight children (only five lived to adulthood) to her and her family members' bouts with illness (don't ask). While museum staff and volunteers are friendly and accommodating, be prepared to spend an hour or two hearing what some might consider TMI about "Lemonade Lucy" (she refused to serve alcohol in the White House).

In direct contrast—although in its own way just as carefully maintained—is the RB Hayes Memorial BP gas station in his birthplace of Delaware (17 William St., 43015). A plaque, several trees, and an American flag honor the nation's nineteenth president, although he might have been a bit perturbed that it is now a gas station owned by a British company responsible for the worst U.S. oil spill in history. But, hey, at least you can come and "go" as you please and fill 'er up at the same time.

★ ★

Really Old School
Genoa

Not many places can boast a twelve-hole brick privy. Of course, many places might not want to, especially one behind a schoolhouse, lending view to all sorts of weird scenarios. But that was then . . . And the

Hello, Jesus

People have claimed to see Jesus everywhere: on a tortilla, in a Pizza Hut sign, on the floor of an auto parts store. Many are rational, normally functioning human beings who hold down jobs and have families.

So it was with drapery installer Rita Ratchen on a warm summer night in 1986. She was minding her own business, driving back from an appointment on Route 12 in Fostoria, when there it was—a large likeness of Jesus Christ on a dimly lit soybean oil tank at the Archer Daniels Midland Company. "It seemed like he was walking on water," she recalled. A small child also appeared to be standing next to him.

And it wasn't like she immediately phoned the *New York Times.* She kept the discovery to herself for several days, slipping out at night to look at the image to make sure she wasn't losing her mind. Finally she took Dorothy Droll, her best friend of thirty-five years, with her, and without prompting, Dorothy immediately recognized the image. Rita told another friend, and then someone said something to someone else and before you knew it, word of the oil tank Jesus spread like, well, a soybean oil fire.

Soon amateur and professional photographers and curiosity-seekers were lining up on Route 12 to capture the image (difficult, since it only was clearly visible at odd hours of the night) or get a

★ ★

pretty little town of Genoa (43430), flush with local pride, wanted to make a name for itself in 1975 for the American bicentennial. Since its oldest building, constructed in the mid-1800s, was built like a brick outhouse and, in fact, was one, albeit with plugged holes and seats removed, the powers-that-be decided to put it on the National Register of Historic Places.

glance (easier), making for a nearly two-hour drive from the local Putt 'N Pond to the tank, only a couple of miles away. Insiders knew where the clearest view was: from the Hi-Lo gas station facing the tank itself.

By the end of summer, thousands of people were flocking from throughout Ohio and elsewhere, tying up roads and frustrating frequent fliers—truck drivers who used the less-patrolled route regularly. Coffee cups and T-shirts bearing the image were sold in town, and a Sandusky ice-cream vendor set up shop to cash in on the phenomenon. The official line at Archer Daniels was that the rust and paint stains were a result of the surrounding sodium vapor security lights. They'd planned on repainting the damned thing, until all hell broke loose and someone organized a "Save the Tank" movement.

Then the inevitable happened: Late September of that year, a Findlay firefighter with what locals described as a fondness for alcohol threw paint-filled balloons on the image, partially obscuring it. He was arrested and charged with a misdemeanor. His excuse, according to a neighbor, was that he was sick of the traffic and disruption. And so corporate America got its way—again—and the tank was repainted.

But it's begun to rust again. And from time to time, people still claim to see stuff, though nothing much has ever come of it. But who knows? Maybe next time it will be an image of Justin Bieber . . .

Never mind that it had become a storage area for the school janitor, its purpose mostly forgotten. Boosters were on a roll, so to speak,
jiggling handles in Washington and convincing the local congressman
it was worth saving. They asked for and received a grant, and now this
twelve-seater is the only outhouse on the National Register.

So if you stop by, ask discreetly for "The Little Building" (310 Main
St.) and they'll know from whence you speak. You can also check out
the town hall, opera house, and Veterans' Memorial, and do some
shopping. And according to the town's website, "Genoa offers a
great place to spend a day or a lifetime," although America's favorite
restored toilet is still a tough handle.

Random Bull, Scuba Diving, and Stinky's
Gilboa

Only in Ohio can you be driving down Route 224, enjoying the flat,
treeless farm scenery and . . . there it is!! A giant fiberglass bull rising seemingly out of nowhere, welcoming all comers to the thriving
metropolis (pop: approx 170) of Gilboa (45875). The "how" and
"why" of the bull's presence remains a mystery; even the town mayor
has no clue as to the reason for its being rounded up from Bowling
Green in the 1970s. Nevertheless it has been well maintained and is
decorated for holidays such as Christmas, despite occasionally being
the object of a low-risk cow tipping.

The bull also serves as a landmark for a somewhat controversial
underground quarry popular with scuba divers and snorkelers. Along
with featuring creepy, slimy submerged attractions such as school-
buses and airplanes and reportedly hungry but nonlethal fish, the
fourteen-acre limestone Gilboa Quarry (3763 Old State Rte. 224, 419-
456-3300, www.divegilboa.com) allows divers to explore depths of up
to 130 feet. However, four deaths in as many months in 2007 and a
few before and after that time make it an even odder choice to risk
life and limb. If you're going to submerge yourself underwater with

Rudolph, the red-nosed rein . . . bull???

only a mouthpiece and a tank of oxygen, at least it could be in the Caribbean or a luxury beach resort.

Just down the street from the bull and again, seemingly random, is Stinky's Country Well (3012 East US 224, 419-456-3271). With a parking lot full of pickups and what looks like a prison transport bus, it's probably a bad choice for an iced tea or bathroom stop. And indeed several of the patrons have been arrested for selling illegal substances, according to police reports.

Now how about those strange-looking objects made from farm equipment down the road from the bull? Maybe it's time to ease on down the road . . .

★ ★

Sure Shot
Greenville

Greenville has spawned several celebrities. There's sharpshooter Annie Oakley, the Lady Gaga of the eighteenth century; Lowell Thomas, who rose to world fame as the voice of CBS radio; and last, but certainly not least, Lieutenant Commander Zachary Lansdowne, who went down with the airship *Shenandoah* (see "Misled Zeppelin" in the Southeast chapter). Memorabilia about their lives and times—and much more—can be found at the Garst Museum and Annie Oakley Center (205 North Broadway 45331, 937-548-5250, www.garst museum.org). This Darke County gem is pretty hip, too. For example, a wall commemorating the signers of the Treaty of Greene Ville in which the Indians ceded most of Ohio to the United States reads: "Class of 1795." That's right, 1795, and includes Tecumseh, Lewis & Clark, General "Mad" Anthony Wayne, Chief Leatherlips, and future president William Henry Harrison. Imagine a reality show with that lineup.

But the majority of visitors come to learn about Phoebe Ann Mosey aka Annie, who, although she died in 1926 at age sixty-six, remains a quick draw. For one thing, the petite, pretty dynamo/crack shot traveled and entertained the world during an era when women weren't allowed to vote or even own property. Decades ahead of her time, she was a generous soul, donating much of her income to charity and fostering ideas about how people, especially women, should be fairly treated. Yet she managed not to piss anybody off—at least not overtly—which also might have been due to the fact that she rarely (if ever) missed.

The museum's comprehensive displays about Annie and her husband Frank Butler range from her gun collection to pictures to costumes to personal effects such as hairpins and diaries to memorabilia that continued to live well past her death (partially due to the musical *Annie Get Your Gun,* which has pretty much been performed in perpetuity since its successful Broadway premiere in 1946). You can also view a demonstration of her skills circa 1894 in one of the first moving

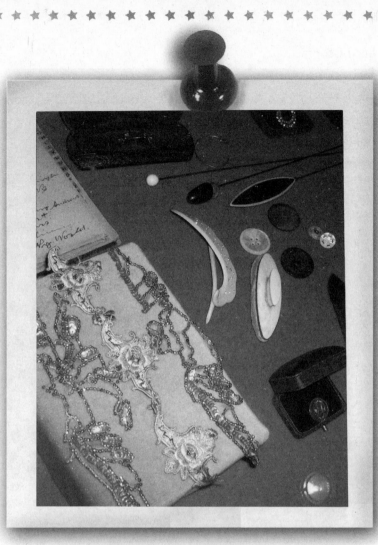

**Even though she could throw one down with
the big boys, Annie got her bling.**

pictures created by Thomas Edison and again thirty years later during her last public appearances. The museum also provides a map to
her birthplace, childhood home, place of death, and gravesite as well
as the park in the center of town which bears a statue in her honor.
When it comes to all things Annie Oakley, Greenville hit the bull's-eye.

Gourd-Ucopia
Greenville

In 1946 Mrs. Howard Hamlin organized a "Gourd Day" at the Ohio State Fair. Nearly every October since, gourd heads—those with a passion for growing and decorating the nonedible first cousins to cucumbers, squash, and melons—have cultivated and displayed their sometimes strange-looking harvest at the Ohio Gourd Show (P.O. Box 664, 45331, 740-965-4661, www.americangourdsociety.org/ohio chapter/Show.html).

People come from far away for our Gourd Day.

Used by primitive peoples as tools and eating utensils, for preparation of food, and even currency (in Haiti, the basic monetary unit is still called the gourde), gourds come in all shapes, sizes, and colors, and lend themselves to artistic and inventive interpretations, from birdhouses and flowers, to masks to musical instruments, to all kinds of animals. There are even "penis sheath" gourds worn by men in certain tribes in New Guinea and Africa, which although they're believed to be more utilitarian than ornamental, really do, er, stand out.

Some gourds are painted and covered with enamel, while others are carved, sculpted, and so changed from their original form that they're hardly recognizable at all. Other folks just like to grow 'em, engaging in intense competitions and discussions as to how to procreate the biggest and the best.

You can see hundreds of different kinds of dried, fresh, and crafty guess-whats at the show and take workshops on making your very own artsy number as well. Since the late 1940s, the event has been organized by the Ohio Gourd Society, an offshoot (so to speak) of what is now the American Gourd Society (AGS). Today the AGS has a presence in some twenty-one states, and claims some four thousand members, although if you look at the map on their website (www .americangourdsociety.org), it looks to be more in the hundreds.

For more than forty years, the show was a tradition in the small town of Mount Gilead. But in 2006 the gourdfathers decided to move it to the Darke County Fairgrounds in Greenville. The new digs allow for more space, with lots of nearby restaurants and motels. Sometimes transplanting does make the thing grow faster.

If You Chew It, They Will Gum
Greenville

Greenville, Ohio: home of the Garst Museum (see above); the Kitchen Aid Experience Store; Bear's Mill, an 1849 water-powered mill and one of the last in the United States; and—drum roll, please—the Wall of Gum!

★ ★

Let's face it: Most tourists come for the unmitigated thrill of being able to put their chewed-up gum on the left side of the Maid-Rite Sandwich Shop (121 North Broadway 45331, 937-547-1938). Thing is, so many people have stopped by to stick it to them that they mucked up the entire wall and now it has proliferated—to the back and front doors, and along the windows where you pick up your order. Yes, the place serves food, its actual purpose not to provide the answer as to

Drop off your gum while picking up your burger.

whether your chewing gum loses its flavor on the bedpost—or in this case, a brick wall—overnight. (It does.)

Yet, incredibly, it isn't just the gross yet fascinatingly colorful kaleidoscope of Bubbilicious, Bazooka, and Chiclets that keeps 'em coming back for more. It's the food, specifically something called the "loose meat sandwich." Or, imagine this postcard or e-mail: "Dear Cousin Billie Sue: Today we went to Greenville for a loose meat sandwich and to put our gum on the wall."

But in all fairness, the sandwich is a sort of Sloppy Joe thing, the concoction of one Fred Angell, "a respected butcher in Muscatine, Iowa [who] combined a special cut and grind of meat with a selected set of spices," according to the franchise website, www.maid-rite .com. In 1926 "as legend goes, Mr. Angell asked a delivery man at his restaurant to taste his newest sandwich creation. After a few bites, the taster exclaimed, 'You know, Fred, this sandwich is just made right.'" Maid-Rite. Get it?

No one seems to know exactly how the sticky tradition started, only that gum has been on the wall of the restaurant since it opened in the early 1930s. So conceivably some pieces could be more than eighty years old!

The place, which is always crowded, also serves beer, which can be a good thing. And not to worry: There's nary a chewed-up wad inside. So eat, drink, and masticate!

Welcome to Bedrock
Kelley's Island

This is the sort of place you drive up to and wonder, "Don't people on Kelley's Island have anything better to do?" It sure doesn't look like much—just a bunch of rocks surrounded by a fence, with lots of tourists milling around.

But, hey man, it's kind of groovy. The Glacial Grooves (north side of Kelley's Island 43438, 419-797-4530) are, according to the Ohio Historical Society website, the largest and most easily accessible remains

Groovy enough to draw tourists from all over Ohio!

of glacial grooves in the world—that is, if you don't take into account ferrying back and forth across Kelley's Island to get to them. Scoured into solid limestone bedrock some eighteen thousand years ago, they were created by a huge slab of ice that passed through North America. What resulted was a narrow, 400-foot-long, 35-foot-wide trough studded with 10- to 15-foot-deep gouges—a prehistoric skateboard park with a half-pipe to challenge all but the most tenderfooted posers.

But wait, there's more: 350- to 400-million-year-old marine fossils embedded in the Devonian limestone. Surrounded by fencing, the grooves are protected by an elevated walkway and stairs, so you may have to really squint to find the fossils. Plus there are other interesting views, such as the rolling, verdant, adjacent quarry, which was responsible for wiping out, in skateboard vernacular, some of the larger grooves.

But nevertheless, you should get a good idea of what it was like back then. And Fred Flintstone would feel right at home.

Swallow This

Lima

What a freak show! In this corner of the Allen County Museum (620 West Market St. 45801, 419-222-9426, www.allencountymuseum.org) is a Buddhist shrine next to a sumo-sized robe that was actually the royal garb of Victorian-era Chinese Dowager Empress Cixi. The ornate fabric was constructed using the enticingly named "forbidden stitch" and was donated by one of the museum's benefactors, a wealthy local family. And over there is a room featuring the dead stuffed animal stylings of one J. E. Grosjean (1892–1920), a normal-looking Lima businessman who loved to arrange them in various tableaux and put them in glass cases. There's a creepy selection of albino creatures (so much red eye, so little time), and if you can find the right employee who knows how to operate the thing, an unbelievably strange reenactment of Noah's Ark with lightning and thunder, marching pairs of dead birds, carved wooden deer, and more, narrated by a sonorous, God-like voice. Gotta love it.

And this is one of the few county museums in Ohio to be accredited by the oh-so-serious American Association of Museums! But with good reason: The two stories of historical collections also include comprehensive exhibits on nineteenth-century pioneer life, the Civil War, and local locomotive heritage, among other subjects, in addition to a separate children's museum, log cabin, and Victorian-era home.

★ ★

But who wants to see that stuff? Let's go find the wall o' swallowed objects! Ironically placed between a water fountain and iron lung, the two-sectioned cabinet was started by father-and-son physicians Estey and Walter Yingling, who collected them—in the most uncomfortable sense of the word—from the esophagi, lungs, and throats of local residents, including patients of the Lima Mental Hospital. Among the hundred or so mostly buttons, pins, and animal bones

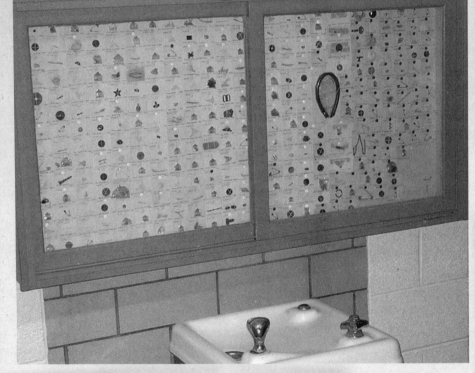

The collection of swallowed objects, with a drinking fountain in case you feel the need for aspirin

are a key, a large screw, and a horseshoe-length piece of rubber hose that prompts the question, "Why?"

The John Dillinger exhibit reenacts arguably the most exciting thing to ever happen in these here parts. While Dillinger languished in the local jail for a robbery in 1933, members of his gang escaped from an Indiana prison and found their way to Allen County, killing Sheriff Jesse Sarber and freeing Public Enemy No. 1. The "calm before the storm" display shows the good peace officer shuffling through papers in his actual chair while Dillinger stands behind bars in the original cell. Other mementoes of the event include guns, handcuffs, and a reproduction of Dillinger's death mask. OK, so the museum uses unorthodox methods in chronicling local history. But when gaggles of teenagers cluster around the Dillinger display jostling for a glimpse, you know you've got 'em hooked.

The Attraction That Time Forgot
Marblehead

For decades Mystery Hill and the Prehistoric Forest (8232 East Harbor Rd. 43440, 419-798-5230, www.mysteryhill.com) have been packing 'em in. That might be a puzzling phenomenon in itself, because the Prehistoric Forest looks to be untouched by time—the early 1950s, that is, when it was first constructed—and not in a totally complimentary way. For instance, the dirt covering the bases of some of the animal statues has been washed away, and in certain areas the paint has worn off. Plus a couple of the dinosaurs have an ironic expression more humanoid than reptilian, made even stranger by the fact that they're surrounded by smiling mini-dinosaurs, apparently their offspring.

Still the Prehistoric Forest has its charms, especially for parents of small children, who would rather not have their kids freak out at scary exhibits. A thirty-five-foot man-made waterfall and cave serve as a "suspenseful" prelude to entering the ten-acre natural woodland. (There's also a "volcano" that is supposed to shake, smoke, and belch

Getting unbalanced at Mystery Hill!

fire, but didn't on the day we visited.) Inside are various "surprises": a dinosaur nest and bones, a Tyrannosaurus Rex, a triceratops, and even an iguanodon, which only barely resembles the scaly fellas you see running around tropical areas today. The animals are featured in various milieus and may make noises and wag their heads. Visitors can also participate in an archeological "dig," uncovering bones, fossils, and footprints.

Mystery Hill is another story entirely. Back when Marblehead was being quarried for its limestone, "workers complained of strange and abnormal events" occurring in a section of rock, according to the attraction's brochure. When a house was built on the plot of land, "the homeowner complained of water running uphill and chairs sticking to walls." The house still stands—actually, leans—and like several other such "mystery hills" sites around the United States, tennis balls roll up instead of down and trees grow in the opposite direction.

Try walking through the structure without the support of a handrail, and it's like failing a DWI test sans alcohol. The physics and electromagnetic force of the field completely mess with your sense of equilibrium. And like the other "mystery hills," a teenage guide usually leads the tour, most probably because that age group is generally unfazed by any physical phenomenon, including something that completely opposes gravity.

Call it a day (and night) by playing at the adjacent, geophysically unbalanced eighteen-hole miniature golf course—eat your heart out, Tiger Woods—the water balloon battle stations, and (but of course) the gift shop and video arcade. Cabins for an overnight stay are also available, but you'll have to brave Brontosaurus and his buddies if you want to take a shower or go pee, as the bathrooms are a few feet from the cabins. Think *Jurassic Park* lite crossed with *Pee Wee's Playhouse*.

★ ★

Eclectic Electric Trains
Marblehead

The result of a runaway obsession, Train-O-Rama—the state's largest operating multigauge, electric train display—had its humble beginnings in the 1940s, in the living room of pipefitter Max Timmons. The entire Timmons family participated, including his wife and two young sons, and the model railroad made tracks into the dining room and the basement, growing to three levels there and threatening to overtake the laundry room. But Mrs. Timmons put the brakes on and said STOP, not unlike the flashing lights and lowered guard rails you see at railroad crossings.

Major "whistle stop" for train aficionados

So in 1972 the Timmons family threw themselves in front of the project and constructed what was to be first of three Train-O-Ramas, each bigger than the last, tracking visitors through a poster board of names and hometowns (and nearly eighty countries) and offering "I Spy" for various types of railcars, bridges, and other scenes for kids of all ages. They moved into their present location (6732 East Harbor Rd. 43440, 419-734-5856, www.trainorama.com) in 1979.

But in the true spirit of "If you build it, they will come," the four-thousand-square-foot display has now overtaken even its present digs. Some forty running trains weave over and under mountains, country-side, rivers, and waterfalls, and through cities, historical and natural panoramas, and much, much more. There's so much to take in, you might want to pretend you're sitting at a crossing waiting for the interminable parade of boxcars to pass and focus on each one. You won't be so derailed by all the bells and whistles, and you'll see a lot more.

With 1,001 lightbulbs and 1,200 pieces of equipment, not to mention countless moving parts, the exhibit must be a real train wreck to repair, and one can only imagine the monthly electric bill. Still, you won't get gauged, er, gouged at the gift shop, which sells a complete line of reasonably priced train sets, accessories, and more.

Holy Relics!
Maria Stein

Not everyone wants to or can go to the Holy Land to see the birth-place of Christianity. You now have an alternative: the National Marian Shrine of the Holy Relics (2291 St. Johns Rd. 45860, 419-925-4532, www.mariasteincenter.org), where you can view more than one thousand relics, the second-largest collection in the United States (the first is St. Anthony's Chapel in Pittsburgh) while minimizing the risk of getting blown up by a terrorist bomb or catching crossfire from an Uzi. And you don't even have to check all your luggage!

★ ★

Although relics are endemic in many Catholic churches, these aren't just any old artifacts. Ninety-five percent of what's in the Maria Stein collection is quantified as first-class, taken from the body of the saint, usually a fragment of bone. (Second-class encompasses physical items such as clothing or a prayerbook, while third-class includes objects touched by the material remains of a saint.) So we're talking a fragment cast of hundreds, from St. Adrian to St. Zita.

But what about the Blessed Virgin Mary and Jesus Himself? Although Mary's items are few, they are impressive—a piece of her veil and belt as well as small portions from her tomb and the House of Loretto, reputed to be her home in Nazareth. The Big Guy's son has a cool dozen, starting with pieces from his crib and the Last Supper table to his crucifixion and beyond—from the whipping post, a thorn from his crown and nail on the cross, his burial clothes, and from the grave (sepulchre) in which he was interred.

So who knew to save all this? That's one question not easily answered, but in 1875 one Father J. Gartner, vicar general from Milwaukee, entrusted his large collection of relics to the Sisters of the Precious Blood at Maria Stein. According to an article in the March 2000 *Catholic Telegraph,* he had obtained the collection in Rome and "had been persuaded to take the items back to the Americas for veneration. At the time, graves and catacombs were being plundered for relics and other church valuables came on the market in overstocked pawnshops."

Results of this sanctified Odd Lots plunder can be found in the main shrine with its ornate woodwork and hand-carved altar, highlighted by stained-glass windows imported from Germany. Adjacent Romanesque chapels boast round arches and vaulted ceilings as well as oil paintings and lots of statuary. You can also see the corpse of St. Victoria, clothed in an ornate red gown, in all her waxy glory. Or, if you're looking for something less intense, the Heritage Museum on the second floor traces the history of early pioneers as well as that of the Sisters. Domestic items, clothing, furniture, and more from this venerable order are on display. They've been in Ohio since the mid-1800s, and although their numbers have diminished, they're still some two hundred–plus strong.

As any good saint would tell you, some habits are just hard to break.

Yes You Can!
Napoleon

It's a combo Andy Warhol/Rachael Ray fantasy: Not only does the Campbell's Soup plant (12773 Township Rd. P3, 43545, 419-592-1010, www.campbellsoup.com) have two, count 'em, two, ginormous LTL soup cans for the world to see, but you can sometimes smell the vegetables cooking, leaving the air redolent with the odor of Chunky Tomato.

The first oversize can is located just outside the factory. While it's appropriately labeled "Tomato"—where's that giant cracker?—the factory also produces V-8 juice. (An oversized V-8 can would probably be a bad idea, since visitors might stand around smacking themselves in the head, thinking they could have had that instead of a fast-food burger.) The second "can" is actually a water tower painted with the Campbell's Soup logo, so if they ever do decide to cook up a whopping batch, all they'll need to do is add the soup and find a really big hotplate.

While the company has been around since 1869, and is still head-quartered in Camden, New Jersey, they are surprisingly au courant, despite their cheesy ad campaigns and preservative-laden products. Along with employing some 1,200 people, the Napoleon factory, which opened in the 1940s, uses produce from area farmers. We're not talking small potatoes, either; they work with locals to obtain lots and lots—as in roughly five hundred thousand pounds—of fresh vegetables per day, including tomatoes, celery, parsley, lettuce, spinach, and carrots. The company also does considerable community outreach with its Stamp Out Hunger food drive, Labels for Education school

Mm, mm, good . . . Don't forget to add water!
PHOTO COURTESY OF CAMPBELL'S SOUP COMPANY

equipment donation, and through encouraging employee volunteer-ism. There's even a Campbell's Soup Foundation that does mm, mm good deeds, helping people improve their living conditions, health care, educational opportunities, and jobs.

The next time you reach for that can of soup or beverage think of all the sustainable healthy veggies that come from this Ohio plant. Unless you're going for Spaghetti-Os, because they don't grow pasta down on the farm.

A Tale of Two Bars

Put-in-Bay

"Tossing a cold one" at the Beer Barrel Saloon (1618 Delaware Ave. 43456, 419-285-7281, www.beerbarrelpib.com) is quite an accom-plishment: The bar alone is 405 feet 10 inches long. According to the saloon's website, that makes it taller than Perry's Monument, the island's other big attraction. What is this, a men's locker room?

Listed in *Guinness World Records* as the World's Longest Bar, it has other attributes, among them 160 bar stools, fifty-six beer taps, and a seating capacity of 1,200, with twenty bartenders employed on busy nights and two "backup bars" at the far corner in event of an over-flow. Of people, that is.

Speaking of which, it's not uncommon to walk in, shoulder your way through the usual jam of revelers, and encounter one or more women who seem to arbitrarily pull up their shirts and bare their breasts. The place just encourages wild-and-crazy carousing, even among folks who should be old enough to know better.

So you just might want to peer in, say to yourself, "OK, now I've seen the World's Longest Bar" (and possibly the most drunken baby boomers in one place), and head toward the Roundhouse Bar (Dela-ware Ave. 43456, 419-285-2323, www.theroundhousebar.com), which along with having excellent acoustics, thanks to a canopy that's been held up by a wooden bicycle wheel for decades, allows for more breath-ing room. Opened in Toledo in 1873 as the Columbia Restaurant, the

Another Thursday morning in Put-in-Bay, where it's always 5 o'clock somewhere!

circular building was cut in half and moved to its present location in 1944. A few years later it was painted its current color of bright red.

OK, so the building is kind of falling apart—the canopy also serves to catch falling plaster from the ceiling—but it is a true original, with most of its wood construction intact and fading funky murals, courtesy of a late artist known as Canoe Bob. But people keep their clothes on, usually a good idea in a public place.

★ ★

Juiced-Up Geodes

Put-in-Bay

It's a winery! It's the world's largest geode! You can't go wrong with this spot; there's something for every age group, including a complimentary glass of wine or grape juice.

Although the cave in Crystal Cave is a misnomer—at thirty feet in diameter, it's more like standing in the middle of a gaggle of glistening white to slightly blue gemstones ranging from eight to eighteen inches—its history sparkles with coincidence and good fortune for Heineman's Winery. The winery was founded in 1888 by Gustav Heineman, an immigrant from Baden-Baden, Germany. Nine years later, when the workers were digging a well for it, they accidentally discovered, forty feet beneath the surface, a cavity lined with strontium sulfate, a blueish mineral also known as celestite. The original hole was much smaller than what appears today, as crystals were harvested and sold for the manufacturing of fireworks.

Although wineries had thrived in the Put-in-Bay area before Prohibition, Heineman's was one of the few to stay afloat, supposedly on the strength of its unfermented "grape juice," a taxi cab service (after drinking too much "juice"), and tours of Crystal Cave.

Today the winery is still operated by the third and fourth generations of the Heineman family, who in conjunction with other local growers, cultivate Concord, Catawba, Delaware, Ives, and Niagara grapes on approximately fifty acres of vineyards on the island. It's also open to the public (978 Catawba St. 43456, 419-285-2811, www.heinemans winery.com). Save your glass of vino for the end of the cave portion of the tour—you wouldn't want to trip over any stray geodes.

Hazard-ous Duty

Put-in-Bay

If not for Admiral Oliver Hazard Perry, we would be subjects of the Crown of England and ending our sentences with "eh?" Today's largely unrecognized hero of the War of 1812—George Washington and Abe Lincoln made better press in the history books—Perry's victory over the British in 1813 marked the first and only occasion their entire fleet was captured. As a result, the Americans took over Lake Erie and the entire Northwest. Not only that, but Perry was only twenty-eight

**"Gee whiz, Mary Lou! We can see
all the way to Cedar Point!"**

years old and had a mere nine ships at his disposal and still had the time to scribble the immortal words, "We have met the enemy, and they are ours." No slacker, he.

Still, Perry does have his own memorial (93 Delaware Ave. 43456, 419-285-2184, www.nps.gov/pevi); at 352 feet, it's the world's largest Doric column and the third-tallest monument in the United States. It's topped off by an eleven-ton bronze urn, and underneath the floor are the remains of three British and three U.S. officers killed in the battle, a sort of karmic kiss-and-make-up. Carved in the rotunda walls are the names of Perry's vessels along with those of the Americans killed or wounded in the battle. If the monument's open, you can climb the thirty-seven circular steps and take the elevator to the top, 317 feet above Lake Erie. On a sunny day, mainland Canada and Cleveland as well as the surrounding islands are clearly and dramatically visible.

If you have the time, you might also want to sojourn to the visitor center, which along with being the home of a rather worn-looking marble statue of Perry—understandable since it was moved and reassembled several times in all kinds of weather since its construction in 1860—is also a repository for all sorts of memorabilia relating to the War of 1812. Rangers will be glad to spend hours discussing cannonades, vessels, and all manner of battle strategies. Bargain hunters will also be happy to know that souvenir musket balls are available from the gift shop for $1.

Circle of Life
Sandusky

If you consider that childhood and old age are similar in many ways, it should come as no surprise that many of the biggest fans of the Merry-Go-Round Museum (301 Jackson St. 44870, 419-626-6111, www.merrygoroundmuseum.org) are in their blue-haired period. More power to them if they can hop on the wooden horses and ride on the fully restored 1930s Allen Herschel carousel located inside the former post office.

★ ★

Going around in circles for the fun of it

This place has come full circle. In 1988 the issuance of four carousel stamps in Sandusky sparked a stampede of enthusiasm from devotees whose lives revolve around carousels (you know who you are). They convinced community leaders that Sandusky needed a museum devoted to the preservation of carousel art, and the horseshoe-shaped former post office had the good luck to be available.

The museum also features the 1867 workshop of master carver Gustav Dentzel, which contains tools, workbenches, and Dentzel's own partially chiseled horses. Other acquisitions include works by carousel-craft superstars like Daniel Muller, M. C. Illions, Charles Loof, and Charles Carmel; a primitive-looking wooden horse that was part of the first merry-go-round in the United States; and a stained-glass replica of a postage-stamp horse.

The museum also has living craftspeople on-site who restore antique carousel figures and related items, using tools similar to those used by master carvers. Visitors can watch them at work. There are also, for lack of a better word, rotating exhibits such as a display on the art and artistry of the aforementioned Daniel Muller.

It's a step back into a simpler time when you could actually see the brass ring you were grasping for.

Tons of Buns
Toledo

Tony Packo's restaurant (1902 Front St. 43605, 419-691-6054, www .tonypacko.com) has the only collection of autographed hot dog buns in the known universe, some one thousand encased in plastic and lin- ing the walls of the venerable eatery, which has been around since the Great Depression. They bear the signatures of Burt Reynolds—who signed the alpha bun—Leslie Uggams, Steve Tyler of Aerosmith, and five U.S. presidents (anything to get a vote).

OK, so they aren't real hot dog buns. They're made of Styrofoam, but you can't tell the difference unless you bite into one (and maybe not even then, if you've had enough to drink). But who would come to a restaurant to see a bunch of moldy hot dog buns, even if they are signed by nearly the entire cast of *The Love Boat* and local news anchors?

Besides, more than celebrity buns and actor Jamie Farr have given staying power to this family-owned enterprise. A former factory worker, Toledo native Tony Packo started a sandwich and ice-cream shop in 1932, only to find that people couldn't afford the full monty sausage. So he split it in half, concocted a special chili sauce and invented the "Hungarian Hot Dog," an anachronism if there ever was

★ ★

one. It was an instant hit, and its popularity spread faster than the heat from the spicy topping itself.

In 1972 Tony's daughter Nancy saw Burt Reynolds in *The Rainmaker* at a local auditorium and sent him a letter, inviting him to the restaurant. Much to everyone's amazement, he showed up, and after he finished his meal was asked for his autograph. No piece of suitable paper could be found, but depending upon which version you're hearing, either the crew or Reynolds came up with the brilliant idea of signing a stale hot dog bun . . . and the rest is history—sort of.

Jamie Farr, another native Toledoan who played Corporal Max Klinger on *M*A*S*H,* mentioned Tony Packo's several times during the lengthy run of the successful TV series. Rumor has it that because of the worldwide exposure, Farr gets free hot dogs for life, which is good because acting can be an uncertain profession, and he'll never starve if he moves back to his hometown. Several walls are devoted to pictures and memorabilia relating to *M*A*S*H* and Farr.

Packo's keeps expanding and adding restaurants throughout northwest Ohio and southern Michigan. Their sauces, hot peppers, and other specialties have become so well liked that they've developed their own line of grocery store products, including variations on another popular menu item, deep-fried pickles. Bet no one ever signed one of those.

Oh, Boy!
Toledo

Before Beavis and Butthead and the Jackass guys there were the Pimps of Pimplyness, a gang of ten teenage boys who, on March 17, 1995, absconded with a six-foot, three hundred–pound Big Boy in front of its namesake restaurant (3537 Secor Rd. 43606, 419-531-5355). The assassins dismembered the statue, cutting it into ten pieces, which were found in various places around town. Each section had a note, "Big Boy is dead," except for one that read, "Big Boy is almost dead. Never mind. Now he's dead."

(Continued on Page 150)

Dead Like Them

Pull up a cold slab and listen to the tale of the Walker Funeral Home, formerly near the intersection of Central and Monroe Streets. The two nondescript white buildings have gone through several incarnations, including stints as a private ambulance company and an insurance firm.

But on October 29, 1960, it was still a funeral home when a plane crashed at the Toledo Airport, killing twenty-two people, including sixteen members of the Cal Poly San Luis Obispo football team, who had just lost to Bowling Green 50–6. After trying to take off in thick fog, the plane only made it in the air about three hundred feet when the left engine sputtered and died. It smashed into an orchard and split in two, resulting in the worst sports-related air tragedy to date.

The victims were brought to the funeral home temporarily and they—along with other dead clients—have been spotted in various incarnations by live ones ever since. Some claimed to encounter the deceased in the basement, walking around or knocking things off the walls. Doors slammed and visitors felt a chill as ghostly presences passed through them.

Many have quite a story to tell. According to a former ambulance driver's testimonial on the website www.forgottenohio.com, he and his partner used to check the parking lot for indigents and saw, on several occasions, a light on the abandoned top floor of one of the buildings. Each time "a young woman in a dress would come to the window and stare at us," he recounts. "One night, after seeing the figure, we got brave and called some law enforcement friends from the area to help us search the building. We went to the room that had the light on expecting to find a vagrant camped out there. The only thing we found was a room that had untouched dust on the floor and no light bulbs in the sockets." It gave them the willies big time, and they never went back there again. But as long as there are "ghosts," there will always be the curious who walk among them.

Oh, the indignities of being a Big Boy in Ohio! Here's another "poser" at Kennedy's Doughnuts in Cambridge.

(Continued from Page 148)

The stunt made news and wire services all over the country, prompting the burning question, "Why?" "We were bored," eighteen-year-old Tom Martinez, the Pimps's spokesman, told the Associated Press. He noted the stunt "was a lot of fun," but "a pretty stupid thing to do." Yes, especially since the not-so-little boys were brought up on charges.

According to some sources, unlike Humpty Dumpty, this Big Boy was put together again, his feet encased in cement shoes, which as Jimmy Hoffa might attest, is no guarantee of anything. According to others, however, the statue was ruined beyond repair, with parts offered as organ donations to other damaged Big Boys. "We still don't talk about it. It was very painful for us," store manager Drema Demers remarked in the *Toledo Blade*. "I know he was happy here. He was always smiling."

But it still didn't deter delinquents from repeating the prank again, in December 1998. This time the fiberglass fella disappeared around 3:00 p.m. on a Sunday on the busy street in broad daylight, leaving only mangled bolts and a pedestal. "One of my managers called me at home and said, 'He's gone,'" continued Ms. Demers, who immediately knew what the manager was talking about.

Apparently this one was returned in better condition, because he's still standing out there on Secor Road in his red-and-white-checked overalls, holding a giant hamburger, waiting for some brawny lad to spirit him away . . . again.

Spaced Out: Part II
Wapakoneta

As with presidents, Ohio seems to have a disproportionate number of astronauts: twenty-four and counting since the inception of the space race in the late 1950s. Unlike the cozy ambience of the John Glenn museum and home in New Concord (see Southeast chapter), the Neil Armstrong Air and Space Museum (500 South Apollo Dr. 45895, 419-738-8811, www.ohiohistory.org/places/armstron) is government-run and resembles something out of *Star Trek*.

Prepare for liftoff by checking out the mockups of the Apollo command module and Gemini spacecraft out front. This may bring to mind such burning questions as: How could those guys stand being in such a confined area 24/7? How did they manage to eat? What did they do if they had to go to the bathroom or, possibly even more embarrassing, pass gas? And you thought being cubicled was bad.

Scattered amid standard exhibits on the development of air travel, Wapakoneta native Armstrong's rise from the family farm to the first man on the moon, and, yes, rocket science, is some truly eclectic

★ ★

Walk in and take a spin . . . not!

memorabilia: displays on Russian cosmonauts and animals in space, an oil portrait of John Glenn, Civil Defense armbands used in 1950s bomb shelter drills, and lots of moon paraphernalia, including rocks, long-armed robotic machines for taking photographs, and even a machete (to ward off green-cheese bearing aliens?). Other exhibits describe how the astronauts ate—sucking through a tube, with everything freeze-dried or cubed, just add water—as well as took care of business at the opposite end, a procedure involving Vaseline, guiding another sort of missile into a sealed plastic bag, then kneading. These guys were dedicated.

Then beam yourself up to the Astro-theater by passing through the twinkling Infinity Room, which looks suspiciously like dozens of holiday lights amid smoked glass and mirrors. The presentation runs every half hour or so, and it's as much watching guys in space suits walk around, defy gravity, and talk to Mission Control as you can handle. Before lifting off, you might want to check out some of the newer exhibits, such as an overview of the NASA space shuttle as well as a tribute to Judith Resnick, the Akron native killed in the 1986 Challenger explosion (hey, where's her museum?). You'll also learn about NASA developments in general use today, such as high-temperature graphite tape and materials used in orthodontics. And if the line isn't too long, try the shuttle landing simulator to see if you have the "right stuff." But first, those heavy, yucky white space suits need a serious fashion makeover.

Small-Town Stonehenge
Wapakoneta

When flying over Wapakoneta, an airline pilot thought he'd made a wrong turn to Peru and was glimpsing the Incan ruins of Machu Picchu. OK, that's a bit of an exaggeration but, like many others who heard about it through word of mouth or glimpsed a snapshot on the Internet, the pilot was intrigued enough to stop by at the Temple of Tolerance (203 South Wood St. 45895, 419-738-4474). After he landed, that is.

This seemingly random conglomeration of rock structures, wrought iron, chairs, utensils, a red barrel the size of an outhouse, and just about anything else you can imagine is the vision of one Jim Bowsher, teacher, historian, writer, speaker and expert on just about everything "Wapa" as the locals call it. Bowsher scoured the region for remains of prehistoric Ice Age boulders; human-cut stones such as obelisks, millstones, steps, and parapets; and different kinds of rocks from granite to limestone to quartz to flint and more.

Each piece has a purpose, documenting local and geological history. "I saw it completed in my mind," Bowsher observed in a recent

★ ★

Rockin' it out at the Temple of Tolerance

YouTube interview. Enlisting the help of troubled youth, he began it in 1995 and finished four years later, constructing the heap de résistance, a giant twenty-foot-high rock conglomeration, complete with large boulders and tributary temples that, according to Bowsher, is safe to climb and play on, regardless of age. "I realized that if kids had a place to go to empower themselves, they would be able to change their lives. It's a place where kids and adults can start over." And indeed it has been the site of at least one wedding as well as impromptu concerts by bluegrass musicians.

The Temple, which is located in the backyard of Bowsher's childhood home and current residence and rambles along several adjacent backyard lots, is practically invisible from the street. There's no parking lot or admission fee although donations of $1 are welcome as long as he's there and/or you can get onto the front porch (the resident cat, who often follows visitors around, seems uninterested in monetary contributions). And like Denny's restaurant, it's always open, and also like Denny's, it might be a good place to hook up, especially if you're a teenager looking for excitement. Er, maybe not.

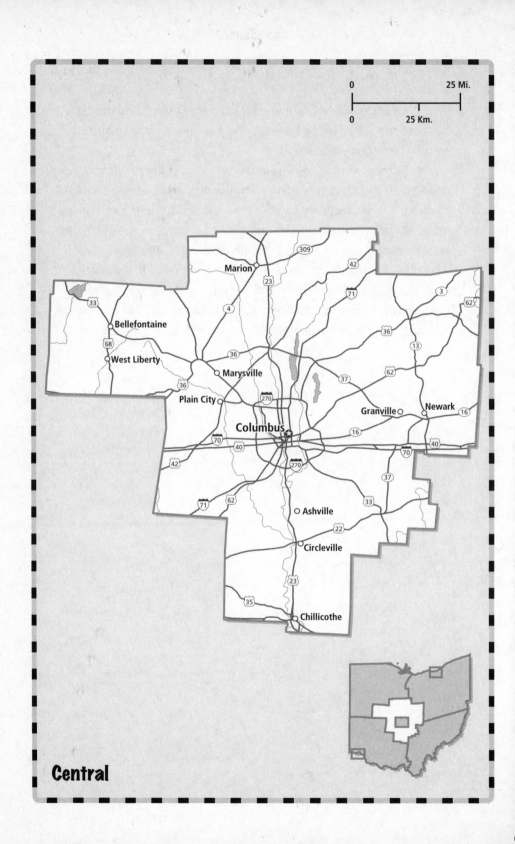

0   25 Mi.

0   25 Km.

Marion

309

42

33

71

3

Bellefontaine

62

68

36

13

West Liberty

36

Marysville

37

62

Plain City

270

Granville

Newark

Columbus

16

16

70

40

40

270

70

42

37

71

62

33

Ashville

22

Circleville

23

35

Chillicothe

Central

4

Central

Mid-Ohio is a *great place to hit the road, in more ways than one. For instance, although the honor of the first actual traffic light in Ohio goes to Cleveland, there's a very cool version in Ashville, a circa 1930s art deco job with a timing device and alternating red and green bulbs. It hung around Ashville for fifty years, until it was retired to the local museum, where it shares exhibit space with the world's smartest (stuffed) rooster, and lost silver nuggets from the Snake Den Mounds.*

Bellefontaine is a veritable hotbed of transportation highlights. Along with having the oldest concrete road in America, it also boasts McKinley Street, allegedly the world's shortest, although there is dispute about both the length and that claim. Here you'll also find Campbell Hill, the highest point in Ohio, a whopping 1,549 feet. Eat your heart out, Colorado!

In the "dead zone," so to speak, are the Granville Inn and the Buxton Inn, which are reputed to be haunted and may share spirits as well as across-the-street addresses; Marion Cemetery, with its "rolling stone" of a grave—the 1880s Charles Merchant family marker that keeps rotating, despite repeated efforts to return it to its original position; and the Newark Earthworks. Constructed sometime between 100 BC and AD 400, this ancient ruin sits squarely in the middle of the golf course at the Moundbuilders Country Club. Better the spirits of Native Americans than grouchy duffers any day!

Going Toward the Light
Ashville

Small towns can be infamous for their lack of entertainment. But if you're going to watch the traffic light change for amusement, Ashville would be the place to do it. Built in 1937 by local inventor Teddy Boor, the odd-shaped, Jetson-esque cylinder has "stop" and "go" lights that rotate clockwise and are timed by a sweeping hand. According to Charlie Cord, one of several older gentlemen/curators who seem to come with Ohio's Small Town Museum (34 Long St. 43103, 740-983-9864, ohiosmalltownmuseum.org), where the light now hangs around, "You knew exactly when it would change, so you could speed up or

One traffic light that's actually interesting to watch

slow down accordingly," taking the guesswork out of making a run for the border of the intersection.

The nation's oldest working traffic light was installed at the corner of Main and Long Streets in Ashville until 1982, when the Ohio Department of Transportation gave the community a strong signal to replace it with a more conventional model. It's still brought out for special occasions such as the Fourth of July, but normally shares exhibit space with such phenomena as the world's smartest rooster, lost silver nuggets from the Snake Den Mounds, and a Victorian-era phonograph that still plays "records" shaped like a jumbo can of green beans.

The rooster, the long gone but fondly remembered Chic-Chic, "would go down to the diner with a dime in his mouth and get a snack," explains Charlie. There's also memorabilia about Buster, the dog that voted Republican, but given the current political situation, perhaps that's not such a reflection of intelligence. Other displays encompass both world wars and sports memorabilia and other souvenirs from local high schools, as well as lots of old-timey stuff and whatever inspires the other curator, also named Charlie, to tell a story about on that particular day.

But the real beacon is the light, and if you're lucky and/or if you have a camera, you'll get to have your picture taken with this luminary that appeared on *Oprah* and *An American Moment* with James Earl Jones.

Mountain Do
Bellefontaine

Colorado has "Fourteeners," and Alaska's Mount McKinley stands a majestic 20,320 feet. Ohio's biggest projection is the 1,549-foot Campbell Hill. Surrounded by flat terrain, it's also the site of the not-so-imaginatively named Ohio Hi-Point Career Center (2280 Rte. 540 43311, 937-599-3010, www.ohp.k12.oh.us/about-ohp/campus-and-facilities. html). And if you want to arrange an expedition, you better call first to make sure the school is open, because it's surrounded by a fence.

★ ★

The good news is there's no altitude sickness, lost climbers, or gla-ciers, at least not during the last few thousand years. And the town of Bellefontaine is proud of its Big Foothill, with signs proclaiming WELCOME TO THE TOP OF OHIO, a dubious honor considering the state is mostly flat with only a few areas of rolling topography. Sometimes inquiries about Campbell Hill are met with puzzled glances, so ask for Hi-Point and they'll direct you right away.

Though hardly a "peak" climbing experience, it's steeper than it looks and elevated enough to have different weather from downtown Bellefontaine. On a clear day you can see as far away as Indian Lake, about fifteen miles to the northwest. Ignore the fence, the radio and water towers, and the United States Geological Survey (USGS) *X* that marks the spot of the actual summit, and you might feel like an actual adventurer. Or not . . .

Before it was a vocational school, Campbell Hill was the site of the Bellefontaine Air Force Station. In the 1950s and 1960s, during the height of the cold war, the 664th Aircraft Control and Warning Squadron monitored the skies for nuclear warheads. No Russian mis-siles came their way, so it became a school in 1970, and though many of the original buildings still remain, it's grown considerably, with a $1.9 million expansion and state-of-the-art technology center.

A geological aberration, Campbell Hill came about during the ice age, when a large deposit of shale rock called the Bellefontaine Outlier became separated from the main body of the glacier. As it retreated, it left behind a large mass of earth and rock debris called an end moraine, which ran perpendicular to the direction of the ice and formed as it melted.

Now it's a place where students can scale the career ladder and become truck drivers, tool and die operators, and cosmetologists, among many other professions.

Concrete Success

Bellefontaine

It's a fact of modern life: Orange barrels seem to barricade the same spots on the freeway, year after year. It's annoying, inconvenient, and a major source of income for local traffic cops. When you see a grinning construction worker holding up a stop sign when you're rushing and late for work, think of Bellefontaine residents George Bartholomew and James C. Wonders.

Road construction workers should build a shrine here.

★ ★

In the late nineteenth century, road conditions were even worse. Streets were getting torn up by vehicles and during dry spells were hard and dusty. When it rained, mud became so thick they could hardly get through. And these were horses, buggies, and wagons—cars hadn't even come into general use yet.

But newbie resident Bartholomew had a concrete solution. He learned about cement production in Germany and in Texas and discovered two of the main ingredients, limestone and clay, in mid-Ohio. So he started his own company, Buckeye Portland Cement Co., and proposed to the city council that they use his "artificial stone," as he called it. But they were reluctant to cement the deal, as it hadn't been tried anywhere in the United States.

But Bartholomew was persistent and in 1891 was authorized to pave an eight-foot section next to two hitching posts near the center of town. It proved to hold fast, and the city council—in a massive gesture of generosity—allowed Bartholomew to pave the square around the Logan County Courthouse, at 101 South Main St., as long as he donated the cement and posted a $5,000 bond that guaranteed that it would last five years. With the help of Logan County engineer Wonders, who designed the construction of the road, he got 'r done and, bolstered by success, was honored at the Chicago International Exposition of 1893. The road is still in use today, more than 110 years later. Talk about long-term investments.

In 1991 Bellefontaine honored George Bartholomew with his own statue, near the original 8-foot section of road. A plaque commemorates the first concrete street in America, whose maintenance and repair for the first fifty years only cost $1,400. Today it shows some wear and tear, but what wouldn't after all that time?

So, what's the deal with the perpetual road construction everyplace else?

Short Street... Sort Of

In brief, Bellefontaine claims to have the shortest street. It's named after Ohio native President William McKinley, who once campaigned there, although no one seems to know exactly how short it is – some accounts say fifteen feet, others seventeen, and even the venerable Ohio Historical Society flip-flops between twenty and thirty feet.

And another thing—it's the shortest street where? Some folks claim that the worldwide honor belongs to Elgin Street in Bacup, Lancashire, England, which is only seventeen feet long. However, boosters of the Bellefontaine boulevard point out that Elgin Street is closed to motor vehicle traffic, whereas driving is permitted on McKinley Street. Plus it goes north and south and serves as a connector between Columbus and Garfield Avenues.

The city website succinctly sidesteps the issue, proclaiming McKinley Street as "the shortest street in America." At the very least, anyway.

Smooth Operator
Chillicothe

Once upon a time, telephones were these clunky black devices with rotary dials, utilizing operators who connected you to the other person and sometimes even listened in (as did neighbors, if it was a shared party line). With its collection of ungreen paper directories dating back over one hundred years and all types of antique communication equipment, the James M. Thomas Telephone Museum (68 East Main St. 45601, 740-772-8200) harks back to the days when calling someone

Dial-up networking, old-school

required total concentration, as opposed to being done while driving, peeing, or otherwise engaged.

Named after telephone pioneer and judge James M. Thomas, this eclectic collection honors his contributions to the industry and community. Although he lived to be only forty-six, Thomas answered the call for independent telephony by enlisting some 2.5 million subscribers by the time of his death in 1904. Along with forming the United States Telephone Company, which provided then practically unheard-of long distance service, he hooked up the Home Telephone Company of Chillicothe, which later became the Chillicothe Telephone Company and today is Horizon (as opposed to Verizon), where the museum is currently located.

Other than a lion's head couch and some papers and photos from Thomas's home, the museum is off the hook with company and telephone history, from huge, clunky-looking operator switchboards to cables and insulators that only engineers or gizmoheads might appreciate to antique office equipment used by longtime employees (Imagine! These people actually had job security!). But the real ringers are the phones themselves—an oak payphone booth (remember those?) that remained functional until 1976; a circa 1895 phone with two separate batteries; and a German rotary model with numbers on either side (good luck figuring that one out), among many others. Admission is free, and the company prides itself on employee longevity and community involvement, something bigger providers might find as obsolete as a crank call.

Hitler Road
Circleville

Yes, Virginia, there really is a Hitler Road in Circleville. In fact, there are three of them: Hitler No. 1 Road (a number, not an opinion, according to one local wag), Hitler No. 2 Road, and Huber-Hitler Road. There's even a Hitler-Ludwig Cemetery in Circleville (1819 Hitler Road 1, 43113, 740-474-2361). Are any Jewish people buried there? "As far

★ ★

No, not *that* **Hitler**

as we know, probably not," observes local historian Wallace "Wally" Higgins.

Before you call the local Anti-Defamation League, consider that the Circleville Hitlers immigrated to the United States in the 1700s and were a prominent farming family and well respected in the community.

"They donated money for education and other local causes," Higgins continues. "Most of them died off or moved, although the last local descendant, Miss Martha Hitler, remained in the area until she passed away in the 1980s."

And der Führer's real moniker wasn't Hitler, anyway. Adolph's father was born out of wedlock to a woman who eventually married a man named Heidler. "The name was misspelled, and it stuck," says Higgins.

The Jewish news service ynetnews.com investigated the phenomenon, pointing out that the Circleville clan was probably the only "real" Hitlers in the world. And they never hurt anyone, so why should they change the name?

The Frankensteins of Canton

Somewhat more mysterious is a gravestone, located about three hours north in Canton (Westlawn Cemetery, 1919 7th St. 44708, 330-455-4021), alleged to be the final resting place of Dr. Frakenstein. Rumor was that the Timken family of Germany—relatives of the American founder of Timken Roller Bearings—arranged for the remains of the body to be flown to Canton because the villagers in Dr. F's "home town" kept defacing the grave. The other story is that it is a family plot of two farmers who moved to Ohio in the early to mid 1800s. Yet, unlike the Hitlers, no descendants or historians seem to have any information about the family.

But Frankenstein was a fictional character . . . wasn't he???

★ ★

Eight-Sided Wonder
Circleville

There's something off-kilter about an eight-sided house in a place called Circleville. But in the mid-nineteenth century, octagon homes were all the rage, especially on the East Coast and in the Midwest, thanks to an 1848 book, *A Home for All; or the Gravel Wall and Octagon Mode of Building* by amateur architect Orson Squire Fowler. A phrenologist by trade who deciphered the contours of the human head, he may have been a few degrees short of a straight angle when he announced that eight-sided homes were roomier, allowing for more wall space and better access through a central stair hall. They were supposedly also healthier, thanks to a cupola that provided improved ventilation and lighting.

Building them could be expensive and a hassle, though, since you had to adapt the structure around the octagon's 135-degree contour. Finding room for stuff could also be challenging—closets and other storage areas were pie-shaped, with sloped ceilings. And forget about privacy: The rooms all opened into each other. Still, in its day, Circleville's Gregg-Crites home was pretty cool-looking, with fourteen-foot-high ceilings, fireplaces in every room, and doors that led to an outer veranda, not to mention a freestanding spiral staircase.

Constructed in 1855 "the house was lived in by only three families," observes local historian Wallace "Wally" Higgins. It sat for 160 years, an undisturbed favorite landmark off Route 23, until development of a certain "big box" superstore threatened its existence. Does Wal-Mart have to be responsible for everything?

Nevertheless, in 2004 a band of devoted preservationists, the Roundtown Conservancy, did a good turn and managed to get the structure—all 480 tons of it—moved a half-mile away to relative safety. So if you really want to find it, contact someone from the conservancy (P.O. Box 501, Circleville 43113, dorothycooper360@frontier.com).

★ ★

Although it's rather dilapidated, they're trying to raise money to restore it as a visual and performing arts center. "It's an outstanding example of the architectural period," adds Higgins. Plus it's reminiscent of the county's first courthouse, also an octagon, which sat in the middle of the original, circular layout of the city. So maybe an octagon in the round isn't such a loopy idea after all.

The house during its Victorian-era glory days
ROUNDTOWN CONSERVANCY, INC., CIRCLEVILLE, OH

★ ★

Orange Crush
Circleville

It's the greatest show on earth—pumpkin show, that is. Local boosters also use the word "free" when referring to the annual Circleville
Pumpkin Show, which takes place the third week of October (43113,
740-474-7000, www.pumpkinshow.com). But don't call it a "festival";
that would brand you a city slicker for sure.

It all started in 1903 when mayor George Haswell invited farmers to
display the fruits of their fall harvest, mostly corn fodder and pumpkins
cut into the shapes of jack-o'-lanterns (somehow "Corn Fodder Show"
lacked resonance). And it's endured almost every year since, except
during the two world wars when it was briefly postponed. Now the
event is a four-day pumpkin-ganza that draws 400,000 plus visitors
from the United States and abroad. Where else can you get pumpkin
pies, pumpkin doughnuts, pumpkin cookies, pumpkin burgers, pump-
kin taffy, pumpkin ice cream, pumpkin cake, pumpkin soups, pumpkin
waffles, pumpkin cream puffs, pumpkin fudge—and all in one place?
And they do grow 'em big. Cultivators compete for the title of Biggest
Pumpkin, some of which have topped 1,110 pounds, and sometimes
rolling into the top spot by only a few pounds. That's a lot of pumpkin
pie, not to mention serious back strain from getting those suckers on
the scale.

There's something for all ages: rides, non-pumpkin food booths,
parades, and a Miss Pumpkin and Little Miss Pumpkin competition in
which even the winners' hair seems to have a slightly orange hue. Or it
could be the reflection from the six-foot, four hundred–pound pumpkin pie baked for the event by Lindsey's Bakery or the water tower,
which is painted to look like—drum roll, please—a giant pumpkin.

You know you're in Circleville when you see
the giant pumpkin water tower.

★ ★

Is Everybody Happy?
Circleville

OK, so his style lacks the bling and flash of, say, MC Hammer or Cher, but the music of Ted Lewis has its own subtle charm. If the tinny recordings emanating from his namesake museum (133 West Main St. 43113, 740-474-3231 or 740-474-3834, www.redhotjazz.com/tedlewis.html) don't intrigue you, perhaps the impeccably refurbished building, the only remaining structure that stands in the original circle after which his hometown is named, might draw you in.

But once you step through the door, you're sucked into the fascinating vortex that was Lewis's life, even though most people under sixty-five barely remember him. Born on June 6, 1890, Theodore Leopold Friedman, a nice Jewish boy, was expected to work the family business, a ladies' emporium called Friedman's Bazaar.

But young Ted was determined to do his own thing and ran away to the Big Apple, changing his last name to Lewis so it would fit on a theater marquee. In 1916 he won his trademark top hat in a dice game, developed his "Is everybody happy?" shtick, and went on to fame and fortune, appearing on the Broadway stage, making records, and performing in front of nine U.S. presidents and King George V. Hits included "When My Baby Smiles at Me," "Sunny Side of the Street," "Me and My Shadow," and many others, including "Tiger Rag," which in 1926 sold five and a half million copies, an astounding figure at the time. And unlike many of today's superstars, he never used a dirty word, nor did he refer to his colleagues as "trolls."

Plus, he remained happily married to Adah Becker, his wife of fifty-six years, in some ways an even more remarkable feat. But Lewis always remembered and respected his hometown roots, appearing in the Pumpkin Show parade and wining and dining locals who had the cojones to go all the way to New York or other far-off places to see one of his shows.

The museum honoring Lewis is a tasteful and elegant array of his stuff, including his original clarinet, top hat, and cane; sheet music;

It's always "sunny" on the street with the Lewis museum.

and oil portraits of Ted and his wife, among other things. Also not to be missed is a short video of his life at the mini-theater bearing his name.

Collectors from Harvard, Yale, and the Smithsonian clamored for the memorabilia, but the always loyal Lewises insisted that it be moved to Ted's hometown, where the family is buried. Was everybody happy? Well, maybe not, but Ted Lewis made a lot of people smile.

★ ★

Casper's Contemporaries
Granville

With its fancy college (Denison University) and upscale New England demeanor, you might not expect Granville to be a hotbed of restless spirits—at least not the dead kind, though there is a rather large population of college students. But Granville does have several ghosts, most notably in Rooms 7 and 9 and in the basement of the Buxton Inn (313 East Broadway 43023, 740-587-0001, www.buxtoninn.com).

Said to be the country's oldest continuously operating inn, the Buxton was built in 1812 by Orin Granger, a native of Massachusetts. Originally a post office and stagecoach stop on the Columbus-Newark line, the restaurant/hotel has seen the likes of famous do-gooders Abraham Lincoln, Harriet Beecher Stowe, and John Kerry, and its patrons and employees have documented sightings of former owners Major Horton Buxton, who oversaw the inn from 1856 to 1905, and Ethel (Bonnie) Bounell. The latter, a singer-actress whose starring role at the Buxton spanned several decades (1934–1960), passed on in her private quarters, now Room 9. She has been glimpsed wandering around in various parts of the inn dressed in her favorite color (blue) and at different stages of her life. Other ghostly encounters include a man, a boy, and a cat, ostensibly the gray feline that adorns the front sign.

According to the current owners, the ghosts are mostly friendly non-folk, floating in and out of the rooms, opening and closing doors, and running around making noise without their bodies on. "We think . . . they are overseeing to make sure we do a good job," general manager Melanie Orr theorized in the *Newark* (Ohio) *Advocate.* "The encounters have always been very ordinary, just casual . . . No customers have ever left here screaming." Well, that's good to know. Or maybe they never left at all . . .

Just across the street is the Granville Inn (314 East Broadway 43023, 888-472-6855, www.granvilleinn.com), a historic and elegant English manor replete with hand-cut oak paneling, native sandstone, and a highly regarded gourmet restaurant. It is rumored to have ghosts as

**The only feline here is a ghost, so folks
with allergies are safe.**

well, although it mostly touts itself as a romantic getaway. If you want
to cover all your otherworldly bases, there's also the Robbins Hunter
Museum (221 East Broadway 43203, 740-587-0430), an antiques-filled
estate allegedly haunted by the last owner. "Doors open and close
when nobody else is here but me, and I've heard footsteps upstairs,"
Bob McDaniel of the museum told the *Advocate*. There are no guaran-
tees, of course, but at least you can get a good meal, a little rest, and
see some really neat old stuff.

★ ★

Presidential Possessions

Marion

Warren G. Harding was president back in the day when more than 49 percent of the public actually liked Republicans. Sure, he buddied up to the old boys, slashed taxes, and imposed limitations on immigration. But as Ohio admirer Harry Daugherty, who promoted him for the 1920 Republican nomination, pointed out, "He looked like a president," and he sure knew how to pack 'em in. So much so that hundreds of thousands made the pilgrimage to his Victorian-style residence (380 Mt. Vernon Ave. 43302, 800-600-6894) to hear him orate from his front porch. Plus, Harding won by a landslide, an unprecedented 60 percent

This front porch saw hundreds of thousands of visitors.

of the popular vote, with nary a single hanging chad or waffling red/blue state.

Harding's home, which is only open to the public in the summertime, contains nearly all of his and wife Florence's original possessions, down to the desiccated chewing tobacco and cigars he was rarely without, and Pete, a stuffed parrot that Florence believed predicted her husband's untimely death of a heart attack on August 2, 1923. Like Nancy Reagan after her, Florence Harding used the services of clairvoyants. An avid advocate of women's rights and an outspoken First Lady before her time, she passed away in late 1924.

Built during Harding's courtship with the former Florence Mabel Kling DeWolfe, and where they were married in 1891, the home also served as the campaign's press headquarters. Eclecticism reigns: cracked leather chairs, a microphone used during the inauguration, and the presidential briefcase share space with Florence's hats and clothes, kitchen utensils, and family portraits. There's even a resident ghost of sorts: The grandfather clock in the hall allegedly stopped on the first anniversary of Harding's death, with various strange occurrences happening around that time in subsequent years.

The Harding regime did not stand up well posthumously. Because of several scandals involving others in his administration—including the notorious Teapot Dome dustup—he gained the reputation as being one of America's least successful presidents, along with being a notorious womanizer. Nevertheless, Florence got the last laugh and is buried alongside her husband in the Harding Memorial, an ornate white marble tomb in the Marion Cemetery on Vernon Heights Boulevard, a few miles away from the home.

Odd Ball
Marion

Even if you're not fond of graveyards—why spend any more time there than necessary?—this one might be worth checking out. Along with the Harding tomb, the sprawling Marion Cemetery, at the corner

**Bowling ball idol worship or very
strange grave markers?**

of Vernon Heights Boulevard and Route 23, boasts a stunning World
War II memorial, upon whose granite and marble walls are inscribed
the names of the six thousand county residents who lost their lives
during that conflict.

Dedicated in 2001 it is one of the more recent additions, joining
statues of women in various poses, a tombstone topped with an elk,
and an urn-shaped gravestone.

But by and far, the oddest attraction that draws the living to the
land of the dead is the gravesite of the wealthy Charles B. Merchant

family, basically a bunch of small black granite spheres that appear to be worshiping at the foot of a 5,200-pound ebony orb atop a large block engraved with C. B.'s name. If there ever was a mecca for bowling balls, this is it.

But wait, it gets weirder. The giant granite globe, which was installed in 1896 and polished after it was put in place, began to move. Nothing dramatic, but one day someone noticed that the unfinished portion of the stone, the part originally in contact with the monument, was now visible. Thinking that it might be a prank, although only Superman could execute such a stunt, the Merchant family hired workers to return the sphere to its original position. But it did it again and again, despite repeated attempts to put it back. At one point the bottom was even sealed with lead. Nothing worked, and that stone kept rolling.

In lieu of moss, the stone gathered curiosity-seekers as well as the media, ranging from Paul Harvey to *Ripley's Believe It or Not!* Scientists examined it, offering theories about heat and cold contractions and gravitational pull. Still others have speculated that a family curse or demonic possession was to blame; after all, a similar ball in another part of the cemetery hadn't moved even a fraction of an inch.

Who knows? The Merchant orb continues to drift an average of two inches a year, with the exposed section working its way up toward the top of the sphere. Maybe there is something extraterrestrial about bowling balls after all. That's as good an explanation as any.

What's Popping?
Marion

Look at it this way: Even if you're uninterested in the world's largest collection of popcorn poppers and peanut roasters, at the very least, admission includes a box of tasty, fresh popcorn from the Wyandot Popcorn Museum (169 East Church St. 43302, 740-387-4255, www .wyandotpopcornmus.com). Plus it tops off a reasonably peculiar array of stuff: the papers of President Warren G. Harding, memorabilia from

A vehicle for fresh popcorn

Miss America 1938, and the collection of former U.S. treasurer Mary Ellen Withrow, the only person ever to hold the office at the local, state, and national level.

Plus, there's Prince Imperial, arguably the world's oldest stuffed horse. Born in 1865 in Napoleon's stables in France, the huge Percheron stallion was given to a local breeder who continued to show him around the region even after his (the horse's) death in 1890. Said to have the longest mane and tail at the time, Prince Imperial still resides in his $6,000 stall, although saddling him up to one of the horse-drawn popcorn wagons might make for an interesting juxtaposition of displays.

Located in the back of the Marion County Historical Society, the popcorn collection—with its chrome, red, and striped fanfare of wagons, trucks, and poppers of all shapes and sizes—has all the big names that most people have never heard of, like Cretors, Stutsman, Kingery,

Dunbar, and Manley, among others. But you'll pick out kernels of knowledge if you read the cards next to the exhibits, most of which are beautifully refurbished. Did you know that the Dunbar 1911 Model 950 wagon was used by Paul Newman to promote his own brand of popcorn and was eventually donated to the museum? (Bet someone had to do some serious buttering up to get that.) And that in the 1911 R.O. Stutsman Ideal, the spring-driven machinery used a white gas called naptha for popping and roasting peanuts and that the peanuts were stored below the popper cabinet to keep them warm?

OK, so it may not be the most fascinating subject in the world, but some of the machines are entertaining in a Rube Goldberg sort of way, with all kinds of bells, whistles, and elaborate machinations for the preparation of seemingly simple popcorn and peanuts. And several actually work, though you'll need a curator to show you how.

For those who want a jumbo-size serving, there's the annual Marion Popcorn Festival. Featured acts have included Gloria Estefan, REO Speedwagon, and—for those who really like life in the slow lane—Myron Floren from *The Lawrence Welk Show*.

Officer Memorex
Marysville

You're on the way to work and running a few minutes late. You're zipping through a school zone, five, OK, maybe ten miles over the speed limit and oh no! There's a cop sitting on the corner! You're sure to get a ticket . . . But wait . . . he must have been on the radio or eating a doughnut or something, because he doesn't even move. Whew, that was close!

Maybe not . . . If you happen to be in Marysville, you may just have had a brush with Deputy Memorex, who's a real dummy. As in an armless, legless mannequin, dismembered so he can fit more neatly into the patrol car. Not only does he work for free, but he's always on duty, except during his days off, which are spent in the trunk of his vehicle. "He's the perfect employee—never complains," Memorex's colleague, Sgt. Chris Skinner told the *Columbus Dispatch.* "He can be kind of unfriendly, though, because he won't wave." He doesn't look too healthy either, what with his pasty complexion and stiff posture.

Use of dummies and cardboard cutouts is a well-kept law-enforcement secret, particularly in the South; Marysville's Memorex is strategically placed in areas where people usually complain about speeders. Powell, a suburb of Columbus, also used a cardboard photo cutout of one of its patrolmen, propping it next to a computerized radar gun, until it (the cutout) deteriorated during a particularly diffi-cult Ohio winter. The real officer is still walking around, however.

However, the next time you see a police car, and start laughing to yourself about the whole "Is it real or is it Memorex?" thing, slow down and forget about running that red or even yellow light. Because the real, live breathing officer who's actually on duty will probably pull you over. Who's the dummy now?

Corporate Headquarters in a Basket
Newark

Martin Luther King, John F. Kennedy, and Mahatma Gandhi all had big dreams. So did the late Dave Longaberger, though his were interwoven with strips of wood. At seven stories high and with two seventy-five-ton handles on the roof, his vision is seen from all direc-tions. Longaberger corporate headquarters (1500 East Main St. 43055, Newark, 740-322-5000, www.longaberger.com) is located inside the mother of all baskets. Along with serving as an office, the vast vessel boasts a thirty-thousand-square-foot atrium, educational tours, and displays of company offerings. Ants are optional.

Un-hampered by a speech impediment, a lack of formal educa-tion, and several enterprises that struggled in the less-than-booming economy of his hometown of Dresden, Dave became convinced that people needed well-crafted items from a bygone era. Specifically, the handmade baskets of his father, J. W. Longaberger, who created them in his spare time while supporting a wife and twelve children.

Work's one giant picnic for Longaberger employees.
KATE MANECKE

In the early 1970s Dave asked his dad to make a dozen samples, and they sold immediately. Soon Dave had his own store, a thriving business, and the idea that home consultants might be the way to go, especially if you bag 'em with your family history and a quality product. By the late 1990s a cult of mostly middle-aged female collectors had grown around Longaberger baskets, and Dresden had become a prosperous Valhalla for the containers, related trinkets, and all things country (www.basketvillageusa.com). Each year a "Basket Bee" was held in nearby Columbus, with thousands of sales associates buzzing around the family-run enterprise like kitsch-infected hornets.

Around the time of Dave's death in 1999, the company was the largest manufacturer of handmade baskets in the United States. And the entire surrounding area was being built up to include a Longaberger Homestead complex with shopping, restaurants, and more, and a Longaberger Golf Club and fine-dining venue, with millions of dollars donated to local and national charities and educational institutions.

Since then, grown daughters Tami and Rachel have worked hard to keep a grip on things, diversifying and expanding offerings to include pottery, wrought iron, fabric accessories, and more. Occasionally there are layoffs, but as everyone knows, big business is no picnic.

A Historic Walk Spoiled
Newark

What a paradox. On the site of the Great Octagon Mound built by the Hopewell tribe in what's now Newark exists that bastion of paleface supremacy: the golf course at the Moundbuilders Country Club (125 North Thirty-third St. 43055, 740-344-9431, www.moundbuilderscc .com). The Octagon is part of the four-square-mile Newark Earthworks, monumental geometric enclosures interconnected by a series of low walls. Like the rest of the compound—the Great Circle (99 Cooper Ave., 800-589-8224, www.ohiohistory.org/places/newarkearthworks/ greatcircle.html), a 1,200-foot-diameter loop used as a ceremonial center, and the Wright Earthworks, a segment of the original complex (near Grant Street and the Route 79 interchange)—it is managed by the Ohio Historical Society (OHS).

How did the world of fairways, foursomes, and sand traps collide with the largest complex of its kind, constructed some two thousand years ago? A site that scientists believe was engineered by ancient tribes, incorporating alignments of moonrises and moonsets in an 18.6-year lunar cycle? And so significant to Native Americans, historians, and concerned citizens that they formed the Friends of the Mounds (FOM), dedicated to preserving the site and promoting public access?

Very easily, thanks to the old-boy network around the turn of the twentieth century, when a Newark High School professor established a six-hole golf course near the mound. Another golf course was added a few years later, and by 1910, claiming lack of public funds, the city leased the property to a newly formed country club. It was supposed to be temporary, but a few months later, a clubhouse had been built and a course designed by golf architect Thomas Bendelow. And the lease continued to be renewed, even when ownership was shifted to the OHS, and has been approved until 2078.

Citing safety concerns (yeah, right), the club strictly limits admittance. The mounds can only be viewed from a wooden stand near the parking lot or a short trail bordering the course. And they mean business: In 2002 Barbara Crandell, a seventy-three-year-old woman of Cherokee ancestry, was arrested for trespassing as she was trying to pray.

In still another irony, Moundbuilders Country Club claims to be proud of its Native American setting. "We have a golf course on an unusual site, older than written history," crows a 1985 anniversary book. "Won't archeologists 2,000 years from now be puzzled as they study the mounds and find all those lost golf balls?" Not to mention the plaques in the trees inscribed with the names of deceased golfers, often near their favorite hole. It's like that cartoon from the *New Yorker,* where a formally dressed father is talking to his young offspring. "I'm sorry, son," he says. "But we WASPs have no tribal wisdom to pass on." So they put their golf courses on Native land instead.

Just a Gigolo
Plain City

This place puts the "sir" in sirloin. The largest bovine artificial insemination (AI) company in North America, Select Sires produces more than seven million units of semen a year for both domestic and iternational breeders. Started in 1965 by a federation of ten farmer-owned cooperatives, they provide, er, services for both dairy cows and beef cattle. They've also raised—so to speak—genetics to a fine art in terms of

(Continued on Page 189)

State Roundup: Mounds Of Joy

Ohio has more Indian mounds and artifacts than Egypt has mummies . . .Well, maybe not, but someone always seems to be unearthing one or claiming a new discovery. Along with the above-mentioned Newark mound and the Miamisburg Mound in the Southwest chapter, here's just a sprinkling. Hey, sometimes you feel like a mound . . .

- **Fort Ancient** (6123 State Rte. 350, 45054, 513-932-4421, www.fortancient.org). Fort Ancient features eighteen thousand feet of earthen walls built a couple of thousand years ago by MacGyver-type Native Americans who used deer shoulder blades, antlers of split elk, and hoes from clam shells for digging. They then carried the soil in 35–40 pound baskets to the mound (OK, so Richard Dean Anderson would have probably figured out an easier way). As with many mounds, portions of the walls were utilized as a calendar to chart movements of the sun and moon. Along with an equally impressive nine-thousand-square-foot museum, the site offers over 2.5 miles of hiking trails, two scenic overlooks, and a picnic area. The museum focuses on fifteen thousand years of native history in addition to hands-on classrooms and exhibits, including a seasonal garden depicting crops grown in ancient times. But make sure you leave when they close at 5 p.m. sharp, otherwise it's just you and a bunch of spooky remains until they open up the next day or you find a sympathetic caretaker who will show you the back entrance.
- **Serpent Mound State Memorial** (3850 State Rte. 73, Peebles 45660, 937-587-2796, www.serpentmound.org). Arguably the largest and finest serpent effigy in the United

States, Ohio's version of the Sphinx runs 1,300 feet along its coils and is about 3 feet high, with jaws wide open (just waiting to snack on an unsuspecting paleface tourist?). In the late nineteenth century, Harvard University archeologist Frederic Ward Putnam excavated Serpent Mound and attributed it to the builders of the two nearby Adena (800 BC–AD 100) burial mounds, which he also uncovered. However, more recent research revealed that it was probably built closer to the time of Fort Ancient culture (AD 1000–1550). Regardless, like its brethren, it is seasonally themed, with the head of the serpent aligned to the summer solstice sunset and the coils pointing to the winter solstice and equinox sunrises. You can also visit the park and adjacent museum, although rangers discourage the use of hallucinogens. So leave the peyote buttons at home.

- **Hopewell Culture National Historic Park** (16062 State Rte. 104, Chillicothe, 45601, 740-774-1126, www.nps.gov/hocu). This sprawled out aggregation consists of 1,200 acres of large geometric earthworks as well as artifacts crafted by the Hopewell culture. The five separate units—Mound City Group, Hopeton Earthworks, Hopewell Mound Group, Seip Earthworks, and High Bank Works—are open for tours at various times, so it's best to coordinate your visit with a park volunteer. While not as dramatic or visibly obvious as the other mounds, you do get a taste of what it might be like to be alive during those times, thanks to rugged, pothole laden trails; insect-filled vegetation; and being cut off from cell phone reception. There's also a visitor center/museum with an educational film and various artifacts.

(Continued on Page 188)

(Continued from Page 187)

- **Adena Indian Burial Mound** (Mound Circle, Enon 45323). Being as it's located in Enon—which is "None" backwards and pretty much sums up the town—this forty-footer is pretty easy to spot (look next to the pioneer house and the library/historical society). It's estimated to contain almost thirteen thousand cubic yards of dirt and rumor has it that early explorers found some remains inside, which nobody's bothered to verify. Bonus: If you go during the Apple Butter Festival in October, you can also indulge in a heap o' goodies (www.enonhistory.com/AppleButterFestival.html).

- **Etna Wanna-be a Mound** (State Rte. 16 and Mink Rd., 43018). Discovered by engineers in 2010 during a preliminary survey by the county, which was developing the site for business and industry, the Hopewell artifacts, including flints, pottery shards, and postholes for huts and wigwams, are probably not enough to stop the bulldozers. OK, so it's not a mound per se, but evidence of day-to-day life from ancient Hopewells as well as early settlers from the 1790s gave historians pause. So they dug up what they could, put it in a plastic bag, and made a presentation to the local historical society. And the show went on, bringing in millions of dollars of construction funding and potentially large payrolls whenever the corporate park is completed. But we know who the land really belongs to . . .

★ ★

(Continued from Page 187)

marketing and controlling the quality of semen, as well as the newest wrinkle, "sexing technology," which determines to more than 90 percent accuracy whether it's a boy or a girl.

It's Brave New World meets Mayberry. Photos of top-producing bulls selling more than half a million units of semen are enshrined in grainy color photos on a wall, with some of the more famous studs being buried on the grounds with granite markers. And workers today have a tough time getting health insurance from their employers . . .

It all started with Elevation, who is also interred out front (you might say he was seminal). "Many bovines today can trace their genetics back to Elevation," states longtime employee Terri Smith. Semen is harvested (oh yeah, baby!) and then can be frozen indefinitely, with specific

What a lineup of studs!

★ ★

breeds and traits being requested. This is done through the Select Mating Service, which bills itself as "the world's most popular mating program, with more than three million recommendations a year," according to company literature. Eat your heart out, Match.com.

Purchasers pick from the bovine equivalent of personal ads, the Beef Sire Directory. In it are vital statistics (age, weight, and so on) and color pictures of the bull. Next to each stud are headlines proclaiming its various assets, which range from the head-scratching "Improves disposition like no other!" to the slightly off-color "Maturing into a powerful, thick-made bull," "Exciting sire of good looks," and a personal favorite "Demand for his daughters keeps growing!" which would make any human father lock his female children up.

Hardly the bovine equivalent of Hugh Hefner, the bulls must work their way to the top (although they never actually are on top, because semen is collected via an artificial vagina that's about fourteen feet long and 2½ feet wide). Of the 1,800 bulls housed in fifty-nine barns, only a few "graduate" to closed, well-ventilated digs, and of those only the elite few get air-conditioned stalls. Still, the bulls are treated well, with specially formulated diets and the most advanced medical attention veterinary science can offer.

Select Sires is not open to the public, but more information about its programs can be obtained by calling (614) 873-4683 or visiting www.selectsires.com.

Big Drip
West Liberty

The weather's fifty-four degrees year-round, and occasionally there are bats. Plus when the lights are turned out, it gets really, really black. And once you start the tour, there is no going back. But as long as the electricity's working and you follow the guide's instructions, there's nothing cold, dark, and scary about Ohio Caverns (2210 East Rte. 245, 43357, 937-465-4017, www.ohiocaverns.com), one of the largest caves of its kind. Really.

It looks much more interesting in person—really.

And you get to see some of the niftiest and most colorful stalagmite (floor) and stalactite (ceiling or wall) formations around. There's the Crystal King, arguably the world's tallest, at nearly five feet and four hundred pounds, an über-stalagmite that looks like a deadly icicle. The forty-five-minute tour also encompasses views of "soda straws" that help feed the various crystals, a slow and ever-evolving process that's about as exciting as watching paint dry, and various "rooms" like the colorful Palace of the Gods and the perhaps slightly exaggerated Fantasyland. Observing the different formations "is like looking at clouds," according to the amiable tour guide. "You can see something new every time." Yes, if you stare at them—or anything—long enough.

Discovered in 1897 by a local farmhand, the caverns quickly became a favorite attraction, with visitors crawling around in the mud to check out the formations (this was before TiVo). Guided tours began in 1925, although it took several decades for workers to clean out the caverns, most of which were about four feet from floor to ceiling. They dug out some of the limestone walls and installed concrete walkways. In the interim, many formations were discolored and ruined by inquiring human hands so a "do not touch" policy is now firmly in place.

Visitors exit through an artificial tunnel, up a few dozen stairs to strains of an appropriately watery version of "Beautiful Ohio," the state song. Then it's out into eye-squinting daylight, to be picked up in a van and driven back to the main office by yet another nice tour guide. It may be chilly in there, but the place exudes Midwestern friendliness.

Sibling Castlery
West Liberty

The Piatt brothers literally made their homes castles. First up is Mac-A-Cheek, aka "Cheek" (10051 Township Rd. 47, 43357, 917-465-2821, www.piattcastles.org). Constructed in the mid-1880s by General Abram S. and Eleanor W. Piatt, it has remained in the family for five generations, a three-story Gothic Revival limestone edifice that sits atop a hill. Although the Piatts no longer reside there, you'll find many of the family heirlooms, pictures, and furniture, along with elegant wood floors, paneling, and staircases, all of which have been lovingly maintained. Standouts include horsehair-stuffed couches and chairs, furniture and military memorabilia dating back to the Revolutionary War, and Native American artifacts.

Round two and just down the road about a mile is the Flemish-style Mac-O-Chee Castle (2319 Rte. 287), aka "Chee." Originally part of the Piatt family home, it was expanded in 1881 by older brother Donn, a well-known journalist and poet, and his wife, Ella. The larger of the two, it is located on top of a higher knoll than Cheek, an architectural nod to the importance of birth order. However, there's no signage for parking, and woe be it to those who make the mistake of driving their vehicle directly up to the home (good luck backing down the narrow driveway).

"Cheek" or "Chee"? You'll just
have to visit to find out.

Because it was out of the family for sixty years, Chee did not receive
the love that makes such family residences living heirlooms, despite the
fact that it has similar woodwork and interior decoration. From 1899
to 1945 it served as a health spa, grain elevator (really!), and finally
an art gallery. Subsequently it's somewhat gloomy, with falling plaster
and other signs of deterioration. Still, there are plenty of nooks and
slightly dusty crannies to explore, and it boasts one of Logan County's
first water closets, a precursor to the flush toilet.

Both castles have imposing architecture and were painted with fres-
coes by noted French artist Oliver Frey. Both are on the National Register of Historic Places and run by the family-owned foundation. And
one castle is decorated for holidays. So which brother got the biggest
toy? It depends upon which Christmas you're talking about.

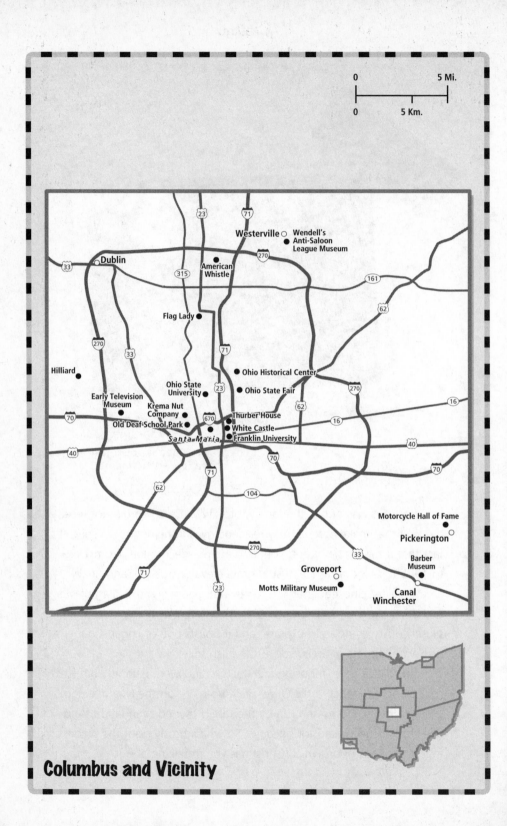

0   5 Mi.

0   5 Km.

Westerville ○   ● Wendell's
                    Anti-Saloon
                    League Museum

American
Whistle ●

Dublin ●

Flag Lady ●

Hilliard ●

Ohio Historical Center ●

Ohio State
University ●   ● Ohio State Fair

Early Television
Museum ●   Krema Nut
            Company ●
Old Deaf School Park ●   ● Thurber House
Santa Maria   ● White Castle
                 ● Franklin University

Motorcycle Hall of Fame ●
            Pickerington ○

Barber
Museum ●

Groveport ○

Motts Military Museum ●

Canal
Winchester ○

Columbus and Vicinity

5

Columbus and Vicinity

College-town Columbus offers *a constellation of educationally weird sights and sounds. Franklin University's ten thousand–pound steel-and-aluminum graduation cap sculpture hangs over a major downtown intersection, a Damoclean reminder to commuters of their mortality. The topiary garden at the Old Deaf School Park is a faithful interpretation of Georges Seurat's* A Sunday Afternoon on the Island of La Grand Jatte, *except for one thing—a cat. And a replica of the* Santa Maria, *launched to honor the 500th anniversary of Columbus's discovery—which was nowhere near the namesake city—is now used as a teaching tool for school kids and for corporate outings.*

You might want to make a "stop" at American Whistle. With the loudest whistle in the world—four decibels higher than the nearest competitor—a tour there can be a real blast. Or if you're feeling red, white, and blue, the Flag Lady's Flag Store sells everything from pins and jewelry to little wavers to jumbo-sized versions.

Columbus also pays homage to its role as a test market for fast food. The corporate headquarters for both White Castle and Wendy's can be found in this area. The Krema Nut factory has stuck around Columbus since 1908 and offers tours. However, don't try to sink your teeth into the Dublin field of corn; it consists of 109 concrete six-foot ears. And for the perfect pit stop, there's Wendell's, which has been nationally recognized for the hygiene and design of its restrooms. You might want to order something, however.

★ ★

Shave and a Haircut—Immortalized
Canal Winchester

In July 2006 Ed Jeffers, the "Godfather of Barbering," passed away at age seventy-eight, leaving his namesake museum without a rudder. Jeffers had shorn thousands of heads in his nearly five decades as a barber, but more importantly he served for many years as the executive director of the Ohio Barber Board and created the Barber Museum (2 1/2 South High St. 43110, 614-837-8400, 614-837-1846, www.edjeffersbarbermuseum.com; tours by appointment only) and Barber Hall of Fame. Started in 1988 with just a few items, this cast of barbershop memorabilia numbers in the thousands: a wall full of shaving mugs, many of which are considered valuable; cases loaded with straight razors, from the ornate to the downright menacing; and colorful poles galore, including an extremely rare striped number with a clock mounted on top. Among the many unusual chairs are a rococo George Archer job made in 1879 and a smaller one for a child with a carved horse head, which might have made Mom nervous had her offspring been the real Godfather's customer.

But no worries—Jeffers was a gentle soul with an extensive knowledge of his museum and the history of barbering. Few people know, for instance, that until the 1800s barbers provided both dental services and surgery, such as bloodletting, as illustrated by the museum's sixteen-lancet spring-loaded device. According to an earlier tour by Jeffers, the red and white stripes of the barber pole were derived from this gruesome practice (as in a blood-streaked cloth). Eeew. Maybe that was too much information.

Among the other oddities in the elegantly laid-out and impeccable collection are a circa 1950s flattop comb that includes a built-in carpenter's level, a complete singeing kit (no split ends here), and a 1920s perm machine that resembles an octopus. You could spend hours examining the rows of ceramics depicting barbers in various poses, wince-inducing dental tools (along with a photo of a man in a barber's chair whose expression is not of someone anticipating a haircut), and

**A museum in need of a good head
(with hair or otherwise)**

something called a Faradic Vibrator, which unfortunately Jeffers, rest his soul, is no longer around to explain.

Hopefully, someone will pick up the gauntlet (or in this case, the razor blade) and continue the tradition of the museum. It costs about $10,000 a year to maintain and is probably tax-deductible.

★ ★

Whistle Stop
Columbus

They're low-tech, durable, and easy to operate. American Whistle (6540 Huntley Rd. 43229, 800-876-2918, www.americanwhistle. com), the only manufacturer of metallic whistles in the United States, has produced them since 1956. It seems everyone has a need to make themselves heard, from sporting types to Boy Scouts to outdoor adventurers (skiers to scuba divers) to the Red Cross to law enforcement. Can you imagine a lifeguard using say, an air horn or kazoo? We don't think so!

And you can tour the facility and see how these noisemakers are made! How's that for a blast? (How many times have they heard that joke?) The forty-five-minute factory tour—which you need an appointment or reservation for—is a combination of the latest machinery and gizmos that look like they might have been cobbled together several decades ago (they were). Production begins with the raw material; then on to coiled brass, thirty-ton presses, and state-of-the-art soldering tables; next comes the polishing and specialized plating processes; and then—at last!—the final touch: putting the ball inside the whistle. Perhaps best of all, everyone leaves with a shiny new American Classic whistle! Talk about a cheap trill!

But American Whistle doesn't, uh, stop there. Although most of the solid brass whistles are plated with nickel, you can get them with bronze or even twenty-four-karat gold. They also make monochromatic nylon lanyards (as opposed to the crazy-quilt kind you used to weave in camp), metallic snake chains, and a hook that pins to the lapel, a must-have accessory for aspiring MPs. Synthetic rubber tips that slip over the mouthpiece of the whistle and protect the teeth and lips also come in a variety of colors, like orange, blue, red, and yellow. Woo-hoo! Now we're making some fashion noise!

Whistles have been around for thousands of years, in some form or another. The modern era "began in 1878 when a whistle was first blown by a referee during a sporting event," states the company's

★ ★

Have a blast at American Whistle.

website. "An English toolmaker—who was fascinated with whistles—fashioned a brass instrument that was used in a match at the Nottingham Forest Soccer Club. This device was found to be superior to the usual referee's signal of waving a handkerchief." The following year, what was known as a "pea whistle," which used a small ball in the air chamber, was invented. It was a precursor to what made this one-note company a success—unless someone blows it and builds a better mousetrap, er, whistle.

★ ★

Flag Waver's Refuge
Columbus

In 1979, during the Iranian hostage crisis, Mary Leavitt, then of Liber-
tyville, Illinois, was looking to display an American flag to honor her
son Andy, who was in the military. "I couldn't find one anywhere,"
she recalls. "I was told to come back during 'flag season'—the Fourth
of July—the only time they stocked American flags."

**Mary Leavitt proving that Old Glory
never goes out of fashion.**

★ ★

Rather than turning red, white, and blue with frustration, she demonstrated her true colors and began peddling American flags from the trunk of her car. Today Leavitt, who comes from a long line of patriots with a history of military service dating from the Revolutionary War, has the Flag Lady's Flag Store (4567 North High St. 43214, 614-263-1776, www.flagladyohio.com), which sells everything from flag pins and jewelry to little wavers you can stick anywhere to jumbo-size versions.

And she doesn't just do it for Old Glory. There are U.S. state flags, military flags, college flags, religious flags, sport flags, seasonal banners, and last but certainly not least Ohio State University flags, of which there are dozens, including a version that's only supposed to be flown by alumni. Does anyone care about such things? "Well, I don't think you'll get in trouble if you fly it and haven't graduated," she observes. On a more serious note, there are also flags in interment cases for deceased soldiers and veterans and grave-marker flags for police officers, firefighters, and other public servants.

A visit involves more than just, say, stopping at the 7-Eleven to pick up a red, white, and blue Slurpee. Along with curiosity-seekers, tourists, and regular customers, people like to, er, hang around "whenever something happens with the U.S., or there's a crisis," Leavitt states. "They want to talk about what's going on and commiserate with others who feel the same way." One man, who lost his son in Iraq, is a frequent patron. "He says it makes him feel better just to come here."

So protesters, leave your peace symbols and antigovernment sentiments at home. Everything's made in the USA, one of the few concepts most Americans stand united on.

Graduation Cap of Damocles
Columbus

Maybe because it's still referred to as "Columbus, Ohio" instead of just "Columbus," the installation of several oversize attractions may be the city's way of compensating for its smaller, uh, image. On South Third Street, at the side of, of all things, a bank, is the world's largest

Capping off downtown traffic

iPod, a twenty-five-foot working model that advertises a local arts magazine. But hey, size isn't everything: It's powered by a tiny iPod shuffle. And if the six hundred–pound, twenty-five-foot, 3-D Columbus Crew soccer ball that looks like it's crashing into the top of a twelve-story condominium complex on North High Street isn't going to stop traffic and get people talking, what is?

Well, that might be the ten thousand–pound steel-and-aluminum graduation cap that literally hangs over the corner of Rich and Grant Avenues, across from Franklin University. Entitled *Commencing,* this mammoth blue sculpture was commissioned to honor the one hundredth anniversary of the college and is meant to symbolize the mortarboard tossed into the air by graduating students. But what goes up . . .

The latter became an issue in late 2002, when the sculpture was newly installed and one of the five poles meant to anchor it (along with thirteen cables) fell a few feet. Everything was fine—the cap stayed stable—but nevertheless the citizenry expressed concern that they or their cars might be pulverized (dare we say beaned?) by the plummeting beanie while walking/driving down the street.

Not to worry, reassure university officials. Not only was the cap engineered by the same folks who brought us the Corporate Headquarters in a Basket (see Central chapter), but its interior is warmed by fourteen heaters, lest ice form on it and then slide off onto passersby or vehicles. Oh, we didn't think of that.

Regardless, the cap is here to stay. The folks at Franklin University are thrilled with the visibility it gives the small but well-respected college, and even Mayor Coleman was enthusiastic about the concept. Plus the governor of Ohio told Franklin president Paul Otte that he enjoys riding his bike under it. Well, if politicians approve, then you know it must be safe!

Sometimes You Really Feel Like a Nut
Columbus

These people have been in the nuthouse since 1898, when the Krema Nut Company opened its doors, making it the oldest commercial peanut butter manufacturer in the United States. Invented a few years earlier by a St. Louis physician, peanut butter was initially used as a substitute for seniors who had trouble chewing meat and other protein. Then someone had the *cojones* to come up with better dentures . . .

But the market for peanut butter had been cracked wide open. Today 83 percent of all Americans ingest the stuff. According to the folks at Krema, this consists of a walloping seven hundred million pounds per annum, enough to cover the entire floor of the Grand

★ ★

Canyon, a rather sticky and ecologically gross mental picture. The average child consumes about 1,500 sandwiches of guess-what by the time he or she finishes high school. And did you know arachibutyrophobia is the scientific term for "fear of peanut butter sticking to the roof of one's mouth"?

A visit to the ten-thousand-square-foot Krema factory/store (1000 West Goodale Blvd. 43214, 800-222-4132, www.krema.com) is a nut lover's equivalent of seventeen virgins in heaven. For one thing, for those taking the factory tour, there's the smell of freshly roasted nuts and the thrill of watching it being made the old-fashioned way, slowly

Nuts for all ages and tastes

ground, in small batches. (Hey, there's even an adults-only peanut butter lovers' fan club, which sounds slightly risqué, until you check out their website, www.peanutbutterlovers.com. It mostly consists of historical and nutritional information, what to do about allergies, and recipes. Bummer.)

Because of liability and insurance reasons, the tour is for large groups and grown-ups only. But, during regular business hours, everyone can partake of the hundreds of different kinds of roasted nuts (salted and plain), raw nuts, dried fruits, mixes, and snacks that overpopulate the shelves. Choose from plain blanched to butter toffee peanuts; giant cashews to mammoth half-pecans (remember these are nuts, so size is relative); and the snooty-sounding country club mix (basically sesame sticks, peanuts, and smoked seasoning) to something called "Can you handle my spicy hot nuts?" And, of course, there's peanut butter, cashew butter, almond butter, and more, all of which are made without salt, sugar, and preservatives.

You can also stop by the snack bar, with a dozen different kinds of peanut butter sandwiches like Grandma's Apple Pie, with homemade chunky fruit spread, as well as several variations of peanut butter milk shakes, ice cream, and sundaes, including the Buckeye, which involves chocolate and extra nuts, and the perennial strawberry. One never truly felt sorry for people who are allergic to nuts until this moment.

History in a Box
Columbus

Along with displaying some weird stuff—including a two-headed calf born in Darke County and an Egyptian mummy—the Ohio Historical Center (1982 Velma Ave. 43211, museum 614-297-2300, archives/library 614-297-2510, www.ohiohistory.org) oversees several dozen historic sites throughout the state and serves as a repository for information on all things Ohio.

The main building, which opened in 1970, looks like an oversize pizza carton on stilts and is a product—some might say victim—of

"I'd like mine with pepperoni and mushrooms, please."

the architectural design known as "Brutalism," described on a related website as "a rational, structuralist, monumental style exported in the early 1950s by French and British architects. Distinguished by its . . . honesty and undisguised, blunt use of materials, Brutalism departed from conventional bourgeois styles." Well, OK, but for some, it just might induce a craving for pepperoni, light on the mushrooms.

The center's archives collects and preserves written and pictorial data about Ohio's history, making it available to the public. It's ideal for those wanting to research their family tree, and for students and academics seeking details about the state not found anywhere else or from long-forgotten eras. There's also a really cool exhibit on war gar-dens in Ohio, so even if you don't find what you need, it's worth the elevator ride up to the third floor.

The center is currently undergoing a renovation, though no one seems to know what's exactly on the menu design-wise. It has gone through some rather dramatic changes in recent years, most nota-bly the downsizing of adjacent Ohio Village, a popular re-creation of several Civil War–era buildings that still occasionally presents live interpreters in period costume and has old-timey baseball games. It is also available for weddings, corporate functions, and bar mitzvahs, although somehow the rugged nineteenth-century rural town and dirt roads seem rather incongruous for the latter.

Museum space was also rearranged to include more "relevant" exhibits, like the display of baby boomer toys. So old favorites such as the Adena Pipe, the Mica Hand, and the Wray Figurine shared space with Mr. Potato Head, Slinky, and Barbie. Not to worry, there's an Ohio connection: Etch A Sketch was manufactured here.

A Slippery Undertaking
Columbus

Some might say the Ohio State Fair (717 East Seventeenth Ave. 43229, 888-646-3976, www.ohiostatefair.com) helps grease the local econ-omy. At the very least, it's a great chance to people-watch those from distant and normally unheard-of corners of the state who only emerge for the fair and who may be just as entertained by seeing you.

And it has provided breading (as in fried food) and especially butter to some. Since the early 1900s Ohio State University and other dairy processors have sponsored butter sculpting contests at the fair. The specific theme was rather slippery until 1903, when A. T. Shelton & Company of Sunbury firmed things up by creating the first butter cow and calf. The fair has had a cow just about every year since.

Since the 1920s the cow and/or cow/calf combo has cooled its/their heels in a forty-five-degree glass display in the Dairy Products building.

★ ★

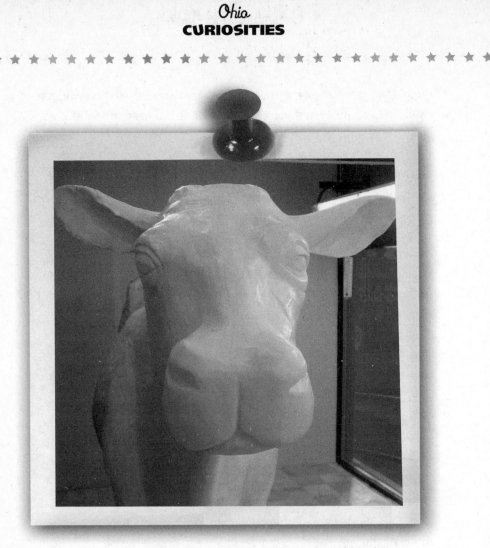

These eyes can butter up even the coldest heart.
AMERICAN DAIRY ASSOCIATION AND DAIRY COUNCIL MIDEAST

Other sculptures are on view as well, an eclectic lineup that has included Jack Nicklaus, Darth Vader, Lewis and Clark, Mr. Monopoly, Bobby Rahal, a tribute to the ninetieth anniversary of the ice-cream cone, a bald eagle, former heavyweight champion Buster Douglas, and last but certainly not least, a Furby (remember those?). If they ever did anything on baseball, they could call it Butter Up!

Approximately half a million people visit the sculptures every year. An added incentive is undoubtedly the ice cream, milk shakes, and other dairy products also sold in the building. They go down easy with elephant ears, deep-fried Twinkies and candy bars, cheesecake bites, and just about anything on a stick. (In all fair-ness, healthy choices are also available, but can you imagine walking down the main drag munching on a veggie wrap or fruit cup? You might be laughed out the front gate.)

In 2006 the *Columbus Dispatch* put a chill on what many believed to be an all-Buckeye undertaking when it revealed that ingredients for the Ohio State Fair butter cow came from—gasp!—Keller's Creamery in Winnsboro, Texas. To make matters worse, a few months earlier, Texas had defeated Ohio State University in a crucial game, melting all hopes for the national football title.

The honorees for 2010 were NFL players Joe Thomas of the Cleveland Browns and Chinedum Ndukwe of the Cincinnati Bengals, separated by a large butter football. So what are the Ohio State Buckeyes, chopped liver? But wait, considering what the football is made of and that both teams—especially the "Bungles"—are known for their fumbles, perhaps that's a slippery slope best avoided . . .

Mr. Excitement
Columbus

Is it a coincidence that the honorees in the Accounting Hall of Fame are all men? And mostly middle-aged white men, at that? What kind of child dreams of being immortalized on one of the brass plaques on the fourth floor of Fisher Hall at Ohio State University (2100 Neil Ave. 43210, 614-292-2529, www.fisher.osu.edu/departments/accounting-and-mis/the-accounting-hall-of-fame)? Certainly not basketball or rap star wannabes or aspiring female pop singers.

Still, accountants can, uh, add a lot to our lives. For one thing, they do our taxes and understand finances, and as any mathematics-impaired individual knows, both are scary propositions best left to those who can balance a ledger and at least explain money markets and tax shelters. OK, so there's the "creative accounting" thing that got a bunch of companies in trouble, but you won't find those guys mentioned in this Hall of Fame.

Should the Queen Not Be Able to Fulfill Her Duties . . .

Move over, Pamela Anderson. You're lucky you weren't around during the reign of Maudine Ormsby.

The 1925 *Ohio State University Monthly* anointed her "the latest star in the Milky way . . . she has represented Ohio State University . . . where she has received honors galore." She also packed 'em in with record crowds during the annual Farmer's Week, where five thousand "paid her tribute," according to the magazine. Is it any wonder that Maudine was elected Homecoming Queen by ardent student fans in the fall of the following year? Never mind that Maudine had four legs instead of two, and at about 1,200 or so pounds (give or take a couple hundred either way), she was a little plus-sized, even for her height. Oh, and did we mention that Maudine Ormsby was a Holstein cow?

Yet Maudine was chosen queen by an overwhelming margin, with votes exceeding the actual number of students enrolled at the university, according to some accounts. The first runner-up, Rosalind Morrison (later Mrs. W. F. Strapp) felt she'd been handed a bum steer and "refused to accept any of the honors at all," as she stated in records maintained by the OSU Archives. "It was quite a blow to all the candidates," although in later years, it had "become quite a joke."

★ ★

Since 1950 a group of qualified peers have nominated and voted in the likes of Arthur Andersen (yes, the one for whom the large firm was named); Sir Henry Alexander Benson of the United Kingdom, the first non-American to be cast in bronze in Fisher Hall; and Yuji Ijiri, the

Stories vary as to what actually transpired, but Maudine was the overwhelming choice of students in the College of Agriculture. Along with being four-year champion, she was the "youngest heifer in the world to produce 22,000 pounds of milk and 984 pounds of butter," raved the article in the *Monthly*. What magnificent teats, and without artificial enhancement!

According to the archives' records, Maudine initially came in second. But the Homecoming Committee got the cow tip after they checked the student directory and couldn't locate her or her photo. However, other irregularities in the election resulted in the divine bovine's catapult to homecoming royalty.

When they heard about her win, Maudine's handlers in the College of Agriculture had a, er, cow. They feared the coronation might curdle her milk, or that she might "zig" when she should "zag" and trample a few revelers. So although she was honored at the Homecoming Parade—two boys in a cow costume rode the float and attended other events—she stayed in the barn during the dance, game, and other hoopla.

Things quickly turned into cow patties after that. Ohio State lost the game to their archrival Michigan by one point, their only defeat of the year, knocking them out of the Big Ten title. By 1929 Maudine had developed brucellosis, a contagious bacterial infection. So like Mary, Queen of Scots, and Charles I of England before her, she became a victim of regicide.

Still, her saga lives on, to the udder amusement of new generations of students at Ohio State.

★ ★

only Asian in the bunch and the only four-time recipient of the AICPA-AAA's Notable Contributions to Accounting Lecturer Award.

There's the late Perry Mason, not the fictive lawyer but rather a Chicago native who was instrumental in the preparation of three indexes for *The Accounting Review*—a possible alternative to Ambien—and who delved into the mystery of rising gas and electric costs in a monograph entitled "Principles of Public-Utility Depreciation." (It was published in 1937, so it's just a little outdated.) Robert Montgomery—the accountant, not the movie star—is perhaps arguably one of the more colorful characters. He never finished high school, served in the Spanish–American War and World War I, and was married three times. He died in 1953.

Each listing discusses the man, his early proclivity toward accounting, his education, career, publications, honors, and so forth. Also included is information about his family and hobbies. It's hardly the stuff of thrillers, but your kids could do a whole lot worse than end up in the Accounting Hall of Fame, which is open whenever Fisher Hall is. It all totals up to one big challenge for female accountants, who have yet to be included.

Lionizing a Literary Lamb
Columbus

James Thurber is proof that, indeed, the meek can inherit the earth, or at least a small piece of it. He and his life are immortalized in Thurber House (77 Jefferson Ave. 43215, 614-464-1032, www.thurberhouse .org), his childhood home, which also serves as a writing center, with a nationwide writer-in-residence program and literary readings and picnics, a national humor award bearing his name, and an active adult and children's writing program. Walter Mitty would be proud, though he, too, was a product of Thurber's active imagination. Daily group tours are available, but if you want to visit, it would be best to call first.

✳ ✳

Born in Columbus in 1894, Thurber lived at this address from 1913 to 1917 while he was a student at Ohio State University. It was here that, on a night in 1915, he encountered the ghost that inspired one of his best-known stories, "The Night the Ghost Got In." (OK, so he wasn't so creative when it came to titles.) The popular theory is that the unearthly visitor was a former inmate of the Ohio Lunatic Asylum, which had burned to the ground on that exact day several decades earlier. Writers-in-residence, Thurber House employees, and others have also encountered mysterious footsteps, moved objects, and other strange happenings.

Otherworldly visitors aside, the original house has been lovingly restored to re-create the time period when the family lived there. The first two floors are open to the public, with original furniture, displays of memorabilia from Thurber's career, and a gift shop where the works of James Thurber and other writers are sold. Other rooms in the house and the Thurber Center Gallery next door also highlight the efforts of visual artists and serve as a meeting place for literary events. Located between the two buildings is the Thurber Reading Garden, the site of the literary picnics and several oversize sculptures of his beloved dogs based on his popular drawings.

It may sound like James Thurber had it easy, but he didn't. Yes, he spent most of his adult life in New York City, a regular among the glittering literati at the famous round table of the Algonquin Hotel. He wrote nearly forty books, including collections of essays, short stories, fables, and children's stories, and even won a Tony Award for his play A Thurber Carnival, which he often starred in as himself. His cartoons and short stories, many of which appeared in the New Yorker, were admired and reprinted. But he suffered from gradual loss of vision, the result of a childhood accident. It greatly hampered his ability to both write and draw. Married twice, he had a lot of health problems, especially later in life. He died of complications from pneumonia in 1961 and is buried in Greenlawn Cemetery (1000 Greenlawn Ave., 614-444-1123). Yet, he's still making people laugh.

★ ★

Painting by Plants
Columbus

What initially looks like a random collection of bushes loosely resembling people, animals, and other not-quite-definable figures is surrounded by an imposing iron fence whose purpose seems to be to keep the seedy, two-legged characters out. But it also contains them.

Just blooming on a Sunday afternoon

* *

In reality the topiary arrangement at the Old Deaf School Park (Town Street and Washington Avenue 43215, 614-645-0197, www.topiarygarden.org) is a reproduction of Georges Seurat's famous 1887 masterwork, A Sunday Afternoon on the Island of La Grande Jatte. The only known topiary interpretation of a painting in existence, the idea germinated, so to speak, when sculptor James T. Mason was visiting a Philadelphia botanical garden in the mid-1980s. "It was late October and kind of a hazy day," he recalled in an article in the Columbus Dispatch. "The gardens reminded me of an Impressionist painting." What he referred to as a "radical interpretation of Seurat . . . becomes a pun—a landscape of a painting of a landscape. The idea is to dim the connections between art, nature and civilization." Whatever.

With the help of his late wife, Elaine, Mason designed, created, and installed the metal frames as well as the living topiaries, which are mostly made out of trimmed and shaped yew trees. The almost eighty figures consist of fifty-four topiary people, eight boats, three dogs, a monkey, and a cat, which isn't in the original painting at all. Seurat's work depicts a bunch of upmarket Parisians in ornate Victorian clothing gazing fixedly at the River Seine, which in this case is represented by a rather cloudy-looking pond, a real stretch of the imagination. The largest figure is twelve feet tall, and depending on when you visit, they either stand out in sharp relief or look as though they need a trim, not unlike their human counterparts.

According to the garden's website, Seurat would have sketched his scene from the top of the easterly hill: "Stand left of the bronze plaque on the stone slab in the path, and you will see 'the painting' as he saw it." But you might have to squint really, really hard. Or you can view the seven-by-ten-foot original at the Art Institute of Chicago and spend your time in the pretty Columbus park (which is open during the daytime) looking for the renegade cat, checking out the gift shop, or going for a leisurely stroll.

Big Not-fun House

Before the glitzy Arena District in Columbus, with its Jumbo-Tron TV and glittering string of clubs and restaurants—not to mention the NHL and other entertainments—there was the Ohio Penitentiary (1834–1979), a grim fortress with a limestone front and barrier walls that extended around Spring Street. The surrounding area was nothing to write home about either, mostly warehouses, light manufacturing, and lots of crime. Today most condos there start at about a quarter-mil. How things have changed!

The prison wasn't even finished when the first 189 guests of the state arrived: "A ragged chain of horse thieves, brawlers and robbers . . . a felons' parade the likes of which Ohio will never see again," wrote David Lore in a *Columbus Dispatch* article proudly reprinted on the Ohio Department of Rehabilitation and Correction website. This was during an era when jailers took no prisoners, so to speak—forget about being or taking a "girlfriend," much less mending your ways. Initially inmates slept on straw mats and were fed corn bread, beans, and bacon, and forced to do manual labor.

But that was hardly the worst of it: "Not only men but women and children were . . . stripped of their clothing, lashed to the cruel posts and whipped until their backs resembled 'raw beef'; then tied face downward on the cold ground while shovels of hot ashes and coals of fire were sprinkled on the raw and bleeding flesh," penned prison superintendent Dan J. Morgan in his 1893 expose, *Lights and Shadows*.

In 1885 the penitentiary became the site for executions, and these included women as well. Twelve years later the electric chair replaced the gallows, resulting in the shocking deaths of some 315 people until 1963, when Ohio temporarily halted the death penalty.

The "Old Pen," as it came to be called, had its share of famous tenants, including Dr. Sam Shepard (the inspiration for the TV series and movie *The Fugitive*); Confederate general John Hunt Morgan and his raiders; and William Sidney Porter, better known as the famous writer O. Henry. But as bad as the place was, due to riots, overcrowding, and corruption, it was about to get worse, thanks to an April 1930 fire, set by three inmates hell-bent on escaping. Instead, it created a conflagration that killed 322, by some accounts the worst prison fire in U.S. history.

By 1955 more than 5,200 inmates were "penned up" in a space designed for 2,000. But the tide was beginning to turn, and public outcry called for reform. Gradually prisoners were transferred to other facilities, with the Southern Ohio Correctional Facility in Lucasville being built in the 1970s to replace the Old Pen. It was finally closed by order of the federal court. Yet nearly two decades passed before it was razed to the ground in 1998, despite objections by some—probably not former inmates—that it should be renovated.

Unlike other places with lurid histories, nary a ghost nor supernatural occurrence has taken place in the Arena District. Or maybe whatever phantoms remain are too busy checking out the bustling bar scene or watching sporting events on the big-screen TV.

★ ★

Fast-Food Nirvana
Columbus

Columbus has a reputation for being one of the fattest cities in the United States, and with good reason. It is the home of both White Castle and the first Wendy's.

First stop would be headquarters for the Albino Bastille, aka White Castle, at 555 West Goodale Blvd. 43215 (www.whitecastle.com). This is one moat you can't bridge; the Porcelain Steel Company, where they actually coordinate the building of the franchise stores, is not open to the public. But you can admire and take pictures of it, and they won't chase you out of the parking lot. Is there a sequel for Harold and Kumar here?

If you want an actual slyder (that's right, it's spelled with a *y*), stop at one of five locations in Columbus, most of which are in and around downtown (there are 380 restaurants nationwide). There's a line of frozen foods as well, but nothing quite equals the ambience (and probable later gastrointestinal distress) of ingesting a hot, greasy double cheeseburger and onion rings while sitting on a trademark uncomfortable seat and inhaling decades of lard work. Hey, they've been doing it since 1921, and have a Slyder Fest, a cook-off, and a Hall of Fame, not to mention (eeew) recipes for quiche, soufflé, and muffins. So it's hard to argue with success.

Wendy's and the story of the late Dave Thomas are perhaps easier to stomach. Thomas, an orphan, never graduated high school but gave millions of dollars to charitable causes, most significantly those addressing adoption. His folksy, humorous ad campaigns were a huge success, and the company hasn't been the same since his death in 2002.

Established in 1969 and named after Thomas's daughter, the first Wendy's was located downtown on East Broad Street, and had the ambience of a shrine—one that serves burgers, Frostys, and chicken nuggets but with a sense of history nonetheless, thanks to memorabilia in glass cases as well as pictures of Thomas with celebrities and

Road trip, anyone?

of earlier restaurants. There was even a small area with the original Tiffany decor and hippie beads. It closed in 2007 due to poor sales, and the artifacts were moved to Wendy's corporate headquarters (1 Dave Thomas Blvd., Dublin 43017, 614-764-3100, www.wendys.com), with the plan being that a museum would be opened. That hasn't happened yet, so in the immortal words of former Wendy's pitch-woman Clara Peller, "Where's the beef?"

Although fast food has its critics, some say Columbus has a Wendy's on every corner, or close to it. If not, there's always McDonald's, Long John Silver's, Rally's, Taco Bell, Pizza Hut . . . and, of course, White Castle.

★ ★

Ship of Schools
Columbus

"In nineteen hundred ninety-two, Columbus sailed the Scioto blue . . . "
Well, that's not exactly how the song goes, but it pretty much
describes the *Santa Maria* (614-645-8670 or 614-645-0351, www
.santamaria.org), a museum-quality replica of the explorer's flagship
that sits at Battelle Riverfront Park, 25 Marconi Blvd. 43215. Do not
go to the *Santa Maria* administrative office on North Fifth Street,
which is what this author did, until she realized that she didn't see the
boat because the river was several blocks west, near the Broad Street
Bridge. Oops.

Anyway, this *Santa Maria* was originally constructed by the Scarano
Boatbuilding Company of Albany, New York, to commemorate the
500th anniversary of Christopher Columbus's transatlantic voyage.
Never mind that the original never actually touched North American
soil and ran aground in what is now Haiti. And that Columbus (the
man, not the city) had it disassembled and used the timbers to build a
fortress.

Or that Columbus (the city, not the man) deployed the replica for
a short time to putter around the Scioto before retiring it as a permanent exhibit favored by school and touring groups. You can even
rent it overnight, which means that everyone has an assigned task and
learns such seaworthy undertakings as rope coiling, map reading, and
ship maintenance, which also may include swabbing the deck (the captain reserves the right to assign this task permanently to misbehaving
crew members). Activities stop just short of visits by unfriendly natives
or pirates, which means your chances of meeting Johnny Depp—or
a reasonable facsimile—are nil. Scurvy, beriberi, and cabin fever not
included.

Most visitors opt for the forty-five-minute guided tour, which dra-
matizes the lives of Columbus and his fellow explorers and allows
you to interact with replicas of their navigational tools, even partaking of the games they played to pass the time. The *Santa Maria* is

Adventures on the high Scioto River
DAVID DAY

what is known as a wooden tall ship, 98 feet long and 89 feet high, and weighing about 130 tons, with the 65-foot main mast made of Douglas fir. It looks impressive, almost modern, until you realize that Columbus and his crew only had the wind and the current for propulsion and the sun and stars for direction. It was the equivalent of space travel today—no GPS, no McDonald's, just endless miles of untouched terrain.

Corporate types also occasionally use it for outings, a change of pace from the cubicle farm.

If You Build It, They Will Laugh
Dublin

This concrete field of dreams—109 human-sized ears of corn (no one seems to know their exact height)—was constructed in 1994. The perfect, perpendicular rows provide an ironic and unintentionally ridiculous-looking contrast to the office buildings, housing developments, and other symbols of urban sprawl that surround it.

In all fairness, the field (4995 Rings Rd. 43017) formerly belonged to Sam Frantz, a pioneer in the development of several hybrid corns. From 1935 to 1963, Frantz farmed the spot in his search for the perfect strain and worked with Ohio State University on several projects. After he was done with the land, he donated it to the city, who

Just add butter and salt—and don't forget the dental floss.

respectfully named it—drum roll, please—Sam and Eulalia Frantz Park. Artist Malcolm Cochran created the field of corn, modeling the ears after a variety known as "Corn Belt Dent Corn," which is the least it would do to you or your car should you try to unearth one of these puppies and take it home as a souvenir. Besides, where would you put it, anyway?

Tucked away in a corner of the park are various signs explaining hybridization as well as the project itself, whose alleged purpose is to "commemorate Dublin's history as a farming community," according to the www.visitdublin.org website. Although most people respect the region's agricultural heritage, they just might say "bite me" to a field of giant concrete corn paid for by public tax dollars.

His Lips Are Sealed
Dublin

Also in Dublin in Scioto Park (off Route 257, 7377 Riverside Dr. 43017) is a twelve-foot-high limestone slab sculpture of what might pass for an abstract representation of former president George W. Bush (the furrowed brow, the aquiline nose, the vacant stare . . .), especially from the side. OK, so it's really Chief Leatherlips (1747–1810), or Shat-eyaronyah, as he was known to his Wyandot tribe. (Try pronouncing that name three times in a row after a couple of rounds of firewater.) The white settlers called him Leatherlips because, unlike the politician he resembles—or many politicians for that matter—he always kept his word.

The statue also lacks a "brain"; you can climb onto the top of its head for a bird's-eye view of whatever's being presented at an adjacent outdoor amphitheater. A Boston artist, Ralph Helmick, created the sculpture in 1990 after it was commissioned by the Dublin Arts Council. It is said to be modeled after the Crazy Horse monument in the Black Hills of South Dakota, although that sculpture of the chief on horseback with his bare chest, six-pack, and flowing hair is much more reminiscent of the covers of romance novels.

★ ★

If he's Leatherlips, where's his mouth?

Regardless, Leatherlips/Shateyaronyah backed the wrong team at the time of his execution in 1810, as he'd been one of the signers of the Treaty of Greenville, which advocated peace with the settlers. After years of bitter intertribal fighting, his rival, Tecumseh, accused him of witchcraft and condemned the old chief to death. Leatherlips was executed by a tomahawk to the head, a few miles north of the monument. For all his headaches, the Wyandot Club, a local fraternal organization, erected a granite grave marker in 1889 at the site where he fell. It still stands today at the corner of what is now Stratford Avenue and Riverside Drive.

Some say Chief Leatherlips took his revenge by causing it to rain during Dublin's annual Muirfield Memorial golf tournament because both the course and the adjacent Muirfield Village are built on sacred grounds. It usually pours at least 50 percent of the time during the tournament, even when they've moved it ahead a week.

But, as usual, Chief Leatherlips isn't talking.

Military Magnet
Groveport

They say "Old soldiers never die, they just fade away." But this is hardly true for the memorabilia they acquire during wartime, much of which has ended up in Motts Military Museum (5075 Hamilton Rd. 43215, 614-836-1500, www.mottsmilitarymuseum.org). Items from this museum have made their way to the middle of Ohio from the far-flung corners of the earth, often under the direst of circumstances.

A lifelong collector and retired professional photographer, Warren Motts started gathering Indian arrowheads as a child and expanded into Civil War relics as he grew older. Before he knew it, he was getting artifacts from the Revolutionary War to Operation Iraqi Freedom from the likes of Arnold Schwarzenegger (an M-47 tank, used by the former Governator while in the Austrian army in the 1960s), Saddam Hussein (a flag and two ornately framed portraits of the deposed dictator), and, indirectly, General Douglas MacArthur (a corncob pipe) and General William Westmoreland (a field uniform), among many others.

The expansion of Operation Motts Museum resulted from a combination of persistence and word of mouth. "People hear about the museum and send me stuff," Motts observes. With the assistance of an influential board of directors, many of whom have a military background, he also actively pursues acquisitions he thinks might be appropriate for the collection.

You could spend hours in this place. There's everything from medical instruments used in the Civil War (including an amputation kit) to blood-stained maps to uniforms and family portraits of Nazi officers.

★ ★

Friend or foe? Hard to tell with that smile.

Mussolini's flag shares exhibit space with a wedding dress made from a parachute and displays commemorating the Holocaust and the Tuskegee airmen. And that's just the inside. The back lot contains tanks from the Vietnam War and World War II as well as helicopters and a full-size, authentic reproduction of Captain Eddie Rickenbacker's boyhood home. The family of the World War One flying ace donated many of the objects. Arnold said "he'd be back" to get his tank, and true to his word, reclaimed it in 2008, although he did allow Motts to take a test drive.

Motts, who created his own exhibits (which are as well designed as any major museum's) has added and expanded exhibits on Operation Desert Storm, NASA, and POWs, among other things.

War may be hell, but it certainly makes fascinating history.

Must-See TVs

Hilliard

Many people believe television sprang full-blown into their living rooms in the 1950s and '60s with *Bonanza, I Love Lucy,* and *Howdy Doody* burning themselves into millions of boomer brains. But actually the creation of TV started before the last century in the late 1900s, with the first images going live in 1926. OK, so the picture was only about an inch or so and produced by a metal disk instead of a tube. But by 1930, mechanical TV as it was known, was being broadcast from over a dozen stations in the United States, with much of Europe following suit. But it didn't last long, since most sets were build 'em yourself and picture quality was poor at best, made up of only 30 to 60 lines compared to the 525 used today.

Although the picture tube for today's electronic TV was invented in the 1920s, it wasn't viable until a several years later when Vladimir Zworkin of RCA Victor came up with the Iconoscope, which produced pictures with a reasonable amount of light. But by then a fellow called Hitler started causing interference, interrupting the scheduling of programs, regular or otherwise. A good thing, since it helped prevent him from becoming as influential as say, Dr. Phil or the folks on *Jersey Shore.* One shudders to think about the potential impact of *Keeping Up with Der Fuhrer.*

The Early Television Museum (5396 Franklin St. 43026, 614-771-0510, www.earlytelevision.com/index.html) provides a unique glimpse into the salad days of what critics later called a vast wasteland. Started by Steve McVoy, a former cable guy—actually he owned a cable company, sold it, and started the nonprofit museum—the collection encompasses over 150 TV sets in a 4,200-square-foot area. They are arranged by era: mechanical TVs from the 1920s and 1930s; pre-1945 British sets from 1936 to 1939; pre-1945 American sets from 1939 to 1941; postwar sets from 1945 to 1958; and early color sets from 1953 to 1957. And many actually work, although attempts to turn them on without permission might result in a "you break it, you buy it"

If you think old cell phones were clunky, try one of these.

scenario far exceeding the modest donation for admission.

Even the mechanically impaired should find entertainment in early TVs that used mirrors to better reflect the image; prehistoric flat screens encased in pleather; and bizarre numbers whose color-producing rotating wheels drowned out sound, among many others. Highlights include a mirrored 1946 "Telejuke," a sort of pay TV/jukebox combo; early studio equipment and cameras, complete with a WGSF Newark truck; and little known and rare models from DuMont, Crosley, and U.S. Television, not to mention numerous DIYs (good luck assembling your own 3-D HD 60" flat screen).

The topic has become so engrossing that for the past several years, the museum has hosted an annual early television convention. It could be more interesting than some of today's programs and, with a $30 registration fee, is a lot cheaper than most cable bills.

Riding High
Pickerington

Motorcycles have come a long way since the chain-and-leather days of movies such as *Savages from Hell, Angry Breed,* and *Under Hot Leather.* Today you'll more likely find doctors, lawyers, and captains of industry astride a Harley than a scuzzy-looking dude and his dentally-impaired "old lady."

Rolex Riders and other weekend warriors can celebrate their hobby at the Motorcycle Hall of Fame Museum (13515 Yarmouth Dr. 43147, 614-856-2222, www.motorcyclemuseum.org). Affiliated with the American Motorcycle Association (AMA), it is more than a bunch of fancy, funny-looking two-wheelers, although there are lots of those, like the 1894 Roper Streamer. Invented by Sylvester H. Roper, it resembles a bicycle with a briefcase stuck between its wheels. It was also his last ride, since the seventy-three-year-old suffered a heart attack while racing it. Talk about dying with your motorcycle boots on . . .

At the other end of the spectrum, some 110 years later, is Chad Reed's 2004 YZ250, a sleek, aerodynamically balanced job that broke that year's records at the Mobile Supercross Series. In between are such classics as no-longer-made Indian and Henderson models, upscale BMWs, and Harley-Davidsons and Hondas, two favorites of what's known in the vernacular as BAMBIs (Born Again Middle-Age Biker Idiots).

The museum's three exhibition halls are also filled with riding gear, photos, literature, sculptures, racetrack reconstructions, dioramas, posters, awards, and more. Major displays change every couple of years and include topics like the history of motocross or various manufacturers, motorcycle-related toys and games, or such innovators as designer Craig Vetter.

The two hundred or so inductees in the Hall of Fame have their own gallery as well, including some familiar names like Evel Knievel and enthusiast/*Tonight Show* host Jay Leno. But there's also Tom Paradise, the hill-climbing champion from the 1930s and 1940s, and Rip Rose, roving editor for *Easyriders* magazine and founder of a charity run for a cure for diabetes. Everything you want to know about the funky, fun, and sometimes bumpy ride of motorcycles is here, and then some.

Bottoms Up!
Westerville

If abstinence makes the heart grow fonder, then the Anti-Saloon League Museum in the Westerville Public Library (126 South State St. 43081, 614-882-7277, www.westervillelibrary.org/antisaloon) can be a lesson to us all. The modern mind may find Prohibition—the abolishment of the manufacture, transportation, import, export, and sale of alcoholic beverages—a difficult concept to grasp, but it was big business from 1893–1933. In 1858 Westerville had distinguished itself by adopting one of the earliest Prohibition ordinances in the state and put its gunpowder where its mouth was by blowing up the saloon of Henry and Phyloxena Corbin. Twice. Some people just can't get the hint.

This sufficiently impressed a temperance group in Oberlin, which later became the Anti-Saloon League of America, the driving force behind Prohibition. When the town fathers of Westerville learned that the league was looking for a location for its burgeoning printing plant, they said "come on down" to the tune of a $10,000 incentive. In 1909 the American Issue Publishing Company was formed, making the village its national headquarters and cementing Westerville's reputation as the Dry Capital of the World. Along with the official newspaper, *The American Issue,* they churned out millions of pages of stories, encyclopedias, cartoons, and more with such titles as *Liquor Octopus, Lou's Cold Bath, A Whiff from Hell!* and *Booze and a Boy.* There was even a barbershop quartet that traveled the country performing at temperance rallies. And the 1960s generation thought *Reefer Madness* was melodramatic.

By 1919 the Eighteenth Amendment, the National Prohibition Act, also known as the Volstead Act, was passed. Obviously it didn't work,

That was then, but now you can stop for a cold one.

given the proliferation of speakeasies, stills, and organized crime. So it was subsequently repealed by the Twenty-first Amendment in 1933.

The museum itself consists of a couple of rooms filled with books, magazines, newspapers, and photos. The curator and other accommodating library personnel help bring this strange period to life with colorful stories and anecdotes. But it can get awfully dry in there and you might find yourself becoming a bit thirsty. So if you're twenty-one and over, alcoholic libations are now available a few blocks away uptown. Westerville became "liquid" on January 1, 2006. Bottoms up!

★ ★

The Well-Groomed Potty
Westerville

Yes, Virginia, there really are people who vote on their favorite public place to go pee. The Cintas Corporation cites a survey claiming that more than 75 percent of respondents said they would not return to a restaurant if the bathrooms were unkempt. (They may have neglected to query bar patrons in most college towns.) In the face of such staggering statistics, Cintas—a leading industrial hygiene supply company and restroom services provider—felt compelled to honor "companies and organizations who go above and beyond the call of duty to present a pleasant, even memorable experience in a public restroom," as stated on their website, www.bestrestroom.com. One wonders if this included highway rest stops at night, or prisons.

"Whether at a restaurant or a rest area, a high-rise office building or a 'nice clean gas station,' everyone at some point makes use of public facilities," continues the site. So in 2001 the good folks at Cintas, which also provides uniforms and other supplies to some seven hundred thousand businesses in North America, created the Best Restroom Award to flush out "businesses across the country that maintain exceptional hygiene, with style, in their public restrooms."

Past winners have included the John Michael Kohler Arts Center in Sheboygan, Wisconsin; the restored Main Building at the University of Notre Dame ("impeccable [with] floors . . . clean enough to eat off!" unless someone has an, uh, accident, and "shinier than the Golden Dome for which Notre Dame is famous!" or perhaps Michael Jordan's bald head); the Grand Casino in Biloxi, Mississippi; and the Fort Smith Regional Airport in Fort Smith, Arkansas ("Beautiful decor and comfortable seating, both inside and outside the stalls. . . . You'll never have to manually flush a toilet or turn on a sink here" or physically move a faucet, God forbid!).

Along with Jungle Jim's grocery store (see listing under "Cincinnati"), a recent winner was—drum roll, please—Wendell's (925 North State St. 43081, 614-818-0400, www.wendells.net) in Westerville. A

Flush with the success of being designated
America's cleanest

popular eatery/sports bar with a great outdoor patio, the bathroom is "always stocked with towels, soap and mouthwash . . . [and has] a classic athletic theme with black and white photos and sleek countertops." Pictures in the stalls help occupy your mind while answering the call of nature. And a tiny waterfall lives next to the sink in the

State Roundup: Drama, Au Naturel

Summer can be a busy time if you like outdoor theater. Along with the Living Word (see Southeast chapter), Ohio offers some distinctive al fresco–themed entertainments. But certain artistic liberties are taken; for example, Chief Blue Jacket was initially believed to be a white man named Marmaduke van Sweringen until 2006 when his DNA remains were definitively found to be Native American. Perhaps that (or maybe the economy) has something to do with the fact that the long-running Blue Jacket drama in Xenia has been indefinitely discontinued, with the website (www.bluejacketdrama.com) stating that a replacement may be forthcoming. Still the show must go on . . .

- (Chillicothe 45601, June through September, 866-775-0700, www .tecumsehdrama.com). "Witness the epic life story of the legendary Shawnee leader as he struggles to defend his sacred homelands in the Ohio country during the late 1700s," proclaims the website. "'Tecumseh!' has been labeled as one of the most mesmerizing dramas in the nation." Well, it was one of the first and is certainly among the noisiest. The huge stage at Sugarloaf Mountain Amphitheatre accommodates a herd of live horses, a booming

★ ★

women's room, a feng shui reminder to wash your hands, if there ever was one.

If you want to check out the "other" restroom, you'll have to trust the observations of companions or strangers of the opposite sex. Management frowns upon dual visits.

cannon, and vivid battle scenes. Plus, if you have relatives in the area, they might be able to get you good seats because they use lots of extras. Hint: Don't speed if you're driving there via State Road 23 because there are cops waiting to give theatergoers another kind of ticket.

- **Trumpet in the Land,** New Philadelphia 44663 (June through August, 330-339-1132, www.trumpetintheland.com). The Revolutionary War–era plot focuses on the founding of Ohio's first settlement, Schoenbrunn, in 1772 and culminates in the slaughter of ninety-six Native Americans who converted to Christianity. Major players include David Zeisberger, the "Moravian missionary who hoped to establish a peaceful Indian settlement along the fiery frontier," according to the website; "Simon Girty, a conniving border renegade who agitated for all-out war in the region"; "Captain Pipe, a young warrior chief whose hatred of all white men for the killing of his father added to the dangers facing the missionaries"; and "John Heckewelder, one of the first explorers of the 'Ohio country.'" As usual the bad boy named Simon—two similar, sometimes misunderstood scoundrels named Legree and Cowell come to mind—ends up with his own spinoff, The White Savage, held on alternate days.

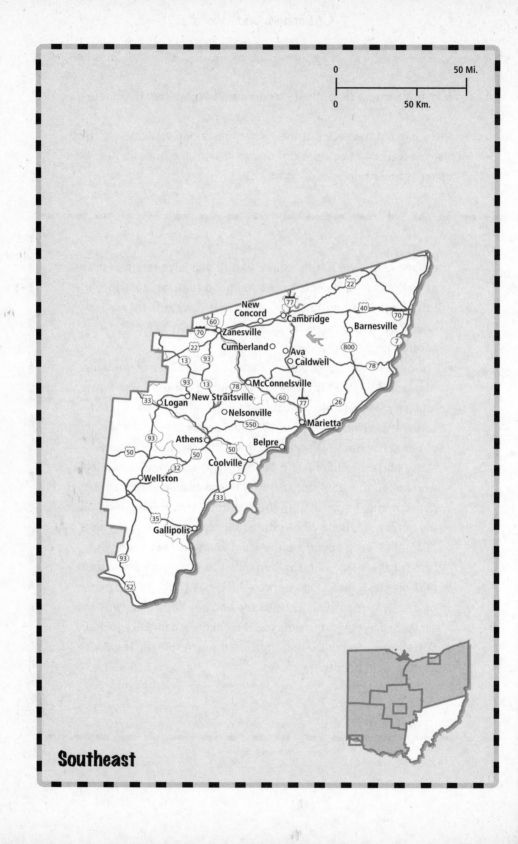

0   50 Mi.

0   50 Km.

New
Concord
77
22
40
70
Cambridge
Barnesville
60
70
Zanesville
7
22
Cumberland
Ava
800
13
93
Caldwell
78
93
13
78
McConnelsville
26
33
Logan
New Straitsville
60
77
Nelsonville
550
Marietta
93
Athens
Belpre
50
50
50
Coolville
32
Wellston
7
33
35
Gallipolis
93
52

Southeast

6

Southeast

From Ava to *Zanesville, the southeastern portion of the state has quality stuff. At the other end of the Prohibition spectrum—in contrast to
the Anti-Saloon League Museum near Columbus—is New Straitsville,
which was renowned throughout the Midwest for its hootch. But "still"
water runs deep—despite its being illegal, moonshine is manufactured
at a festival held there every year. Bottoms up!*

*Zanesville has its share of "zany" attractions as well. For over two
hundred years, its "Y" Bridge has crossed both the Licking and Musk-
ingham Rivers, the only bridge in the United States where you can
end up on the same side of the river that you started on. A few miles
away in McConnelsville is the Big Muskie scoop, a remnant of the largest single-bucket digging machine ever made, a twenty-seven million
pound groundbreaker. At 220 cubic yards and 325 tons, it's not exactly
chopped liver in the size department, either.*

*You can get a different kind of "scoop" in Ava, which commemo-
rates the 1925 crash of the airship USS* Shenandoah *through monuments on several sites where the dirigible disintegrated. It all comes
together at the Shenandoah memorial museum, arguably the only collection of its kind in a trailer. Then swing around to the golf ball house
in Logan. Known as Stewart's Folly after the builder (Stewart, not folly)
it was constructed in the 1970s with the idea of being hurricane- and
fire-proof, and was never lived in. Fore heaven's sake!*

★ ★

Art in a Barn
Athens

They say artists can be a little crazy . . . OK, maybe more than a little.
So it's kind of fitting that the Dairy Barn Cultural Arts Center (8000
Dairy Lane 45701, 740-592-4981, www.dairybarn.org) building was
at one point a state-owned mental health facility, in addition to being
a home for cows, chickens, and other farm animals. Built in 1914 the
barn had served as part of the activities therapy program—for the
humans, of course.

By the mid-1970s, however, it was like, well, living in a barn,
and was slated for demolition by the state. But instead of seeing a

Like farm animals, the art in the barn takes on its own life.
PHOTO COURTESY OF THE DAIRY BARN ARTS CENTER

run-down structure with a gutted floor, rows of stalls, and a residual smell of methane gas (we are talking about bovines after all), a group of local artists and others, led by boosters Harriet and Ora Anderson, had a vision of "a lovely example of early twentieth-century architecture sitting quietly on the crest of a gently sloping hill," according to www.quiltnational.com, a related website. Situated on thirty-six acres, "the natural amphitheater formed by the hills and trees behind the barn created a backdrop of serenity and beauty." It was also down the street from Ohio University, so assorted intellectuals and visiting academics could stop by and bask in the pastoral aura of flyover country.

The governor granted a stay of execution nine days before the barn was to be torn down. A group of ambitious quilters held the first Quilt National there in 1979, which went on to become a world-renowned exhibition of art quilts held during odd-numbered years. If you miss the quilts, you can always check out the Bead International and Basketry International shows. And to think these used to be standard hobbies for the elderly, infirm, and/or mentally incapacitated.

Consisting of a 6,500-square-foot exhibition area, the main building is now an upscale art gallery with climate control, security systems, and sophisticated lighting and displays. It also serves as a showcase for the visual and literary arts, festivals, and live performances, such as concerts. They also have really cool openings, usually with a decent spread. So like the cows before them, participants can stand around chewing their cuds and laying on the bull.

Misled Zeppelin

Ava

They say breaking up is hard to do, and no one would know better than Lieutenant Commander Zachary Lansdowne, captain of the USS *Shenandoah*, "the strongest airship in America." He perished, along with thirteen of the forty-three-member crew, when the blimp crashed into a zillion pieces during a thunderstorm on September 3, 1925, amid the rolling hills of Noble County.

★ ★

The first rigid airship built in the United States and the first in the world to be inflated with helium, the *Shenandoah* was made of a new alloy that supposedly combined the strength of steel with the lightness of aluminum. And it was a big 'un: 680 feet long, with a maximum diameter of 78.7 feet and maximum height of 93 feet. Its five 300-horsepower, 6-cylinder Packard engines reached a top speed

One Old Soldier

From the dry and dusty history books emerges the ghost of one John Gray. Born on George Washington's plantation in 1764, he actually was friends with Washington, served in the Revolutionary War, and was present during the Battle of Yorktown. After the war he moved to Ohio to claim land and start a farm. He became the war's oldest survivor, though that was subject to debate at the time.

Still, Uncle Sam did not recompense him for helping to create the United States until journalist and Civil War veteran J. L. Dalzell fought to prove Gray actually was a veteran. So at the ripe young age of 103, Gray finally got a pension from the military, only to die a year later, in 1868. All that for less than a measly fifty bucks a month (probably not all that bad, given the time period). He is buried near where his cabin once stood, preceded in death by three wives and at least four children.

But a book by James Dalzell, *Private Dalzell: His Autobiography, Poems and Comic War Papers; Sketch of John Gray, Washington's Last Soldier, Etc.*, published in 1888, puts a spin on the real John Gray: "I was a mighty tough kind of boy in them days, I tell you," Gray told Dalzell of his youth on Washington's plantation. "I saw big, heavy men give out, but I never lagged a foot behind. My family were

★ ★

of 60 miles per hour—pretty darn fast for the Roaring Twenties—and could carry a 33-ton load.

It's not the *Titanic,* or even the *Hindenburg,* but you can do the *Shenandoah* circuit without leaving Noble County. Start at the *Shenandoah* memorial, along Route 821 in the tiny village of Ava 43711 (since it's near the Methodist Church, it should be easy to spot).

mighty poor. . . . So . . . I had to go to work to support them. There was eight children of us. I used to take my dog, and go out and catch rabbits. It was all we had to eat sometimes."

Shortly after the war, Gray moved to Morgantown, Virginia. He told Dalzell, "We had our things in a wagon. I took a notion we would go down to Kentucky. So I built a boat, and put my family and horses aboard. . . . There was a salt-lick up on Duck Creek [now near Belle Valley in Noble County, Ohio, where he lived for the remaining several decades of his life] and we used to come up and hunt of winters. I saw Indians, plenty of them. I remember the year of Wayne's defeat. I tell you, the settlement was badly skeered of them. I may have shot one or two red-skins—no matter." Back then, they didn't like us much either.

You can take the easy way and stop by the modern-day monument dedicated to Gray at a roadside park near Route 821 south of Belle Valley 43717 (www.noblecountyohio.com/johngray.html). Or you could schlep to the difficult-to-find graveyard near Brookfield Township Road 1130. There you will find three—count 'em, three—markers. John Gray would have undoubtedly appreciated that, and also your visit to the grave of someone who actually rubbed shoulders with the father of our country, false teeth and all.

Crashing with the Zeppelin
COURTESY OF THE NAVAL HISTORICAL CENTER

Originally located in a secluded wooded area where the stern section of the *Shenandoah* crashed, it was moved by the good folks of Ava, who wanted to make it accessible to the thundering herds of tourists. Along with listing the names of the dead on a bronze plaque, there's a replica of the *Shenandoah* amid swirling metal thunderclouds.

Then it's on to the "official" crash sites. No. 1, in Buffalo Township, where the initial crash took place, is demarcated by an early fieldstone and granite marker where Zachary Lansdowne's body was found. Site No. 2, where the stern came to rest, is a half-mile southeast across Interstate 77 in Noble Township. The rough outline of the stern is delineated by a series of concrete blocks and a sign marking the site. No. 3, approximately six miles southwest in Sharon Township at the northern edge of Route 78, is the spot where the *Shenandoah*'s bow landed. An Ohio historical marker describing the wreck appears at the rest area on I-77 southbound, approximately fifteen miles south of Cambridge.

But the best is yet to come . . . the Shenandoah Memorial Trailer (50495 Rte. 821, 43711, Ava; 740-732-2624). The life's work of Bryan and Theresa Rayner—Bryan's family owned one of the farms where the blimp crashed—it is usually parked outside the garage. But to be sure, call first. Inside you'll find sheet music entitled "The Wreck of the Shenandoah"; a 78-rpm record, "The End of the Shenandoah"; a bottle of Zep Up carbonated beverage; bolts received from Charles McNutt (get it?); and Captain Lansdowne's cuff links. The Rayners are so dedicated that they once went to New Jersey to meet a man who had ridden on the Shenandoah, but he died before they got there.

Confused? This author recommends visiting www.noblecountyohio.com/shenandoah.html or contacting Bryan Rayner (see above) or John Powell at (740) 732-2341 to arrange a tour. It should help keep things on an even keel.

Stud Bull
Barnesville

Ohio lionizes its cattle. You have your Select Sires in Plain City (see Central chapter), Maudine Ormsby (see Columbus and Vicinity), the Dairy Barn in Athens, and now Texas Longhorn #215182, aka The Shadow. He is immortalized via a stone marker just outside the corral at the Dickinson Cattle Ranch (35000 Muskrat Rd. 43713, 740-758-5050, www.texaslonghorn.net). His lovingly polished and preserved skull (yuck!) is on display at the Longhorns Head to Tail Store on the grounds, though given his, uh, contributions, perhaps another part might be more apropos.

His owners had no idea that the lil' bovine born on June 6, 1991, would become so prolific. He soon weighed more than a ton and had an amazing horn spread of eighty-two inches. Originally called "The Veep"—as in Vice President, an appropriate name for a bull if there ever was one—his owners were steered into the new moniker because his large, imposing figure seemed to cast a silhouette, even in the bright sunlight.

★ ★

And he was undoubtedly well-endowed someplace else: The Shadow's first large group of calves arrived in the spring of 1998, producing horn spreads and body configurations similar to dear old Dad's. And thanks to the wonders of artificial insemination, his semen has been distributed more than any other longhorn bull of the last decade. At a whopping $25 per one-half-cc straw, it's three times more expensive than a comparative amount of gold.

But he paid dearly for life in the fast lane ("fast" being a relative term here). In 1999 he punctured his right front outer toe, and it had to be removed. Then arthritis began to interfere with his "activities." According to the Dickinson website, special pain medications were used daily to keep him in service. (At this point, even a human male might begin to complain.) In 2002 his left hind toe was broken completely off, ending his career and perhaps disappointing many cows, but even more so, their owners. Since only his right leg supported his massive weight, Shadow met the light and passed away on April 24, 2003.

He was given full honors, including a memorial service, a eulogy, and a psalm, 112:9c, ". . . his horns shall be exalted with honor." And hundreds, if not thousands, will carry on his name for time immemorial—Shadowizm, Shadow Savvy, Shadow Rula, Shadow's Reflection, Prickly Shadow, Shakey Shadow, and so on. "He will live forever in pedigree, [through] his progeny, who will continue to be born annually as a result of the miracle of frozen semen," according to the company website. Yeah, but as Shadow would undoubtedly tell you if he could talk, it's not quite the same as the real thing.

Dueling Doll Makers
Belpre and Coolville

Usually in a marital breakup, the fight is over kids, household items, and pets. With the Middletons, it was dolls—in this case, it was Lloyd Middleton starting his own doll-making company after divorcing his artist wife, Lee. This may be the first time actual plastic (as opposed to credit cards) was the subject of dispute.

As with many such situations, there are two different versions of events. According to the Lloyd Middleton Dolls (24924 Brimstone Rd., Coolville 45723, 740-667-3555, www.lloydmiddleton.com) website, Lloyd started Middleton Doll Company in 1979. But based on the Lee Middleton Dolls (1301 Washington Blvd., Belpre 45714, 740-423-1481 or 800-233-7479, www.leemiddleton.com) Web history, it didn't actually get off the ground until four years later, though Lee had begun sculpting dolls earlier in her kitchen, with the first two being the likenesses of the Middleton children. By 1991 the split had occurred and Middleton Dolls became Lee Middleton, while a year earlier Lloyd founded the Royal Vienna Doll Company (later Lloyd Middleton Dolls) with his new wife, Janice. Lee passed away in 1997. Well that certainly clears things up.

Belpre was declared the Baby Doll Capital of the World, although "Valley of the Dolls" might have been more fitting given the drama involved. "Ours are happy babies, and his are crying," sniped a Lee Middleton employee of the ATHENSi.com website. Though you can get both in Belpre and tours of Lee's factory are available, the Lloyd Middleton plant is located 15 miles away in Coolville.

Lee's versions are life-size, realistic infants, molded, hand-painted, and assembled in a fifty-thousand-square-foot facility. There's even a "newborn" nursery and plenty of new additions to choose from, along with an annual convention of collectors called (really) the Baby Bunch.

With detailed outfits and various hairstyles and eye colors, Lloyd's kids are a little bit older. Some of the dolls have actual tears. You can also have a doll made in your child's/grandchild's image, using molds, body types, hair/eye color, even his/her clothes. You get a certificate with your handpicked offspring's name, re-creating all the pleasure and none of the hassle of the actual kid.

The Lee Middleton people lay it on pretty thick as well. A recent offering in the "Not Fair" series includes "Peas & Carrots" in which Baby is trussed up in an outfit with appliquéd peas and carrots, with a pissed-off look on its face, or as the company website coos,

★ ★

"Remember trying to convince your little one that vegetables taste good? That little lip begins to pout as small mounds of green vegetables peek between baby's lips . . . " Where is Chucky when you really need him?

Snake Oil
Caldwell

Not many people realize that Caldwell is the site of the first—well, allegedly the first—oil well in the United States (Junction of Hwy. 78 and Hwy. 564, 43724). While Ohio is hardly in the same league as say, Texas or Saudi Arabia, oil was pretty useless in 1814 when settlers Silas Thorla and Robert McKee noticed two deer licking a spot on the ground. (There wasn't even electricity and the invention of the gas engine was over fifty years away.) They figured, correctly, that it was salt brine, drilled a well and made hay, so to speak, selling it to folks who used it for livestock and to preserve meats. Early settlers had bigger things to worry about than sodium intake and chemical additives.

Unfortunately, mixed in with the salt was this yucky, greasy black stuff that the two men had to drain off. Eventually, they bottled and sold it as a digestive elixir named Seneca Oil (talk about artificial ingredients . . .). By the time "black gold" really became valuable in America, Thorla and McKee had gone to the big oil rig in the sky.

The town of Caldwell benefited, however. During the last two decades of the nineteenth century, it boasted four newspaper offices, three churches, and a bank, as well as several manufacturers, including the town's largest employer, Caldwell Woolen Mills.

Unfortunately, nothing lasts forever, and the oil reserves depleted, with residents and industry declining accordingly. Today the region is one of the most sparsely populated in Ohio.

Which probably explains why the site itself is fairly deserted and, aside from the park where it's located, appears somewhat neglected. (Even the neighboring cows look suspiciously upon visitors.) You'll have to walk pretty far back to see the thing, just past an abandoned,

Don't expect any wars over this oil field.

creepy-looking shack and a seemingly random caboose. The well—or what's left of it—is located inside what might loosely pass for a batting cage, except for the winch, pulley, and large wooden stick that extends several feet above the ground. A faded sign explains how drilling took place in bygone years.

OK, so it's not much to look at, but it is an oil well that's practically in your own backyard. And who can beat that, with gas prices these days?

Jesus on a Wire
Cambridge

There's something comforting about the Greatest Story Ever Told, even if you're a non-Christian or atheist. Millions of believers can't be wrong, eh? (Well, maybe; that's how wars begin.)

Perhaps seeing Ohio's only outdoor passion play, the Living Word Outdoor Drama (6010 College Hill Rd. 43725, 740-439-2761, www .livingworddrama.org) will help solidify one's spiritual persuasion. In the summer, usually until the end of September, they put on the show on Friday and Saturday evenings.

Here, Jesus is more grounded.
PHOTO COURTESY OF LIVING WORD AND DAVID CATER

★ ★

It's sort of *The Rocky Horror Picture Show* for the devout, without the risqué elements, of course. The audience participates at various points by waving palm fronds while the plot follows Jesus from the manger to the Resurrection, with familiar scenes like the Sermon on the Mount and the Last Supper. The impressive four hundred–foot set includes lots of live action with Roman soldiers, chariots, and assorted livestock. Everything culminates in the Ascension of Jesus into Heaven; in this case, several feet in the air on a wire.

Founded and authored by the late Frank and Hazel Harvey of Cambridge, the durable drama has been around since 1975. The gift shop also sells chicken sandwiches, bratwurst, hamburgers, and ice cream. Praise the Lord and pass the popcorn!

Glass House
Cambridge

If it wasn't for gas, Cambridge might not have glass. Natural gas that is, and coal needed by the Cambridge Glass Company to blow that first pitcher in 1902 and the subsequent table sets, jugs, bowls, tumblers, lamps and many more exquisite works of art on display at the National Museum of Cambridge Glass (136 South 9th St. 43725, 740-432-4245, www.cambridgeglass.org).

And this wasn't just any old line of products, haphazardly produced. "The designers were acutely aware of trends, and the fact that Cambridge products were expected to be unique and of high quality," observes museum director Cindy Arent. The result is an almost overwhelming display of designs and colors arranged by period and hue that encompass several decades. So you might see ash trays and brandy snifters that appeared in 1930s Hollywood movies alongside centerpieces and candlesticks used by 1950s housewives for dinner parties. And in a period of mostly plain and pastel "Depression era" glass Cambridge churned out such colors as Carmen, Royal Blue, Crown Tuscan, Heatherbloom and Forest Green as well as new dinnerware lines and etchings such as Rose Point.

And that's only the mint green!

So what caused the meltdown that closed the plant in 1954? "Basically competition from foreign and machine-made glass," continues Arent, citing variations on a theme that has happened many times before and in other industries. But the art of glass-making lives on today, in both its glittering collections as well as displays and demonstrations on how glass was made. The Sample Room features the door and shelving from the original factory, and a dining room display shows off a table setting and period furniture much as it would have appeared in the early 1900s. Guests can do their own rubbings from original etching plates in the Education Center, and view a movie made in the 1940s by the Cambridge Glass Company.

Arent and her troop of volunteers clean and shine all six thousand pieces and their display cases during the winter months when the museum is closed (it's open from April to October). And if a piece or two breaks, then it ends up as a necklace or a pair of earrings for sale in the gift shop. Well, you don't need a crystal ball to see that one coming.

A Ride on the Wild Side
Cumberland

What a concept: The animals are outside, while you're in an enclosed space. Talk about karma (car-ma?); in this case, an open-air bus that takes you on safari through the Wilds (14000 International Rd. 43732, 740-638-5030, www.thewilds.org), 14 square miles of rolling hills, valleys, tall wavy grasses, and lakes that twenty-five mostly endangered Asian, African, and North American species call home. It's the Serengeti in Ohio, dude.

Started in 1986 as a public-private partnership between the Ohio Department of National Resources (ODNR), zoos, and other enterprises, most of the land consists of a former surface coal mine donated by American Electric Power. The grounds also contain an extensive veterinary clinic, although much of the work is done directly in the field, using portable fences and equipment. Several colleges and zoos utilize the facility for research as well.

The animals roam freely through large multispecies habitats, developing their own social systems and behaviors, much as they would do in their natural environments. Though they don't know it, they're also involved in research and breeding programs, which raises questions as to who exactly might be watching us.

Existential inquiries aside, visitors can get up close and personal with the critters, who come right up to the buses or basically keep on keepin' on whatever they're doing. Antelope, rhinoceroses, camels, and other species graze in groups across grasslands or browse in restored woodlands. You'll see sika deer from the forests of Vietnam, double-humped Bactrian camels from the Gobi Desert, and red-crowned cranes from Siberia, to mention a few.

Knowledgeable guides share the animals' stories: Some have virtually been hunted to death, or their habitats destroyed by deforestation or other advances of so-called civilization. Others were neglected or slated for euthanasia and have been rescued for rehabilitation. It's a jungle out there, albeit one in Middle America.

Curses!
Gallipolis

Some people believe that the December 15, 1967 collapse of the Silver Bridge linking Point Pleasant, West Virginia and Kanauga, Ohio was a direct result of a two-hundred-year-old jinx from Shawnee Chief Keigh-tugh-gua, aka Cornstalk. And he had good reason to be ticked off: Despite his many efforts to help the colonists during the Revolutionary War, even providing them maps and turning against his own tribe members who wanted to fight for the redcoats, the rebel soldiers *still* murdered him, his son, and two hostages. So as the big guy lay dying—he was over six feet, very tall for those times—he put an equally large curse from the Great Spirit upon the land.

After that, things did not go well. Along with being partially destroyed by a fire in 1880, Point Pleasant and the surrounding region where the tribes had lived and hunted were plagued with an abnormal number of floods, tornados, mining disasters, plane crashes, and other mishaps. But none was creepier than the Silver Bridge collapse: not only because it killed forty-six people during evening rush hour and caused dozens of cars to plunge into the frigid, murky Ohio River, but also because it was preceded by strange visitations and sightings of what became known as "Mothman." (Yes, the same one from the book *Mothman Prophecies* starring Richard Gere.)

According to witness accounts—and there were many—Mothman was a very large grayish-brown bird-type creature with angel-type wings, glowing eyes, and an eerie screech. So he pretty much stood out wherever he went. Nor was he shy, allegedly following people around, peering into their windows, and taking up residence at an abandoned TNT plant in Point Pleasant, an explosive combination if there ever was one. In fact, between November 1966 and November 1967, the entire area became a hotbed of UFO and poltergeist sightings, encounters with men in black, and other bizarre happenings.

However, by the time the bridge collapsed a few weeks later, Mothman had begun to flutter into obscurity. But as the media descended upon the area, the eerie lights, flashings, and sightings around his alleged nest came back with a vengeance. According to an account on the website prairieghosts.com, a suspicious-looking guy who resembled Mothman even showed up to speak with a local reporter who brushed him off because she was too busy covering the bridge tragedy. How he managed to disguise his wings was never addressed.

But there's lots of speculation about these events. John Keel, author of *The Mothman Prophecies* and similar books, theorized that the region was a "window" area, a sort of magnet for strange goings-on. Others tied the whole mess to Chief Cornstalk's curse. Still others claimed that Mothman was a sandhill crane from Canada whose malfunctioning GPS had brought him to the area. And engineers blamed the bridge collapse on corrosion and structural failure.

You can revisit the whole scenario at the Silver Bridge Memorial in Gallipolis

★ ★

(State Rte. 7 North 45631) located two miles north of the replacement bridge. And it's probably safe to drive over if you want to stop at historical sites at Point Pleasant, such as the eighty-six-foot-tall monument built to honor the men who died in the battle that defeated the Indians. OK, so it was struck by lightning twice, once in 1908 when it was dedicated and again in 1941. A not-so-gentle reminder that karma, the Great Spirit, or whatever you want to call it usually has the last word.

Cleaning Up
Logan

Consider the humble washboard: Hardly anyone, except perhaps the Amish, uses them these days, although they're still around. Chances are most people under thirty don't even know what it is; they're undoubtedly more familiar with motherboards than the square utensil with wavy corrugated steel designed to scrub clothes.

In fact, the Columbus Washboard Company (14 Gallagher Ave. 43138, 740-380-3828, www.columbuswashboard.com; tours available by appointment) isn't even located in Columbus anymore. Established in 1895 by Frederic Martin Sr., who started building washboards in his backyard to sell, the company sold fewer than 1,000 during its first thirty years of operation.

Still, they managed to clean up, selling twenty-three million washboards from 1926 until the late 1980s, not only to those who either had no electricity or chose not to use it, but additionally as decorative items providing a touch of the past to laundry and family rooms and kitchens. (Ah, the good old days, when women spent all their time doing housework . . .)

Washboards also serve as musical instruments, with entire bands centered around them, like the Juggernaut Jug Band, the Boondockers, and the Buffalo Ridge Band. These groups and others have played at the Washboard Music Festival, an annual event held each June in Logan that features tours, street vendors, and all manner of good, clean fun.

★ ★

In keeping with the manual tradition, the washboard manufacturing is done by hand, though various models are spiffed up and even customized with colorful designs on the wooden handle. Most are made from Ohio-grown white pine and tulip poplar, with rubbing surfaces including metal, stainless steel, brass, and glass in addition to the classic galvanized steel.

Columbus is the last washboard company standing, thanks to the diversity of their offerings and because investor George K. Richards formed a partnership with six friends and purchased the business in the late 1990s, moving it to Logan to reduce labor costs, and because it was closer for co-owner/factory manager Jacqui Barnett. And they didn't even need to buy new equipment. Low tech: It can be a good thing.

Fore!
Logan

It sits in the middle of an overgrown stand of trees, looking as if its sole purpose is to be whacked by a giant golf club. However, should the impact come in the form of a hurricane or tornado, the golf ball house, which also came to be known as Stewart's Folly (31628 Chieftain Dr. 43138; not open to the public) after the man who built it, was specifically designed for the rough, to withstand such forces of nature.

Constructed over a two-year period in the early 1970s using two wooden shells and poured concrete, this fire- and wind-resistant orb has neither corners nor flat outside surfaces. The walls are eight inches thick at the base and five inches in the sphere, and the windows are made of Lexan. Mr. Stewart had covered any contingency inside as well, including escape hatches. The only thing it lacks, it seems, are dimples and the word Titleist on the exterior.

Still, it's your basic two-floor layout, with a basement, garage, and porch. Shortly before it was finished, someone offered Mr. Stewart $350,000 for it, which he declined. Back in the 1970s that was a small fortune, and he could have joined a real country club and played actual golf.

✦ ✦

What he didn't plan for was that the house would never be completed or wired for electricity, because he died of heart disease and diabetes before he and his family ever moved in. Nor would anyone else be able to duplicate it, as the original blueprints and design notes were lost in a fire. Talk about hitting a sand trap.

Today it's a shell of its former self, destroyed by time and vandals and overrun by underbrush and graffiti, though Mr. Stewart's son does stop by to check on it occasionally. But in a sense, the golf ball house has scored a mulligan, because "dome homes" of similar size and shape are now used around the world for residential, industrial, military, and other applications.

Drag(line) Queen
McConnelsville

Here's the scoop: According to a website maintained by preservationist Blake Malkamaki (http://cletrac.org), "She dwells in the coal-rich hills of southeast Ohio, near the small town of Cumberland. She is a big girl. Her name is Big Muskie and she is the biggest machine that has ever walked on the face of the earth." Amazing how technology can strike poetry in a man's soul.

The only model 4250-W Bucyrus-Erie dragline ever built, this groundbreaker weighed in at twenty-seven million pounds, with a height of 222 feet 6 inches and a width equal to an eight-lane highway (151 feet 6 inches). With a bucket capacity of a twelve-car garage (220 cubic yards, 325 tons), she was the largest single–bucket digging machine ever created.

During Big Muskie's illustrious career (1969–1991) she removed more than 608 million cubic yards of earth—twice the amount of the Panama Canal—uncovering twenty million–plus tons of coal. Let's hear it for the depletion of our natural resources!

Built and maintained by American Electric Power (AEP), she was put out to pasture, so to speak, due to a reduction in demand for high-sulfur coal. But tourists came to this machine-mountain and wandered through her innards, having their pictures taken and buying postcards. In 1999, however, the Surface Mining Reclamation Act required that all machines be removed on abandoned strip mines. Those dang conservationists!

Despite efforts to save her, she was scrapped. And AEP literally lowered the boom, using high explosives to destroy the thick cables that held up Big Muskie's, an effect similar to cutting Dolly Parton's bra straps, on a much larger scale, of course.

But AEP kept the giant cup, er, bucket intact, moving it to Miner's Memorial Park and ReCreation Land (State Rte. 78 E, 43756, 740-962-1205 or 740-962-4909). And at 460,000 pounds empty, it's not exactly chopped liver in the size department either.

Nor is the park itself, Ohio's largest privately owned recreation area (Re-Creation Land, get it?). Over 30,000 acres of reclaimed surface mines include 300 ponds and endless miles of trails, a natural for fishing, hiking, mountain biking, and other outdoor pursuits. There are also interpretative photos and stories about Big Muskie, proving that even multinational utilities can have a heart.

Chain Saw Massacres
Nelsonville

If you're ever stumped about the perfect gift, and tired of cruising the information highway for purchases, try pulling over on a real one on the west side of Route 33, just north of Nelsonville. You may make a different high-speed connection with Rob Nixon, chain saw artiste extraordinaire, at his modest roadside stand. Since 2002 he has carved bears, foxes, eagles, dolphins, wizards, and other figures, usually from white pine logs, running the chain saw some six hours a day. It's generating such a buzz that sculptures start at $100, and he often has several on backorder.

Nixon, who told the *Columbus Dispatch* that he makes enough money to live off the proceeds of his craft, learned the basics from a friend, who taught him how to carve a bear, the most popular item (the bear has a

★ ★

fish in its mouth, adding the rugged Appalachian touch that city slickers seem to like so much). He's doing so well, in fact, that he enlisted another buddy, who recently began selling his sculptures there, too.

So when you "log on" to Nixon's roadside stand, you get something original.

State Roundup: Underground Ohio

Ohio's deep involvement in civil rights and the Underground Railroad has been well documented. According to the Ohio Underground Railroad Association (www.ohioundergroundrailroad.org), there are some 700 Underground Railroad sites, with more being added. Following are some places that spotlight history. (For information about the National Underground Railroad Freedom Center in Cincinnati, see the Cincinnati chapter.)

Lorain County was a major stop on the Underground Railroad, and was home to Oberlin, the first college to admit women and among the first to enroll African Americans. Along with Westwood Cemetery, the final resting place for runaway slaves and abolitionists, it boasts the railroad tracks to nowhere and Martin Luther King Jr. Park, with its several monuments, including one honoring three Oberlinites who were killed in John Brown's raid on Harper's Ferry. Another memorial, the Underground Railroad Monument, tells the story of Lee Harold Dobbins, a four-year-old slave child who died in 1853 on his way to Canada. Churches, museums, and homes relating to the era can also be found.

★ ★

It's a Wonderful Life
New Concord

Like Will Rogers and Caesar's wife, few if anyone has anything bad to say about former astronaut and U.S. senator John Glenn. Could it be because he has the right stuff? You have a chance to discover the

Southwest Ohio. The Paul Laurence Dunbar House in Dayton is a high point, and the National Afro-American Museum and Cultural Center in Wilberforce, about a half-hour away, provides a more current insight into the pre–Civil Rights era with *From Victory to Freedom: Afro-American Life in the Fifties.* Along with clothes, jewelry, consumer products, sports equipment, and other artifacts, there's a period barbershop, beauty salon, and a complete church interior with recorded speaking voices and music. Among other things, you can also view a film tracing the origins of black music from its roots in Africa to gospel, jazz, bebop, classical, and protest. Then journey another hour and forty-five minutes to the Ohio–Kentucky border town of Ripley and the home of John Rankin, the Presbyterian minister reputed to have been one of Ohio's first and most active "conductors" on the Underground Railroad. From 1822 to 1865 Rankin and his family assisted some two thousand escaped slaves. One of the first stations on the Underground Railroad, Ripley's many stops included the residence of former slave John Parker, who planned rescue attempts of slaves in Kentucky.

★ ★

origins of this font of goodwill at the John and Annie Glenn Museum and Home (72 West Main St. 43762, 740-826-3305). Built in 1923 by Glenn's father, it was originally located on a gravel street and had four upstairs rooms that could be rented to students at nearby Muskingum College. Rather than having it razed, the Glenns opted to move the house to its current address in the 1940s when the state widened National Road. Perhaps they had an intuition about the future fame of their only and New Concord's favorite son.

His life reads like a script from a Judy Garland–Mickey Rooney movie. Of his wonder years, Glenn has said, "A boy could not have had a more idyllic early childhood than I did." In New Concord he developed an interest in science and flying and also met his future wife, Annie, his high school sweetheart. After becoming a war hero and then a test pilot, Glenn was selected by NASA as one of the first seven astronauts in the U.S. space program. On February 20, 1962, he became the first American to orbit Earth.

Never one to rest on his laurels, Glenn ran for the U.S. Senate several times, finally winning the Democratic seat in 1975 and retiring in 1999. He tried to run for president, but his 1984 bid failed. (Hey, even happy films have complications.) Shortly before he left the Senate, NASA invited him to rejoin their ranks, and on October 29, 1998, he became the oldest person ever to venture into space. In 1999 Glenn donated the house to Muskingum College, and it was opened to the public three years later. What a guy!

Through the miracle of reenactors, you can meet Glenn's mother, Clara; his father, Herschel; a young couple who boarded in the childhood home; and even the family paperboy. The first floor is devoted to the Glenn home in 1936, while other galleries center around John and Annie's upbringing in Ohio and how New Concord and southeastern Ohio reacted to instant fame. You can also visit John's boyhood bedroom, complete with model airplanes and a crystal radio set.

There's even a twenty-minute video narrated by former *20/20* host Hugh Downs. It's about John Glenn's life . . . so far. As Glenn himself says, "You can start here and go anywhere."

* *

Hootch Heaven
New Straitsville

At the other end of the Prohibition spectrum, and unlike Westerville with its Anti-Saloon League legacy (see Columbus and Vicinity chapter), is New Straitsville, the self-proclaimed Moonshine Capital.

In fact, the bootleg whiskey made during the Depression era was so popular that during Prohibition, people asked for "Straitsville Special" by name at speakeasies throughout the Midwest. Maybe it was something in the water that made for such a smooth-tasting yet potent concoction, or perhaps alcohol production ran in the blood of the English, Irish, and other British Isles folks who immigrated to the region. They call it Scotch for a reason, you know.

And the area's wooded, hilly terrain—with its "hollers," coal mines, caves, and other crevices—made it ideal for hiding stills. And when "revenuers" (aka federal agents) came to town, the locals, even non-drinkers, pulled a Colonel Klink. Sometimes it's best to "know nothing" if it puts food on the table and pays the bills, especially if there are no jobs.

Today New Straitsville celebrates its hootch heritage through a Moonshine Festival (43766, 740-394-2838), usually held around Memorial Day. Only they make the stuff legally, having been granted a special permit from the state to concoct no more than 250 gallons. The working still is one of the festival's biggest attractions, and though you're allowed to smell it, no sampling allowed! Perhaps tragically for some, the freshly brewed whiskey is dumped at the end of each day.

Of course, there are plenty of other things to do. Along with partaking of carnival rides and listening to entertainers, you can visit the local history museum, haggle with flea market vendors, and sample moonshine cuisine, including whiskey-flavored burgers, hot dogs, and moonshine pie, which can actually be tastier than imbibing the hootch straight up. Hmm, maybe they don't destroy every single ounce . . .

Blast from the Past
Wellston

OK, so it may not leave you burning with excitement, but Ohio's only restored charcoal furnace (123 Buckeye Park Rd. 45692, 740-384-3537, www.buckeyefurnace.com), built in 1852 and used for the last time in 1894, harks back to the glory days of iron production in the Hanging Rock region. The discovery of richer and more easily transported iron ore in the Lake Superior area resulted in the region's decline.) On this self-guided tour you will:

Visit the 270-acre site! It's in the middle of Appalachia—not the genteel Hocking Hills region, but the real shoot-the-revenuers,

**Hot times at the Buckeye State's only
restored charcoal furnace**
MICHAEL E. HILL

same-last-name, financially impaired section of the country—so you'll get a taste of poverty without having to travel to, say, Mexico or India. Plus there are two nature trails with plenty of places to explore.

See where iron was made! This includes not only the blast furnace and original stack, but also the casting shed and the charging loft where iron ore, limestone, and charcoal were loaded, as well as the engine house with its steam-powered compressor. There's even a company store with nineteenth-century items. The laborers were paid in scrip, rather than cash. Scrip could only be used at the store or for company lodging, leaving some workers continually in debt. Can you say "credit card"?

Learn about the back-breaking, laborious production process! Raw materials such as iron ore, limestone, and charcoal were brought uphill by wagon. Workers then mixed and poured huge quantities of materials into the top of the furnace. Each day, tens of thousands of pounds were measured and loaded, with temperatures reaching six hundred degrees, burning off impurities and producing a waste product called slag. Then the hot, heavy, liquid iron was removed by opening dams at the bottom of the furnace and allowing it to flow into molds. And this went on twenty-four hours a day, in two twelve-hour shifts. Are we having fun yet?

At the very least, you might leave with an appreciation of your current employment, even if it is of the cubicle farm or "What would you like on your pizza?" variety.

Existential Bridge
Zanesville

It seems fitting that something as zany as a Y-shaped bridge would be in a place called Zanesville (43701). Although it crosses both the Licking and Muskingum Rivers, some say it leads to nowhere.

To get the full flavor, drive onto it from the east on U.S. Highway 40, go down about halfway, and then suddenly you're faced with a choice: left or right? Which leads to the burning question, "Y?" er, "Why?"

★ ★

According to the Museum of the Open Road website (www.road museum.org), "The city of Zanesville is divided into three segments. One is to the east of the Muskingum River; one is to the west of the Muskingum and north of the Licking River; and one is to the west of the Muskingum and south of the Licking River. So if you're building a bridge across the Muskingum, does the bridge empty out north of the Licking River, thereby leaving the southern community bereft? Or do you have the bridge end up south of the Licking, leaving the north bereft?"

Constructed of wooden trestles and stone with logs and planks, the first bridge was built in 1814 and fell into the river five years later. A second bridge was thrown together but condemned as unsafe due to heavy traffic. At that time Zanesville was a major thoroughfare and part of the National Road.

The town parents built the third bridge in 1832, and it lasted until 1900. The fourth went up in 1902, only to be blown up in 1979 after being deemed unsafe, making for one cool explosion that was even televised. The fifth, completed in 1984, still stands today and is made of steel and concrete.

It's also arguably the only bridge in the United States that you can cross and still be on the same side of the river that you started on. So you are going nowhere, in the sense of the sound of one hand clapping.

State Roundup: Cavalcade of Caverns

Ohio has a veritable cornucopia of caverns. From Ash Cave to Zane Caverns, just about every part of the state has something to spelunk.

Hocking Hills State Park (20160 State Rte. 664, Logan 43138, 740-385-6841, www.ohiostateparks.org). Forged from sandstone and shale deposited over 350 million years ago, this mother of all state parks boasts a variety of cavities—ones in the ground, that is. Terrain ranges from the soft, loosely cemented grain-like dirt found in Ash Cave to razor-sharp hard layers at Old Man's Cave. The effect of the glaciers can still be felt in certain regions of the park, which have retained a moist, cool environment. Among others, you'll find:

Old Man's Cave. The most well-trod of all the Hocking areas, this area has deep-cut gorges, impressive waterfalls, and in one section, a 150-foot-thick slice of rock that allows visitors to look into the earth's subsurface. In the late 1700s/early 1800s, it was also inhabited by two brothers, then an elderly hermit, all of whom are buried there. Although recently renovated, the trails still require climbing, and are a honeycomb of rocks and carved steps.

Ash Cave. The largest recess of its kind in the state—seven hundred feet from end to end and one hundred feet deep—this cave is surrounded by hemlocks, beech trees, and hardwoods, as well as wildflowers. Named after the ashes found by the original settlers, it remains in use today for various gatherings, thanks to excellent acoustics and handicap accessibility. Pulpit Rock, at the entrance, was once used for Sunday worship, and there's a spectacular water geyser.

Rock House. The only "true" cave in the park, this natural phenomenon consists of a two-hundred-foot-long, twenty-five-foot-wide tunnel-like passage with a twenty-five-foot-high "ceiling." Man-made additions like water troughs and nooks for cooking can also be found.

(Continued on Page 266)

(Continued from Page 265)
Native Americans, explorers, and even horse thieves and bootleg-
gers decamped here; at one point it had the nickname "Robber's
Roost."

Olentangy Indian Caverns (1779 Home Rd., Delaware 43015,
740-548-7917, www.olentangyindiancaverns.com). Formed millions of years ago by an underground river, these caverns are
a"maze"ing, with all their winding passages and underground
rooms. According to the website, the Wyandot Indians used them
as a haven from the weather and from their enemies, even making the rocks part of their tribal ceremonies. And of course J. M.
Adams, the first white man believed to have entered the caverns
in 1821, just had to carve his name and date on the wall. The Cave
House on top of the entrance is accessible to almost everyone
although you'll have to descend 55 feet down concrete stairways
to the natural passages and rooms occupying three different levels. Discovering the reasons behind the names alone is worth the
exploration—"Indian Lover's Bench," "Battleship Rock," "The
Crystal Room," and "Fat Man's Misery," although the fourth level
and other passages have yet to be fully plumbed.

Perry's Cave (979 Catawba Ave., Put-in-Bay 43456, 419-285-
2405, www.perryscave.com). Take a break from the drunken
revelry that can be Put-in-Bay and "go underground" to Perry's
Cave, a limestone cavern 52 feet below the surface of the island.
Commodore Oliver Hazard Perry supposedly discovered the cave
in 1813, yet another one of his amazing feats. And it's a cool fifty
degrees year-round, thanks to the constant drip, drip, drip of
water, resulting in a 208-foot by 165-foot accumulation of calcium
carbonate. An underground pond rises and falls in accordance with
Lake Erie. Tours take about twenty minutes, then you can partake

of such family-friendly add-ons as a rock climbing wall, gemstone mine, butterfly house, miniature golf, and more. Or you can go back to the bars.

Seneca Caverns (15248 East Thompson, TR178, Bellevue 44811, 419-483-6711, www.senecacavernsohio.com). In 1872 in a scene straight out of Alice in Wonderland, while pursuing a rabbit, two boys and their dog fell through a sinkhole into what eventually became known as Seneca Caverns. But first, since Emmanuel Good owned the farm where it was located, they called it—drum roll here—"Good's Cave." Then in 1931 Don Bell discovered "a series of passageways and rooms not previously known to exist, which led to an underground river, the water table," according to the caverns' website. By 1933 it was opened to the public, and offers a unique experience in that it remains much the way it was after Peter Rutan, Henry Homer, and their pooch, whose name is lost to memory, lived to tell the tale.

Zane Shawnee Caverns (7092 Hwy. 540, Bellefontaine 43311, 937-592-9592, www.zaneshawneecaverns.net). Talk about Indian givers. This is one of the few attractions in Ohio owned by Native Americans, in this case the Shawnee Nation-United Remnant Band, who bought it back in 1995. The nearly half-mile tour takes forty-five minutes and features all the usual suspects: stalactites, stalagmites, soda straws, flow stones, and more. Bonus: You can also see cave pearls, supposedly found in no other place in Ohio. The bad news: Although they look like the real thing, they're simply calcite precipitates formed around various items in the cave. While there you can also explore Shawnee Village; a Colonial Village and Native American Woodland Museum; and even camp, fish, swim, and hike.

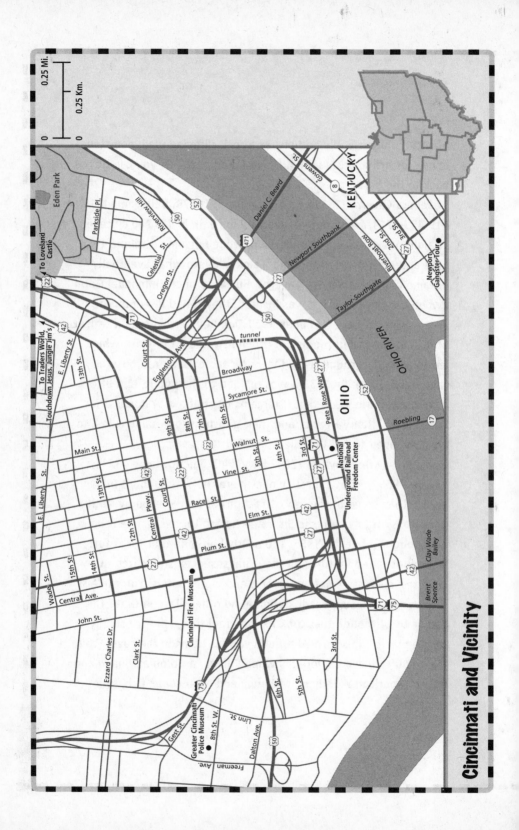

Cincinnati and Vicinity

Cincinnati and Vicinity

The Queen City *offers a hard-to-beat combination of funky, conservative, and gangster. At the edge of questionable is Loveland's castle, Chateau Laroche. Started in 1929 by lifelong bachelor Harry Andrews, it took him over thirty years to construct a retreat for his teenaged friends, so they could swim, camp, fish, and "have little parties." Also outside of the law (and just over the bridge) is the Newport Gangster tour, although they offer related tours in Cincy as well. More underground excitement can be found in the never-used but constantly on the verge of reinvention subway, with an altogether different kind of transportation chronicled at the National Underground Railroad Freedom Center. Law and order types can justify their trip by stopping by the Cincinnati Fire Museum and the Greater Cincinnati Police Museum. And then there's Jerry Springer, who defies categorization . . .*

★ ★

Hall of Flame
Cincinnati

Just about every kid at some time wants to be a firefighter, and 9/11 reaffirmed the courage of these dedicated and brave civil servants. In addition to having lots of "hot" memorabilia, the Cincinnati Fire Museum (315 West Court St. 45202, 513-621-5553) claims to be the only museum that saves lives. And the firefighters themselves aren't bad-looking either.

Located in a 1907 National Register firehouse, it chronicles more than two hundred years of firefighting history, with leather fire buckets, silver trumpets, a gigantic 1808 fire drum, and the oldest surviving fire engine in Cincinnati, an 1836 Hunneman hand pumper. "The Fox," a shiny red fire engine made by Ahrens Fox of Cincinnati, "seems about to leap through the doors and dash to a fire," according to the museum's website. You can also learn about the bomb squad, chemical spills, and the Jaws of Life through interactive computers.

Of the twenty-five thousand visitors a year, more than half of them are children. And while they're more likely to slide down the pole; turn on the lights, siren, and bell for all those exciting special effects; and "drive" a modern Emergency One fire engine cab than, say, Grandma and Grandpa, more importantly they get to learn about safety.

During the museum's education program and tour, young visitors are briefed on proper exit procedures, participate in an old-time "hands-on" bucket brigade, and visit the Safe Home. Here they'll come to understand not to hide under the bed or in the closet during fire rescue efforts; how to "stop, drop, and roll"; and not to play with matches or lighters or put Fluffy in the microwave.

OK, maybe not that last thing, but after visiting this museum, sitting down with family members and figuring out an emergency exit plan is in order. And that goes for you grown-ups, too.

★ ★

A Slave to Freedom

Cincinnati

Not all curiosities are odd or even funny. Some are just downright wrong, such as slavery. Yet they are worth exploring, especially if it helps teach how to avoid repeating history. So be prepared for an education at the National Underground Railroad Freedom Center (50 East Freedom Way 45202, Cincinnati, 513-333-7500 or 877-648-4838, www.freedomcenter.org).

Most visits start with a short film depicting slavery and the Underground Railroad; there's also *Brothers of the Borderland,* a longer, experiential movie with smoke and other effects dramatizing one woman's

Inside the real world of Uncle Tom's cabin

★ ★

flight to freedom across the Ohio River. Next stop: a circa 1800 slave pen, and not the kind for writing. Recovered from a Kentucky farm less than sixty miles away from the museum, the barn-like structure was used to hold slaves in abeyance until they could be moved further south. Although it's spiffy and refurbished, the chains and rough hewn second floor sleeping and living quarters provide a chilling reminder. ESCAPE! Freedom Seekers and the Underground Railroad utilizes storytelling, role-playing, and hands-on activities to re-create the Abolitionist period of 1830 to 1865. Still other exhibits portray three centuries of slavery from its introduction into the Americas until the end of the Civil War; how slavery still takes many forms and guises; and cutting-edge and interactive stories of human trafficking around the world.

You can take a break from the intensity at the North Star Café or adjacent gift shop. Or just leave your cell phone on. There's nothing like a call from a child or significant other to jar you into the present when the interactive exhibit is pressuring you to decide whether to shelter the young family that's trying to flee the slave hunters.

Phantom Subway
Cincinnati

Not many cities can claim a perfectly good but unused subway system beneath their feet. But Cincinnati does, although actually getting to see it can be quite a challenge, because the only obvious way to get a tour of the thing is through Facebook (see Cincinnati Abandoned Subway/Subway tour information).

According to the City of Cincinnati website (www.cincinnati-oh .gov), city planners first unearthed the concept for a subway in 1884 when the newspaper of the day, the *Graphic,* printed drawings illustrating a practical use for the dried-up old canals, which being mosquito-infested, were also a health hazard. As Cincy was one of the biggest cities in the country at the time, it seemed like a great idea, so in 1912 city officials drew up plans to build the subway system, a sixteen-mile transit loop, with a portion going underground and

✮ ★ ✮ ★ ✮ ★ ✮ ★ ✮ ★ ✮ ★ ✮ ★ ✮ ★ ✮ ★ ✮ ★ ✮ ★ ✮ ★ ✮ ★ ✮ ✮

heading downtown. It would surface at Brighton and Saint Bernard and run aboveground along the Ohio River.

Although the citizens approved an initial budget of $6 million, actual work didn't begin until after World War I. Then Murphy's Law took hold—corrupt politicians drained the coffers, inflation kicked in, and costs began to mount, even though the Walnut Street station and the two-mile underground portion were completed by 1923.

Then with the addition of another estimated $10 million in the throwing-good-money-after-bad tradition of city/county government, Central Parkway was added on top of the underground tunnels and opened in 1928, just in time for the Great Depression, which mothballed the entire thing, though there were various proposals for using the tunnels, such as trolleys (the cars were too long for the subway's bends) and auto traffic (but then the tunnels had to be retrofitted, costing money that wasn't there and maybe never had been).

A 1948 study finally hammered the final nail into the public-transit coffin, though the city didn't pay off the $13 million debt until eighteen years later. But the ideas still kept coming. In the 1950s it was decided that the tunnels would make perfect bomb shelters, so Uncle Sam renovated one of the stations and installed toilets, running water, heat, and canned goods, to be utilized "in event of a disaster situation involving fallout," according to the city government's history of the subway.

The Diocese of Southern Ohio wanted to use it for religious services; a local winery hoped to utilize a portion to process vino; a local group even suggested turning it into retail shops and nightclubs a la "Underground Atlanta." Zero, zilch, nada.

A 2008 study found the tunnels to be in relatively good shape, holding up remarkably well against vandals and water leakage. Sections of the original structure still remain, including all four stations put in during initial construction. The city has maintained the subway, hoping that someday, maybe . . .

Should that occur, however, they'll undoubtedly need to do something with the moldy canned goods that were supposed to get folks through the long nuclear winter.

★ ★

Uncuffed
Cincinnati

Crime may not pay but it certainly is fascinating, considering how many cities have a police museum or at least a collection of memorabilia (see the Cleveland Police Historical Society entry in the Cleveland section). The Greater Cincinnati Police Museum (959 W. 8th St., Suite 201, 45203, 513-300-3664, www.gcphs.com) offers the whole enchilada, including Handsome, the city's first police dog, memorialized via taxidermy for eternity or at least the past one hundred or so years. He stands proudly in his glass case and looks pretty good for his age, considering.

According to their website, the museum "collects, displays, and presents history and artifacts of more than one hundred municipal, county, state, and federal law enforcement agencies who have, for more than two centuries, served Boone, Butler, Campbell, Clermont, Dearborn, Hamilton, Kenton, and Warren Counties of Indiana, Kentucky, and Ohio." That's a mouthful of stuff crammed into some 4,500 square feet. Uniforms (winter, summer, dress, everyday), badges, guns of all shapes and sizes, vehicles, lie detectors, fingerprint and mug shot kits, call boxes, radios and more all trace the development and evolution of police work.

Other highlights include the "Found not guilty" weapon collection of local defense attorney William Foster Hopkins, author of the bestselling *Murder Is My Business.* Among the various hammers, bayonets, bombs, guns and other weapons labeled "Love Car Murder," "The Bedroom Murder," and so forth is a broken lawn mower handle used in the "Ulm Sex Murder." Enough said. An anonymous person donated what's arguably the world's largest collection of restraints, although only a portion of the handcuffs and leg irons are on display. Also on view are the custom-made truncheons of Cincinnati officer Ernie Porter, described as especially resistant to breakage (unless of course you are on the receiving end).

This collection of uniforms gives new meaning to "fashion police."

The Wall of Honor does justice to those brave officers who made the ultimate sacrifice. It's a stretch from the mindset of the inner-city and Vietnam protest riots of the late '60s and early '70s, which are also represented (the author herself had a run-in with Butler County's finest during the April 1970 takeover of the Miami University ROTC building, but that's another book entirely). But when faced with a criminal or other threat, it's best to know and respect which side of the law your bread is buttered on.

★ ★

Springer Sprung
Cincinnati

Would you believe that Jerry Springer was . . . mayor of Cincinnati? Yes, Springer was elected mayor of that bastion of conservatism, known for indicting an arts center and arresting its director for displaying photographs by controversial artist Robert Mapplethorpe, and home of antiporn crusader Charles Keating, he of the savings and loan debacle who cheated thousands of elderly folks out of their life savings. And perhaps even more paradoxically, voters elected Springer after he was busted for paying for the "services" (wink, wink, nod, nod) of a "health club" with a personal check! And he was married at the time. Talk about a place not being able to make up its mind!

But before there was the *Jerry Springer Show* and all the incest, phone sex, and trailer-park high drama that entails, there was Jerry Springer, the human being, whose parents were refugees from Hitler's Germany and who was born in an Underground tube station in London toward the end of World War II. After he and his family emigrated to the United States in 1949, like many people he went to college, graduated, and got a law degree. At one point he even worked for Bobby Kennedy; after Kennedy was assassinated, he joined a Cincinnati law firm.

It was there that Springer's passion for politics really kicked in. After being at the forefront of a successful movement to lower Ohio's voting age, he ran for Congress in 1970 and lost, but a year later snagged a bid for the Cincinnati City Council. In 1974, after being caught with his hand in the cookie jar, so to speak, his public apology was carried live on local TV, even garnering grudging respect from his opponents. Not only did he get his seat back in the next election, but in 1977 was elected mayor.

And it wasn't all that bad. Springer utilized his liberal clout to establish rec centers for disadvantaged youths and health clinics in low-income neighborhoods. He resigned from the office of mayor in the early 1980s to run for governor but came in last in the Democratic primary, so he turned his talents to TV, quickly becoming a popular news anchor and winning top ratings and local Emmys before starting his own *Jerry Springer Show* in 1991.

The show initially was supposed to have a serious, political format, but Springer found that the more outrageous and over the top the guests, the higher the ratings. Although the show has made him wealthy, it has destroyed his credibility as a serious journalist and social commentator. Nevertheless, Jerry Springer remains heavily involved in the Democratic Party, contributing to campaigns and also to charitable causes concerned with birth defects, disabled access, and AIDS, among others (his only daughter, Katie, is partially disabled). And he still talks about running for various offices—and people listen.

Let's face it: Politics and "bread and circuses" are closely related. Just ask the two former wrestlers who were governors of Minnesota and California. So why not the "Ringmaster"?

Welcome to the Jungle
Fairfield

Most of us find a trip to the grocery story pretty routine. Not so at Jungle Jim's International Market (5440 Dixie Hwy. 45014, 513-674-6000, www.junglejims.com), a 310,000-square-foot, four-acre food fun house that features specialty items from seventy-five countries, drawing some fifty thousand shoppers a week from as far away as Indianapolis and Lexington, Kentucky. And we're not talking just gourmands and the culinary elite: Pop Tarts and Oscar Meyer hot dogs share shelf space with smoked pheasant and truffle pâté.

So what's the big deal? Well, for starters, the moment you pull up, it's a jungle out there, with a waterfall and pond surrounded by mountain gorillas, giraffes, elephants, birds, snakes, and appropriate sounds—all fake, of course. Animal antics continue with giant plastic chimps hanging over oversize faux fruit; "Bearvis," an animatronic Elvis bear who sings various hits; and a couple of electronic crows (who's counting?) that periodically burst into "Rockin' Robin."

★ ★

There's a method to this madness: An exhibit with a full-size horse-drawn buggy pulls customers toward the Amish-style meats and groceries section; a 1952 fire truck shrieks the location of the hot sauce; and Robin Hood and his band of merry men point an arrow to the English groceries. You can delve into the Olive Bar, with dozens of selections, or "cut the cheese" in the section that features a six-hundred-plus-pound piece in its own aging box. The boys at Busch Mountains would undoubtedly appreciate studying in the "beer library," and wine lovers have their own "stacks" as well. The latest addition, a five-foot Campbell's soup can suspended above the—you guessed it—soups, is a real swinger, in the sense that it goes back and forth on one, talking and singing as it swings. Hey, it could be worse—it could have been the Pillsbury Doughboy.

All this marketing madness is courtesy of one Jim Bonaminio, a college dropout who built this freak show (in the most positive sense of the term) from a small roadside stand in 1971. A combination of P. T. Barnum and Sam Walton, his corporate philosophy is simple, as stated on the store's website: "The first rule is to treat customers like gold. The second is to have fun doing it."

So if you're looking to be entertained while picking up rattlesnake meat or ostrich, choosing among forty varieties of rice and seventy-eight olive oils, or simply trying to get a buzz from exotic honeys or the walk-in humidor, Kroger's or Wal-Mart simply won't do.

Castle de la Strange

Loveland

Loveland Castle, aka Chateau Laroche (12025 Shore Dr. 45140, 513-683-4686, www.lovelandcastle.com), has never known a woman's touch. And by the time lifelong bachelor Harry Andrews had it mostly completed—a task that took him more than three decades—he had received fifty-plus proposals of marriage from "widows and old maids" (his words) who wanted to move into the medieval-style structure picturesquely situated on one-and-a-half acres. It had many of the amenities of a modern home, in addition to thirty-inch-thick walls, several towers, and a two-story dungeon so secure that it was declared the safest bomb shelter in the state of Ohio.

Its only nod to the fairer sex was a small room in the tallest tower, which, again in Harry's words, "was used to imprison women" back in the good old days of the sixteenth century. Looks like the casserole brigade should have stormed another male bastion.

An architect by training, Harry designed and built the castle himself, using bricks made from concrete, formed by quart-size paper milk cartons. He was nothing if not anal, keeping impeccable records of exactly how much stuff it took: 2,600 sacks of cement for the bricks, some of which contain lightbulbs or tin cans to provide cheap insulation, and fifty-six thousand pails of stones hauled from the nearby river in five-gallon buckets of sixty-five pounds each. It took Harry twenty-three thousand hours of hard labor, which included building a road to the castle and flattening all the land around it for a garden, orchard, drainage system, and moat. It only cost him $12,000, a deal since he lived there from 1955 to 1981. Pictures of Harry show a fit, slim guy. No wonder.

Harry's other thing was that he really enjoyed the company of young men, and taught Sunday school and worked with Boy Scouts during much of his adult life. In the late 1920s he bought some land for his teenage friends, so they could swim, camp, fish, and "have little parties" (Harry's words again). As if this wasn't Michael Jackson-esque enough, he dubbed the group the Knights of the Golden Trail and vowed to build them a castle there.

"Nothing that God ever made on the earth is more awe-inspiring and heart warming than the sight of a noble youth just budding into manhood," Harry wrote in his self-published booklet, *Chateau La Roche*. "Any man of high ideals who wishes to help save civilization is invited to become a member of the Knights of the Golden Trail." Nevertheless, most of the Knights did not deign to help Harry realize his dream, as by his own account, he did 99 percent of the work, and he died basically alone in his nineties from complications of burns when he accidentally set his pants on fire.

Harry willed the castle to the Knights, however, and today it is open to the public for tours and overnight visits. You can even see the

Even Weirder . . .

The one-fifth-scale replica of the real Château de La Roche in France—where Harry Andrews had been stationed during World War I and which served as the inspiration for Loveland Castle—was the end result of an even more bizarre occurrence in a life studded with strange events. During the War to End All Wars, young Harry "was one of the 7,000 soldiers at Camp Dix, New Jersey, who were cut down by an outbreak of deadly cerebrospinal meningitis," according to an account by Lori Jareo that can be found at www. worldwar1.com/sfroche.htm. "Andrews' motionless body was moved to a morgue, and his records were marked 'deceased' and sent to Washington.

"Harry Andrews was on the slab for some time," continues the article. "The body was then taken back to the hospital for dissection. Doctors opened the mouth, cutting away tissue from the upper palate for bacterial cultures. One of the doctors said, 'Let's see if we can start his heart with this new stuff.' The 'new stuff' was adrenaline. A

secret room built by Harry: "It was only discovered after it collapsed from years of neglect . . . even the Knights didn't know it was there!" exclaims the castle's website. Or maybe they did, and don't want to talk about it.

needle pierced his heart and the doctors punched his chest. Then his heart began to beat again." Shades of Dr. Frankenstein!

"Andrews was blind and paralyzed, and no one expected him to live. After a few weeks, he could sit up and eat. He weighed eighty-nine pounds and was fed six times daily, sometimes gaining two or three pounds a day. Andrews' sight came back, but he had to wear glasses. Later, doctors removed his blood to obtain meningococcus antibodies, and he became a blood bank to save others from the disease. Only one other Camp Dix soldier survived the initial outbreak." And a reverse vampire, too!

While in France, Andrews was stationed in an army hospital and worked as a medic. When he returned to the States, he brought back souvenirs: his nurse's cap, his mess kit, and some postcards, which are on display at the castle. When he "applied for his Army pension, he had to convince the Pentagon that he wasn't dead," no mean feat when you're talking about the government. But he received his pension for twenty-three years, and it ran out shortly before he died, this time for real.

★ ★

Gangsta's Paradise

Newport, Kentucky

Sometimes you have to travel just a bit further afield for some excitement. And that would be across the bridge linking Ohio to Kentucky for the Newport Gangster tour (www.newportgangsters.com). The seasonal tour starts and ends, fittingly, at the Gangsters Dueling Piano Bar (56 East 5th St. 41071, 859-951-8560), a few blocks away from the hopping but apparently legal bars and restaurants at Newport on the Levy.

Proceedings start with a briefing from "West Side Joey," "The Hit Man," or one of the other black-clad, muscular guides. But there's safety in numbers here, as long as you don't ask too many questions. Seriously, though, Newport was akin to Vegas in the 1920s, when that place was a dusty twinkle in vice's eye and Prohibition (and moonshine) were at its height. And with gambling, girls, and booze galore, Newport's Beverly Hills Country Club served as a prototype for many a casino, as well as attracting top tier entertainers.

Initially run by local gangsters, the town also got the attention of national crime syndicates. By the late 1950s, "Newport Vice" was so obvious that magazines such as *Time,* the *Saturday Evening Post,* and *Esquire* published stories that shocked the nation. Yet its dangerous, glittering patina drew visitors by the thousands looking to brush shoulders with celebrities as well as notorious mobsters.

During the eight-block walking tour you'll be treated to a cornucopia of syndicate lore about buildings that that once housed casinos, strip clubs, speakeasies, and brothels. Some are still standing, although the gangsters who ran them are mostly lost to legend, despite the fact that the guide repeatedly states, "I swear it's true." Stories abound about "Mr. Las Vegas," "Sparkle Plenty," "The Kit Kat Club," and Dixie Chili that had its origins in Newport but is still wildly popular in Vegas. They are also peppered with familiar names: Frank Sinatra, Dean Martin, Jerry Lee Lewis, and even Bobby Kennedy, who visited to allegedly wipe out crime (but wasn't big brother JFK friends with members of the above-mentioned "Rat Pack"?).

**Faded but not forgotten—one of the few
remaining signs from the gangster era**

Not unlike their predecessors, tour organizers have their fingers in
several other enterprises—haunted tours in both Cincinnati and Newport, a Queen City Underground Tour (not the subway, but its illegal
activities) and Civil War Tour. But if you want to get your Mafia on,
Newport is da bomb.

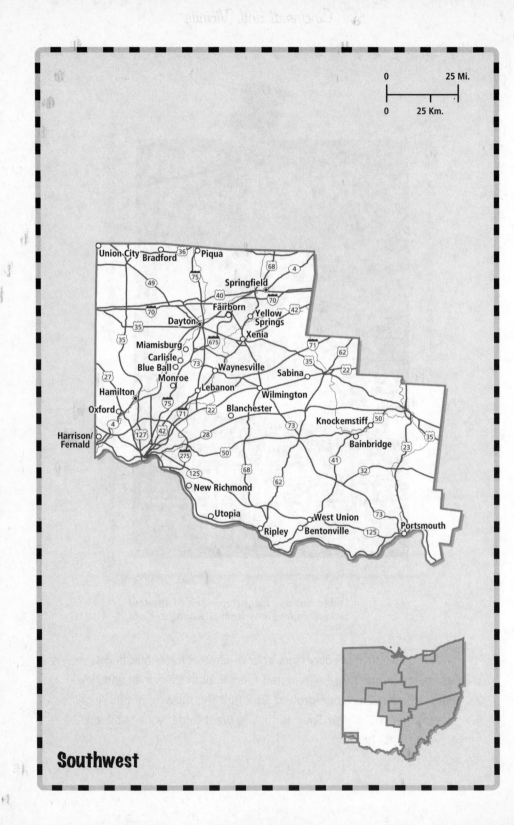

0 25 Mi.

0 25 Km.

Union City Bradford 36 Piqua
68 4
49 75
Springfield
40 70 42
Fairborn
70 Yellow
Dayton Springs
35 Xenia
35 71
Miamisburg 675 62
Carlisle 73
Blue Ball Waynesville Sabina 22
Monroe 35
Lebanon Wilmington
Hamilton 75
Oxford Blanchester 73 Knockemstiff 50
4 71 22
Harrison/ 127 42 28 Bainbridge 23 35
Fernald 275 50 41 32
125
68 62
New Richmond
Utopia West Union 73
Ripley Bentonville 125 Portsmouth

Southwest

8

Southwest

People in this portion of the state certainly enjoy unusual living. Although it looks like a giant UFO—or a dining room chandelier owned by this author in the early 1990s—the "Martian House" in Carlisle is actually two prefabricated homes connected by a silver pipe breezeway. Apparently the occupants came in peace, because it's a private residence.

Back to earth—sort of—is Pyramid Park in Hamilton. The owner, a former lawyer, cleared the initial forty acres of land and coordinated the design and construction of the seven-thousand-square-foot underground house topped by a glassed-in pyramid. Then he decided to add another 220 acres, and turn it into an art park, opening it to the public, even though he still lives there.

The region also has a predilection for bizarre names. In the 1850s when Blue Ball was established, many people couldn't read, so it was designated by a blue metal sphere where the coach stop stood. Today it is a favorite of adolescent minds everywhere. There are several versions of how Knockemstiff got its moniker, and the basically deserted area is a "ghost" town in more ways than one, as it's reputed to be haunted.

You'll also find little pockets of political incorrectness. Although smoking is banned in public places in Ohio, the Ohio Tobacco Festival in Ripley keeps on puffin', with a tobacco spitting contest and (cough, cough) beauty pageant. Back in 1929 when an unidentified black man was found dead in Sabina, they named him Eugene, embalmed him, and put him on display for thirty years. A sort-of precursor to Weekend at Bernie's, he was once "kidnapped" by a fraternity at Ohio State. Party on!

★ ★

Bite on This
Bainbridge

Some memories are painful to the touch, and for most of us, a visit to the dentist can be one of them. But if you want to "open up" to two hundred years of dental history, there's the John Harris Dental Museum (208 West Main St. 45612, 740-634-2246 or 634-2228).

The small town of Bainbridge calls itself the "Cradle of Dental Education," a dubious honor at best. Nevertheless, John Harris, a medical doctor from Cincinnati who settled in the area in the 1820s, began teaching classes in his home "preparatory to . . . entering a medical college," according to the museum website, with an emphasis on dentistry, a specialty in his practice. At the time, most medical schools failed to cover dentistry—for an aching tooth, a string and a slammed door mostly did the trick—and thus Bainbridge became the home of the first dental school in the country. At least an informal one, anyway.

Harris was viewed as the father of dental education in the United States, and many of his students went on to establish "official" dental schools, including John's brother Chapin, who pioneered the world's first, the Baltimore College of Dental Surgery in 1840, and John Allen, who founded the Ohio College of Dental Surgery in Cincinnati five years later.

Harris also helped put the squeeze on modern toothpaste, adding chalk as an abrasive to help clean teeth. You can experience all this history and more via the thorough library with its yellowed, musty dental books and manuscripts—no artificial whitening here—as well as period equipment used to extract, repair, and drill teeth. Highlights include a display of ancient Japanese dental tools and a pair of forceps used on Abraham Lincoln's choppers. There's also a wall o' false teeth, adding to the sense that you've stumbled onto a medieval yet strangely benign torture chamber. It's enough to make you numb, or at least brush and floss twice a day.

Taking a Horse Bite Out of Crime

Bentonville

In this age of hybrids and Harley-Davidsons, why would anyone want to belong to the Bentonville Anti-Horse Thief Society? Well, for one thing, a lifetime membership only costs a dollar, and they have a banquet in the cafeteria at the Burning Heart Campground the last Saturday in April (www.adamscountytravel.org/allevents.php), where you don't have to dress up. Even better, you don't even need to own a horse!

This isn't a joke: In 1880 the State of Ohio granted the society, which formed in 1853, a charter. Back then, few things were lower than a horse thief; since people used them for transportation, and not everyone had one, it was equivalent to stealing a car today. Only you didn't need a key, and if you got caught, you were hanged.

Since there was little in the way of law enforcement in the sparsely populated Bentonville area, a group of property owners decided to band together and rein in matters themselves. Whenever someone's equine was ripped off, the trustees chose a captain and several riders to rope in the thief and return the steed to its rightful owner. Each member of the search party received ten dollars from the treasury if they were successful in their quest, and were fined five if they declined the mission.

By the early 1900s horse thievery was no longer a social problem, but instead of disbanding, the former vigilantes took a kinder, gentler tack and became a social club, raising funds for local organizations. In 1961 the hamlet of Bentonville honored the group with a monument on Route 41, and an Ohio historical marker denoting its longevity and history was erected in the town in 2003.

You should join! Thousands of people all over the country have, with their very own lifetime membership card. Send your dollar to the Anti-Horse Thief Society c/o Mrs. Verna Naylor, Bentonville, OH 45105. She's the town postmaster and the post office is in her home, so she'll get it for sure. And not to worry: They don't hang horse thieves anymore. But if you've ever stolen a horse, or considered doing so, an auto club might be a safer bet.

Bite Me

Blanchester

Feeling crabby? A visit to the World's Largest Horseshoe Crab (664 W. Main St. 45107, 513-256-5437) might lift your spirits. Not only because it's one of the top five roadside attraction sites according to CNN and RoadsideAmerica.com but because it's located at the Freedom Worship Baptist Church. So you can get a little religion, too, if you're so inclined.

In fact it was Pastor Jim Rankin who welcomed the bright orange sixty-eight-footer with open arms into the flock, to mix a metaphor or two. Originally constructed by Academy Award–winning designers Faren & Associates for the Baltimore Maritime Museum in Maryland, Crabby, as he is affectionately called, was then purchased by the Creation Museum in Hebron, Kentucky, for a display on evolution. However, the latter soon realized they had bitten off more than they could chew, size-wise, and since Rankin just happened to be giving a talk there, well, the rest is divine intervention. "Five semis drove up and dropped it," off in the church parking lot, Rankin told RoadsideAmerica.com. "It was nine huge pieces. We had no drawing, no nothing." Undaunted, the intrepid man of God brought horseshoe crab shells from home and used them as a blueprint. The end result was also twenty-eight feet wide with a maximum capacity of sixty-five people.

Since then, Crabby's attracted thousands of visitors from the United States and abroad, including bus tours and, according to Rankin, folks from Germany who made the pilgrimage to see the giant crustacean their first priority (Okaay . . .). In 2008, the church hosted its first annual CrabFest; born-again stunt driver Gene Sullivan jumped over Crabby on a motorcycle, smashed through the burning "Gates of Hell," coming to a safe halt on the other side, praise Jesus! The feat has been part of the CrabFest ever since. In 2010, an image of Crabby was also featured in *Eclipse,* the third film in the "Twilight" series. Naturally the church held a reception to celebrate it (the film's) release in June, with a special marker erected for occasion.

**Crabby . . . making friends and influencing all
who cross his path**

If the church is open, visitors can also check out its Freedom Biblical Museum with Roman dice, Greek coins, and other eclectic artifacts, including a seemingly paradoxical scourging whip and Crown of Thorns. And miniature plush versions of Crabby are available for purchase as well. Outside, you can wander 24/7 around the sculpture garden while your clothes dry at the Scrubbing Bubbles laundromat next door (it's a car wash too!).

Crabby's always available for photos and his insulation and fiberglass design make him perfect for year-round functions such as meetings, movies, and weddings, although bar or bat mitzvahs may be out. He's a shellfish at a church, for God's sake!

★ ★

By Any Other Name . . .

Blue Ball

When this author was in college, one of her closest friends always made a point of trying to find Blue Ball (45005) on the way back to Miami University in Oxford. He wasn't always able to do so, but when he did, he erupted into hysterical laughter and off-color speculation as to how the place got its name.

In this case, the truth is a lot less entertaining. Established in 1820 at the intersection of Dixie Highway (later US 25) and what eventually became Route 122, it originally bore the name Guilford, after a prominent local politician, and was a stop along the stagecoach route between Cincinnati and Dayton. In those days most drivers were illiterate and thus could not read place names. So the citizens—unaware of what they would bring to generations of teenage males later—hung a large blue metal ball at the town's main intersection, and drivers were instructed to stop at the "blue ball." How easy was that?

Time passed, and people stopped calling Guilford "Guilford." In 1862 the name was officially changed to Blue Ball. It was annexed to Middletown in 1993, undoubtedly generating yet another raft of jokes. It didn't help that one of the nearby tributaries was once called Naked Creek.

You can find Blue Ball on Route 122, between Interstate 75 and Route 4. Most visitors are on their way to someplace else, but you can stop and have your picture taken underneath the most recent incarnation of the large blue ball that remains prominently displayed in town (the previous one was damaged when workers were installing a new traffic signal). Up until the 1980s it was mostly a collection of older wooden houses, a gas station, some churches and bars, and at one point, a post office, but that has long since closed. Since then, however, Blue Ball's location between Butler and Warren Counties has made it a desirable piece of real estate, close enough to the cities of Cincinnati and Dayton but far enough away to provide a rural flavor.

The original "blue balls" are gone, but the town's
name still retains its mystique.

There's even been a book published about the town, The Epoch of
Blue Ball, Ohio, written by the Blue Ball Historical Society.

So it looks like Blue Ball is here to stay . . . in all senses of the word.

★ ★

Fountain of Mayberry
Bradford

"It's not a whim anymore if you put on clean underwear."
—Barney Fife

Yes, that Barney Fife, deputy sheriff of the clean-livin', God-lovin', life-in-the-slow-lane small town of Mayberry. Even though the show ended its run several decades ago, it lives on in perpetuity in the hearts and minds of thousands of active members of *The Andy Griffith Show* Rerun Watchers Club (TAGSRWC; www.mayberry.com) and through several related websites devoted to followers of all things Andy. These people are serious, with newsletters, annual gatherings, and even episode analyses they refer to as "Bible Studies." As Gomer would say, gollee!

A TAGSRWC shrine extraordinaire can be found at Bob Scheib's home, aka Wally's Filling Station (10870 Sugar Grove–Circle Hill Rd. 45308, 937-473-5606). Bob is a regular guy, with a wife, kids, and a steady job, the sort you'd expect to meet if the show was an actual place instead of a state of mind. But like many TAGSRWC members, he's got this thing for Mayberry, only his obsession centered on re-creating Wally's Filling Station, which was "owned" by Goober and Gomer. So instead of refurbishing a '65 Ford that he'd happened across and giving it to his wife, he thought, "Why not make it into a squad car?" to complement his rapidly growing accumulation of vintage gas pumps; soda, cigarette, and candy machines; signs; and other memorabilia.

His wife gently suggested that he move the collection, which was taking over the family home, into a nearby shed. Thus Wally's Filling Station was reborn, with gen-u-ine Acme gas pumps, a fishing pole, a wicker basket (presumably stocked with Aunt Bee's picnic lunch), and, of course, the black-and-white, topped with a cherry siren light, as well as three other classic police vehicles. The exterior is a faithful re-creation as well, with a rocking chair, Coke cooler, and other accoutrements.

★ ★

There's even a black-and-white TV inside to catch reruns (a sort of "show within a show" Andy Griffith existentialism). You can go to Floyd's Barber Shop in the barn next door and sit in the antique chair, or get "locked up" in one of the jail cells with their comfortable-looking cots and mirrors. Hey, it's Mayberry, not San Quentin.

It's no surprise that Scheib's efforts spawned an annual Squad Car Rendezvous that drew thousands of the faithful, along with actors and others involved with the show. Unfortunately, it was discontinued several years ago, but Scheib is willing to entertain visitors if they want to come and set a spell. Just make sure to call first.

Flying Saucer Hookup
Carlisle

Carlisle and Blue Ball are so close as to share the same ZIP code (45005). Coincidence? Perhaps not, because on Central Avenue and Chamberlain Road, near the intersection of Routes 73 and 123, you'll find not one but two flying saucers. And it looks like . . . they're mating!!

Fans of UFOs may be disappointed to learn that, rather than being an extraterrestrial love dance—or scientific exhibition of same—it's actually two prefabricated homes connected by a silver pipe breezeway. Perhaps even more strange, the rocket, er, residence is privately owned by a family—presumably *Homo sapiens*—who actually live there, and it has the human conveniences of a kitchen and central air and heating.

And they are not alone . . . There's a whole X-file full of these aptly named Futuro homes, many of which are documented on the website www.futuro-house.net. Most—about a dozen—are located in New Zealand, though there are a few around the United States, including one in Pensacola, Florida, that survived Hurricane Ivan, supposedly because of its aerodynamics.

Designed in the 1960s by Finnish architect Matti Suuronen, the eleven-by-twenty-six-foot structures were made out of reinforced plastic and were initially intended to be used as ski cabins or getaway homes, with the space-age concept that you could take it with you wherever you decided to vacation. At between $12,000 and $14,000, the things were cheap, even for back then, and came in sixteen pieces that could easily be assembled.

OK, so you needed a helicopter or other heavy-duty method of transport, but, hey, anything was possible in the era of the Jetsons. Although the compact interior—which supposedly could accommodate eight, but only had six plastic bed-chair combinations, along with a central fireplace, tiny kitchenette, and single bathroom—would have definitely cramped dad George's style, not to mention teenage daughter Judy's.

All the space-age dreamin' came to an end during the oil crisis of the 1970s, which sent plastic prices into the stratosphere, resulting in the crashing and burning of plans for mass production. But those who own Futuros continue to pay homage to their idealistic history, often by decorating them with such kitschy touches as lava lamps, plastic chairs, and 1970s television sets shaped like space suit helmets, which are probably as difficult to locate as the homes themselves.

Next to the Carlisle Futuro is a big satellite dish. Is it there to pick up transmissions from the mother ship, or is it yet another takeover by DirectTV in the ongoing war to replace cable? Either way, as they say in the movies, resistance is futile.

Is There a Doctor in the House?
Dayton

If you were a member of the David Bernie family in the 1970s, the answer would be "yes" ten times over. And that doesn't even include David's in-laws and assorted cousins and other relatives. In fact, there were so many Bernie MDs that they were listed in the 1976 *Guinness Book of World Records* as having the most physicians in a single family. Except for Sanford Wolfe, husband of daughter Karen, who was a DO (Doctor of Osteopathy). But we're splitting hairs with a scalpel here.

So what inspired all this medical mania? It probably began when Helen Kuhr met David Bernie, back in the 1930s when nobody had much money. Helen's brother, Abe, was a family doctor who made house calls, delivered babies, and was on call around the clock. Abe himself was married to a doctor, Hortense Schmitz, who specialized in pulmonary medicine. Then Dave, who at the time was a general practitioner, wed Helen and they had eight children, which in conservative Dayton was pretty amazing in itself. And they weren't even Catholic— they were Jewish!

After the kids were born, Dave decided he wanted to spend more time with his family, so he went back to school to get a degree in ophthalmology, a specialty that didn't require long hours and weekends. This necessitated going to Case Western Reserve in Cleveland to get additional training. So rather than leave Helen at home with the entire brood, he took the three oldest children with him. Thus they experienced medical training firsthand and caught the "bug," so to speak. In fact, Dave's passion and enthusiasm for the healing arts infected all of his offspring.

Helen and Dave had three daughters: Marianne, Vicki, and Karen. Marianne married a rheumatologist; Vicki, who herself became a radiologist, wed an orthopedic surgeon; and the youngest, Karen, married another rheumatologist, the aforementioned DO. The Bernie "boys"— William, Steven, Jan, Bruce, and Howard—work in specialties ranging from gastroenterology to urology. In fact, you would be hard-pressed to find a body part that the Bernie family (or relative) does not cover.

In a perfect world, all of David's fifteen grandchildren would be doctors. But only about five or so are either physicians or in training, including an orthodontist. And—gasp!—some are even lawyers.

★ ★

Hell's Bells
Dayton

Hell's bells indeed . . . well, maybe if you live on top of Carillon Histori-cal Park (1000 Carillon Blvd. 45409, 937-293-2841, www.dayton history.org) and have to hear them every time they ring, supposedly every quarter hour or so, if they're working properly that day. Still, it could be worse; it could be noise from a construction site or an out-door venue that specializes in heavy metal bands.

And in its own way, the Art Moderne tower—at 151 feet tall and with fifty-seven bells, the largest carillon in Ohio—is a real chimer. Built in 1942 by Colonel Edward and Edith Deeds, it stands at the entrance to the sixty-five-acre park, which opened to the public in 1950. When the tower was built, each bell was inscribed with the name of a fam-ily member, with the "silent" bells bearing the names of deceased ones and the ringing bells cast with the monikers of the then-living. In 1988, in a nod to reverse technology, it was retrofitted from an elec-tronic carillon to a traditional, mechanical one. So every Sunday during the summer months, live concerts are performed by a carillonneur; that is, someone who plays a carillon.

For decades the park was just that—a big bell tower and a bunch of old buildings, trees, and pathways near the Miami River and a fun place to go on a picnic. But then someone got the bright idea of mak-ing it into a historical exhibit, and before you knew it, it became an "infotainment" center with twenty-five structures bursting with arti-facts and displays like an 1835 B&O Grasshopper steam locomotive, the first automobile self-starter, and an array that always signals the sound of money: National Cash Registers, which were manufactured in Dayton and sold around the world. Also on the grounds is Newcom Tavern, Dayton's oldest standing building, which was also used as a courtroom and has many of the original items; a restored canal lock and covered bridge; and a replica of the Wright brothers' bicycle shop.

But the real ringer is the 1905 Wright Flyer III, the first plane the famous brothers built that was actually capable of sustained, maneuverable flight. Weighing 855 pounds, it stayed aloft for thirty-nine minutes and was described by Orville Wright as the plane he and Wilbur learned to fly in; Orville even supervised the initial restoration. Don't you dare drop your peanut butter sandwich on that.

Religion for Art's Sake
Dayton

Although Dayton is considered small by some, it does have a mighty impressive Art Institute (456 Belmonte Park North 45405, 937-223-5277, www.daytonartinstitute.org). We're talking major exhibits here,

Art for everyone's sake
DAYTON ART INSTITUTE

★ ★

everything from the treasures of ancient Egypt—the largest selection of antiquities ever loaned by that country—to the photographs of Ansel Adams to a coup that drew Anglophiles from several states: the final U.S. engagement of the Princess Di show, a display of nearly 150 of her heirlooms, personal mementos, paintings, and childhood home movies and photos. Not to mention almost thirty designer dresses, including the 1981 Royal Wedding gown.

Founded in 1919 as the Dayton Museum of Fine Arts by such major players as Orville Wright and the Patterson brothers, founders of National Cash Register, it was originally located in a large mansion downtown. But it quickly outgrew its home, and a $2 million donation by Julie Shaw Carnell resulted in the decision to pattern the new structure, built in 1930, after two sixteenth-century Italian Renaissance villas. Part of the interior mimics a Gothic church, though services were never held there. So is it art for religion's sake or vice versa?

Nevertheless, the displays worship at the altar of diversity, ranging from Oceanic to Asian to American fine and decorative collections to Native American art. Baroque paintings share exhibit space with primitive works, and communities from the underserved to the elite are entertained by special programs and tony fund-raising balls, respectively. The institute also offers art classes to the public; Experience-center, an interactive showcase, is geared toward the entire family. So everyone can reap the fruits of artistic endeavors, even if they can't draw a straight line.

Iconic Brain Trust
Dayton

It could have been a Hallmark Hall of Fame movie, and probably should be. Despite differences in socioeconomic class and race, and the fact that it was the late 1800s, African-American poet Paul Laurence Dunbar and white flight co-inventor Orville Wright became lifelong friends.

They met as children, probably because Paul's mother occasionally cleaned house for Orville's family. They were also in the same high

★ ★

school class. Although the only African American, Dunbar became the head of the literary society and was so well liked that he was elected senior class president, along with becoming editor of the newspaper.

Orville was more of a jock; he dropped out of high school to pursue the latest fad, bicycling, and became a champion cyclist. He also opened a print shop with his brother Wilbur, the ultimate silent partner, at least historically (see sidebar). So it was natural that wordsmith Paul would drop by the print shop to have his short-lived newspaper, the *Dayton Tattler,* published.

The rest is history, of course, and the two men went on to their respective destinies. Being a black poet in a white world was a tough road for Dunbar, who at one time worked as an elevator operator to support his writing habit. But he prevailed and won national publication and acclaim, becoming an "overnight" success that took several years. He married Alice Ruth Moore, another black poet, and took a job as an assistant librarian with the Library of Congress in Washington, D.C.

Then Dunbar contracted tuberculosis, but instead of bed rest, he spent his time working and reciting his poetry. One of his last stops was Dayton, where his old buddy Orville and Orville's sister Katherine had intended to hear him speak. But by then Dunbar was so ill he had to cancel the appearance and spent the last several months of his life in Dayton with his mother, Matilda, who took care of him. He struggled with alcoholism, and his marriage deteriorated. Paul died in his mother's arms on February 9, 1906, at the age of thirty-three. In his short life he produced twelve books of poetry, four books of short stories, a play, and five novels, more than many writers during careers twice as long.

You can see the house where this transpired, even the bed where Paul passed and the dresser where his last poem was written, lost forever because his mother left it out for visitors to see, causing the ink to fade. Established in 1938 and the first ever to honor an African American, the Dunbar House State Memorial (219 North Paul Laurence

★ ★

Dunbar St. 45402, 937-224-7061, www.ohiohistory.org/places/dunbar) boasts a bicycle given to him by the Wrights in addition to many other of his personal and family possessions.

And in a sense, even death—always the great leveler—failed to sever their closeness. Dunbar and Wright are buried not far from each other in Woodland Cemetery (118 Woodland Ave. 45409, 937-228-3221, www.woodlandcemetery.org).

Theater with Nine Lives
Dayton

That would be the Victoria Theatre (138 North Main St. 45402, 937-228-7591, www.victoriatheatre.com), which has survived fires, floods, and near misses with the wrecking ball. And it allegedly has three—count 'em, three—ghosts! Plus it's really cool inside, with lavish period touches like green marble accents and gold gilt trim, not to mention an impressive stage with excellent acoustics.

But if these walls could talk . . . Opened in 1866 as the Turner Opera House (well before Ted's time), it was an instant success, until a blaze consumed the hall. It took two years to rebuild. Then the Great Flood of 1913 did a number on both the theater and the city, but (obviously) both survived and were restored. In 1918 there was yet another conflagration, and it reopened a few months later as the Victory Theatre, a name it kept in honor of World War I until the "Hell no, we won't go!" late 1960s, when it was marked for demolition. Even Houdini made a "great escape" here in 1925, by using the theater's vents (and we thought that device was invented by the writers of the *Voyage to the Bottom of the Sea* TV series).

By the 1930s or so it became progressively seedier, starting out by showing first-run movies and some live shows and deteriorating to shall we say, less family-friendly fare which may have resulted in performances kept under a raincoat. By the 1970s, city parents were talking parking lot but some civic-minded folks formed the Victory Theatre Association, raising millions of dollars to refurbish and restore the lady

★ ★

instead, reopening in 1989 as the Victoria. Today the theater is home to the Dayton opera, ballet, contemporary dance company, and others; as well as Broadway Series and Humana plays and other nationally known entertainers.

Now about those ghosts. . . . The first, Vickie (get it?) is, according to legend, a young actress, wearing a 1900s black taffeta dress, who likes to show up behind the glass and bronze entryway and also has a thing for mirrors. In the middle of the production, Vickie supposedly forgot a fan she needed in the next scene and never returned. Could she have possibly meant a different kind of fan, as in a stage door Johnny? You can ask her if you hear the sound of footsteps, the ruffle of taffeta, or the scent of rose perfume (and these things always seem to wear rose perfume).

The other ghosts include Lucille, who according to www.forgotten oh.com, "was assaulted in the privacy box . . . and lived to be an old woman, but it's said that [you can] feel the anguish Lucille felt during her attack." The box, which faces the stage, supposedly turns chilly if you enter in a bad mood or are angry, so make sure you're thinking happy thoughts if you sit there. The face of the third ghost could be seen on the backstage curtains "before they were replaced with doors. He is supposed to be that of a suicide who impaled himself on a knife fastened to the back of a seat." Nice. Not many places where you can catch a performance, both live and dead.

"Scareborn"
Fairborn

Since 1929, when it opened a couple of weeks before the stock market crashed, Foy's Variety Store (18 E. Main St. 45324, 937-878-0671) has been supplying local citizens with, in addition to all manner of housewares and dry goods, barrels of fun in the form of Boston Baked Beans, wax lips, marbles, and giant gumballs, to mention a very few.

But penny candy and nostalgia can only take you so far—especially in the era of Meijer, Big Lots, and Family Dollar—so the Foy family, now in its third generation of ownership, decided to capitalize on sales of seasonal items: in particular, Halloween (see: www.foyshalloween store.com). So from mid-September to the first of November, the old-school five and dime becomes The Thing That Ate Fairborn, taking two city blocks—a good chunk of downtown—with six Halloween-themed Foy's stores, plus a restaurant and a residential "haunted mansion."

First stop: the Main Store with wooden floors and stuff crammed in every nook and cranny, even a pet section that sells fish. For the duration, however, it's home to thousands of different Halloween masks, along with seasonal and party items. Each year, Mike Foy, the present owner, aka "Mr. Halloween," picks up a little something to freak out the customers, such as an animatronic Headless Horseman. There's even a free haunted house in the rear.

Next stop: the Haunted House Store, which peddles everything from life-sized monsters to spare body parts, must-haves for every serious spook-out (or weirdo, depending upon your point of view). We're talking major cash here: according to an article in the *Springfield News-Sun,* it's not uncommon for folks to drop a cool $2 to 3 grand on a yard display. Bonus: A couple of working electric chairs that go off every hour, on the hour, a real buzz-kill if you can't get close enough to see them because of the weekend crowds.

But as they say in the TV ad: Wait, there's more! This would be the adult costume store with its sexy to scary outfits staffed by a manager named (really!) Vicki Fox. The adjacent kids' store has "Hero" getups for superbabies up to complete pirate gear for twelve-year-olds. Foy's Haunted Museum and Glow Store, the only building that charges admission, features glow-in-the-dark and black-light items. Your three bucks will get you a visit with scary monsters, both fake and breathing (as in teenaged actors), a torture chamber and "The Black Hole," a spinning tunnel. Such a deal! A couple of blocks away on 208 West Main St. is a Halloween Store West that houses overflow props,

★ ★

ranging from strobe lights to caskets, which are cheaper to rent by the day ($50) than purchase for $899. Why rush things, anyway?

These folks just love Halloween. Foy's draws customers from as far away as Florida, New York, and Wisconsin, accounting for about 35 percent of their annual business. And once you get like-minded visitors to a small burg like Fairborn, selling them stuff is like shooting fish in a barrel. And Foy's has plenty of both.

Every day is Halloween.

Where's Wilbur?

It seems that in just about every reference to Dayton, other than the actual invention of the airplane, you hear "Orville" this and "Orville" that. That is only partially due to the fact that Wilbur (April 16, 1867–May 30, 1912) died several decades before his younger brother Orville (August 19, 1871–January 30, 1948) of typhoid fever.

Even Wilbur's dad, Bishop Milton Wright, wrote of his son, "In memory and intellect, there was none like him. He systemized every thing. His wit was quick and keen. He could say or write anything he wanted to. He was not very talkative. His temper could hardly be stirred. He wrote much."

Wilbur's reticence may be partially attributable to a mishap during his teenage years. Accidentally struck in the face by a hockey stick while ice-skating with friends, he had been vigorous and athletic until then, and initially appeared to be fine. But eventually he became withdrawn and did not attend Yale as planned, spending the next few years housebound, caring for his terminally ill mother, Susan, who had contracted tuberculosis. Nevertheless, Wilbur was an avid reader and (obviously) a mechanical genius.

And he wasn't that much of a wimp. In 1908 when the brothers were out promoting their "flying machine," Wilbur went to Europe (on a ship) to do a demonstration at a horse-racing track near the town of Le Mans, France, a sort of a turn-of-the-twentieth-century *Planes, Trains and Automobiles.* He impressed onlookers, including wannabe French aviators, by doing figure eights and other technically challenging moves while airborne. He also flew the first female passenger, Edith Berg, the wife of the brothers' European business agent, an act of courage back then, considering that it was socially accepted and even expected for women to freak out at the littlest things (think "vapors" and fainting chairs).

Who knows what Wilbur might have accomplished had he lived? After the brothers became famous, Orville got the longest and most visible ride by default.

★ ★

If They Told You, They'd Have to Send You into Outer Space
Fairborn

Just the facts, ma'am, about mysterious Hangar 18 and UFO investigations at Wright-Patterson Air Force Base (WPAFB) according to the book *Above Top Secret,* by Timothy Good and other sources:

- While head of the U.S. Air Force's Air Technical Intelligence Center (ATIC) "Project Blue Book," Captain Edward Ruppelt was stationed at WPAFB. From 1947 to 1969, the Air Force investigated UFOs under this project. Of the 12,618 sightings reported, 701 remained "unidentified."

- Some believe Wright-Patterson to be a 24/7 Top Secret UFO monitoring and research station.

- After the July 2, 1947 crash of a UFO at Roswell, New Mexico, the wreckage of the craft was loaded onto a B-29 and shipped directly to WPAFB.

- Wright Field (as it was formerly known) was the headquarters for the Air Materiel Command (AMC). General Nathan Twining was the Commanding General of the AMC back in 1947. He is also implicated as being a member of the original "MJ-12" secret committee, allegedly part of the "conspiracy theory" of an ongoing government cover-up of UFO information.

- In 1948, a one-hundred-foot saucer with sixteen dead aliens aboard allegedly crashed near Aztec, New Mexico. The remains were sent to Wright-Pat.

- Tommy Blann, a researcher, interviewed a Colonel "X" who said, "In the earlier years they had taken some bodies to this base, but later it depended on where they were found. They had a hell of a time setting up procedures for this operation, as well as getting craft out of the area without it being observed. Usually this was done at nighttime." Colonel "X" also told Blann that he believed the bodies were flown outside the United States to a secret naval installation on an island in the Pacific. That could explain the strange-looking beings on the *Survivor* TV series . . .

★ ★

OK, so maybe it's more speculation than hard data. And if you actually tried to infiltrate Hangar 18 or any other top-secret area at WPAFB, they might kill you, or at the very least drag you off to Guantanamo Bay for some Homeland Security–type interrogation. So you might be better off visiting the National Museum of the U.S. Air Force (1100 Spaatz St., Wright-Patterson AFB, 937-522-3252, www.national museum.af.mil) instead. It's free and you won't "alien"-ate anyone.

No More Warheads!
Fernald/Harrison

The unintentionally hilarious sign reads future site of a former uranium production plant, a classic example of governmental doublespeak. But that's only the tip of the warhead. Since the early 1950s, the Fernald Feed Materials Plant had been making the world unsafe for anything by creating uranium metals for reactors at Hanford, Washington, and other Department of Energy (DOE) weapons facilities, resulting in the proliferation of nuclear waste and poisonous radon gas. In calling itself a "feed materials production center" and painting its water tower with a red-and-white-checkerboard Purina-esque pattern, it lulled the neighbors into thinking it was manufacturing cat chow instead of contaminating the air, ground, and water. Bad government; bad, bad government!

As they say, you can fool some of the people . . . but by the 1980s a group calling itself FRESH (Fernald Residents for Environmental Safety and Health) had reached critical mass and demanded that the plant clean up its act—after the DOE accidentally released nearly three hundred pounds of enriched uranium oxide into the environment, in addition to contaminating three off-site wells.

FRESH sued, and Uncle Sam ponied up $73 million for "emotional distress, medical monitoring, residential real property diminution and legal and administrative costs," plus an additional $5 million for "commercial and industrial real property diminution claims . . . within a five-mile radius of the Fernald site," according to the plant website.

★ ★

Your tax dollars at work

But even more fallout was to come. By 1989, and neatly coinciding with the near-end of the cold war, the plant closed and was slated for a massive environmental cleanup, with the task being assigned to Fluor, an independent contractor. "A 1992 government report fore-casted completion in 2019 at a cost of $12.2 billion. Today's [October 30, 2006] achievement carves twelve years off that schedule with

★ ★

a final cleanup cost of $4.4 billion," crowed a Fluor press release announcing the completion of the overhaul. Such a deal! Now we can pour the unused billions into making even more weapons!

And fusion seems to have replaced fission, at least where FRESH is concerned. "I thought this day would never come," Lisa Crawford, longtime president of FRESH and a member of the affiliated Citizens Advisory Board, said in the release. "But we saw that DOE and Fluor were just as committed to fixing what had happened as we were. Over time we came to trust each other." A scary thought, indeed!

Today the re-branded (so to speak) Stoller Fernald Preserve (Visitor Center, 10995 Hamilton Cleves Hwy., Harrison 45030, 513-648-4899) is home to over 170 varieties of birds including waterfowl, shorebirds, and songbirds as well as 1,050 acres of what can pass for native Ohio grasses and trees, prairie, and savannah. The Department of Energy monitors it closely, constantly checking radiation levels. But while you can walk, run, and birdwatch, any activities involving your dog, picnicking, camping and even picking up rocks are prohibited. And if the plants and wildlife look a little off and glow in the dark, at least Uncle Sam is trying.

Deconstructing Harry
Hamilton

Hamilton certainly is a place of extremes. In 2000 then-governor Bob Taft recognized it as "The City of Sculpture," and not because of the dilapidated "Hollow Earth" installation (see sidebar). It was more along the lines of Pyramid Hill (1763 Hamilton-Cleves Rd./Rte. 128, 45013, 513-887-9514, www.pyramidhill.org), which, when it opened in 1996 with its dozens of outdoor sculptures by local and nationally known artists, was touted as the "most beautiful natural setting of any art park in the country" by none other than the *Atlantic Monthly*.

Perhaps even more eclectically, Pyramid Hill also serves as the not-so-humble abode of Harry T. Wilks, a retired lawyer who made millions of dollars by investing in real estate and stocks. Set amid winding hiking trails, numerous gardens, and seven lakes, the 265-acre sculpture park and outdoor museum came about rather circuitously. In 1982, when Wilks bought the initial forty acres to build his home, it was a jungle out there: a dense forest, full of brambles and vines, and virtually impassable. Undaunted, Harry cleared the land and coordinated the design and construction of the seven-thousand-square-foot underground house.

Crowned with a blue glass pyramid that also doubles as an observation tower, it rises some twenty-seven feet above the ground and is furnished with antiquities from Rome, Greece, and Egypt, dating back to 2000 BC. Even though Wilks did most of the planning and decorating himself, it's been recognized by architects and other building professionals as a feat of outstanding engineering and was even featured on HGTV.

Still, Harry wasn't satisfied. "I got worried that if I died, all that I had built would be torn up again," he told the *Cincinnati Enquirer*. Fearing that the land might be used for subdivisions or soccer fields, he decided to create a sculpture park for the public, donating it to a charitable foundation, with the underground house becoming a public museum, upon his passing.

Its mission may be lofty—"eventual establishment of a collection which will demonstrate the complete history of sculpture, making Pyramid Hill the only art park in the world working on the accomplishment," according to the park website—but it's really geared for the "great washed"; that is, the public that enjoys educational programs about art, horticulture, and related subjects; art fairs and holiday light displays; concerts; and other civilized pursuits. Pyramid Hill also challenges artists to express themselves in unique ways, such as painting golf carts in their particular style.

Though visitors can explore a nineteenth-century pioneer house, a tearoom, the amphitheater, and other buildings, the park is designed so you can view all sculptures from a car. But there's something special about walking through the grounds and experiencing avant-garde endeavors au naturel. And you never know: You might run into Harry, who may offer his own interpretations.

★ ★

Made Ya Look!
Knockemstiff

You likely wouldn't be as interested if the town was called Glenn
Shade or Shady Glenn, which was actually the original name. Located
near Bourneville in Huntington Township in Ross County (west of Chillicothe), it's actually no longer a physical entity, given that the only bar
and general store closed a while back.

Hollow Words

Everyone has an opinion. If
you have enough money and
political clout you might actually get Congress to listen to your ideas.

Such was the case of John Cleves Symmes. A veteran of the
War of 1812 and businessman, he signed an affidavit in 1818 stating the Earth was hollow and that the North and South Poles were
entrances, four thousand and six thousand miles wide, respectively,
that led to the interior, sort of like a giant hamster ball with a tunnel
down the middle. He also attached a document attesting to his san-
ity, an act which itself lends to speculation.

It wasn't entirely a crackpot theory, given that in 1692 English
astronomer Edmund Halley—he who pinpointed the return of his
famous namesake comet—proposed that the Earth consisted of several magnetic fields, within which there were increasingly smaller
spheres, a planetary matrioshka nesting doll, if you will. Others,
such as Swiss mathematician Leonhard Euler, saw it as more of an
Atomic Fireball: a single hollow sphere that contained a six-hun-
dred-mile sun for an (obviously very tanned) advanced civilization
that lived there. Later, Scottish mathematician Sir John Leslie elabo-
rated on this, proposing two inside suns. So that's where George
Hamilton came from.

Legends vary as to how Knockemstiff got its moniker. One involves the fighting ability of the young men at the local tavern, while another centers on the advice a preacher gave to a woman who asked how to get her cheating husband to stay home. "Knock 'em stiff," the good pastor allegedly replied, which if you think about it, could be interpreted in more ways than one. The most plausible theory is that it was

Symmes dedicated much of his life to advancing his theory. He began to lecture throughout the Midwest, and by 1822, had garnered enough support to pressure Congress into funding an expedition to the South Pole. It was never approved—at least not then—but he did catch the attention of Jeremiah Reynolds, a newspaper editor, who sold his shares of the publication to help Symmes promote his theory.

The two men continued with their grueling schedule of lectures, packing them in at 50 cents a pop, the cost equivalent of a ticket to a Rolling Stones concert today. Eventually Symmes took ill and went back to his Hamilton farm where he died in 1829.

Reynolds kept on gathering moss, however, and eventually got some wealthy backers. Although his 1829 expedition reached the Antarctic shore, it returned almost immediately due to perilous weather and a mutinous crew so nothing was proved. The Great U.S. Exploring Expedition of 1838–1842 finally punctured Symmes' theory.

Nevertheless his son, Americus Vespucci Symmes, thought enough of his dad to erect a monument in his honor in the 1840s. The "Hollow Earth" replica (Ludlow Park, Sycamore and 3rd Streets) consists of a stone with a hole in it on top of a pedestal. It's worse for the wear, and basically ignored by locals who use the park and, for the most part, have no idea what it is. But it's a testament that any voice can be heard, even if there are huge holes in their logic.

★ ★

slang for the moonshine coming from the area, which supposedly had quite a kick.

Additional local flavor can be found in stories of periodic flashes of light that appear in the sky on certain nights, as well as these ghosts reported by www.forgottenohio.com:

Devil's Leap. "Located behind the old McComis property, these cliffs are haunted by the ghost of a suicide who supposedly leapt from the top when he was haunted by the voice of the devil in his head. You are supposed to be able to hear him scream all the way down," states the site. What fun!

Foggymoore. "One night a lady and her daughter were driving home and happened upon a man lying in the road on his side with one hand propping up his head, smoking a cigarette. Instead of getting up and moving, the guy simply floated away, still in the lying-down position." Or maybe it wasn't just a "cigarette"?

Donald's Pond. "It's not the pond that's haunted so much as the forgotten cemetery behind it, which dates to the 1700s. Locals report all sorts of weird occurrences in the old boneyard." Maybe they lack a sense of humor about the area's name.

Lindy Sue. The ghost of a girl whose body was found strangled after she had been out in a carriage with her boyfriend, supposedly named Clem Slatterson, or according to some accounts, Jason. The horse was found literally scared to death, and Lindy Sue can still be heard crying out in terror. Clem/Jason was never seen or heard from again. Sounds like a bad country-western song or maybe a plot from *Friday the 13th.*

There's not much information as to exactly where these hauntings can be found, but then ghosts generally don't leave forwarding addresses. And besides, the area is more a state of mind anyway, a bunch of houses spread amid rolling hills. Still, if you really want to say you've been to Knockemstiff, set your GPS to ZIP code 45601 (the intersection of Black Run Road/County Rd. 156 and Shady Glen Road) and have at it.

Sleeping with Dead Presidents

Lebanon

And that includes a live one as well—in the sense of being physically alive but not particularly lively, add George W. Bush to the lineup of POTUSes (Presidents of the United States) who might have slobbered on the pillows of the Golden Lamb (27 South Broadway 45036, 513-932-5065, www.goldenlamb.com). The dozing dozen also includes Garfield, McKinley, J. Q. Adams, Harrison, Harding, Taft, Harrison, Grant, Van Buren, Hayes, and Reagan.

Other celebrities, such as Mark Twain and Charles Dickens, visited there as well, though the latter complained bitterly when he found out that the tavern did not serve "spirits." Hey, after the end of a hard day, we can relate. And as empirical proof of the "squeaky wheel" theory, the most expensive room in the inn is named for Dickens; it's a reproduction of the Lincoln bedroom at the White House. Speaking of which, there's even a George W. Bush room that, while tastefully done, has fittingly nondescript furnishings and a view of the gazebo park next door for empty gazing.

Ohio's oldest inn is more versatile than you might expect. Established in 1803 by Jonas Seaman, as a "house of public entertainment" (no, not that kind of house), it started out as a two-story log cabin. Seaman's wife was an excellent cook, and soon herds of folks were coming to the tavern for good eats as well.

In 1926 Robert H. Jones started remodeling, a project that would eventually help turn the Golden Lamb into an internationally acclaimed destination, with four floors, a lobby, several large public and private dining rooms, a gift shop, and forty modern guest rooms. A colonial porch and second- and third-floor balconies serve as a reminder of its early American origins. In 1969 it was purchased by Lee and Michael Comisar of Cincinnati's Maisonette—Mobil Travel Guide's longest-running five-star restaurant in the country—who helped ramp up the menu of the adjacent Black Horse Inn to include flavorful, complex fare.

★ ★

And for "shear" historical value, there's the Shaker Museum located on the fourth floor, with pieces from Union Village, a nearby defunct burg where the former religious community lived until their practice of celibacy guaranteed their extinction. Like the Amish, their furnishings are simple and functional, with rope beds (no need for sturdiness here, for obvious reasons), plain chairs and rockers, and other assorted household goods. There's even a child's bedroom—Sarah Stubb's—furnished as it had been when the young girl lived at the inn more than a hundred years ago.

If you plan to visit, make reservations in advance, as people flock to the place. No amount of "ramming" will help get you in if they're booked.

Take Me to Your Leader
Miamisburg

They say the ancient Adena Indians built the Miamisburg Mound (1 mile south of Route 725 on East Mound Ave. 45342, 937-866-4532, www.ohiohistory.org/places/miamisbg). But who were they, really? It's estimated they roamed the earth from 800 BC to AD 100 and buried their dead by accumulating bodies and then covering them with dirt, resulting in a "mound." Their name resulted from the discovery of the first mound on the property of former governor Thomas Worthington near Chillicothe. Excavation revealed an earthen jar, bracelets and rings of copper, and a clay pipe in the image of a human. Or maybe a not-quite-human . . .

There's even uncertainty as to the mound's exact dimensions: Some sources say it's 68 feet high with a circumference of almost 900 feet, while others claim it to be 65 feet tall and 800 feet around, while still others state it's 70 by 877 feet. To get the answer you'd need a really big tape measure, and even then time continues to erode the proportions—or maybe there's another explanation (cue *Twilight Zone* soundtrack here). Regardless, the mound contains 54,000 cubic yards of earth, the equivalent of 3,400 dump truck loads, and is the largest

★ ★

Climbing the mound—with a little help from modern technology.

conical burial mound in the state of Ohio and possibly the entire east-ern United States. The other is Grave Creek Mound in West Virginia.

Anyway, what they do believe is that it was constructed in several stages, sometime during the nine hundred–year period that the Adena roamed the earth (well, that narrows it down). And that the base has two burial vaults, which served as cemeteries for several generations of Native Americans. At one point the mound may have had a stone face and possibly marked the boundaries of tribal territories. But, who knows, really?

As recently as 2004 crop circles were found near the Miamisburg Mound. One thing's for sure: The pictures of the circles look real. According to an article on the Web by Jeffrey Wilson, director of the Independent Crop Circle Researchers' Association (ICCRA), "The formation is in 7–8 foot corn (maize) and is swirled generally clockwise. The formation is approximately 200 ft in length (exact measurements are in progress). The formation . . . looks to be tangent to the mound on the eastern side. The corn stalks in the formation were found lying flat to the ground but unbroken, without any scuff marks on any stalks discovered (no mechanical damage discovered so far)." It has to be true—it's on the Internet!

Nestled in a thirty-seven-acre park with picnic tables and a playground, the mound is built on a one-hundred-foot-high bluff and has 116 easily countable and literally breathtaking steps from its base to the summit. But the view from the top is worth the huffing and puffing. And you might see something that's not of this Earth: say, another crop circle. Jeff's cell phone number and e-mail address are on the website, or you can contact the ICCRA through www.cropcircle-news.com. Operators are standing by.

Touchdown Jesus No More
Monroe

You're barreling down I-75, thinking about breaking the speed limit, or worse, the Golden Rule. Then suddenly, there he is, the King of Kings—and we're not talking Elvis here—all sixty-two feet of head with flowing hair and shoulders with arms outstretched forty-two feet wide, welcoming you home. The rest of him is submerged, waiting for the Second Coming, to rise up God-zilla–like into a frenzy of smashing passing cars and stomping out sinners at the nearby adult bookstore or hot sheet hotel, or doing heaven-knows-what at the trucker rest area.

The object of speculation and endless practical jokes ("Giant Jesus Erupts From The Earth!" screams a fake headline, accompanied by photos of "passing heathens" giving him the high five), this Super

Savior lords it over the baptismal pool at the Solid Rock Church (904 North Union Rd. 45050, 513-423-7040, www.solidrockchurch.org). Founded by evangelists Darlene and Lawrence Bishop, the three thousand–member nondenominational congregation boasts a huge sanctuary more befitting a football game or rock concert, a digital marquee flashing the next godly event, an outdoor theater, and assorted "missions," including a home for unwed mothers and homeless teens. The multitalented Bishops also sell their own CDs as well as that of the church's Fire Choir, hell-raising music to burn your soul.

The Bishops commissioned Florida artist James Lynch to render the fiberglass-and-Styrofoam-over-metal-frame depiction of Big J. Lynch, who has created worldly mammoths in Las Vegas and Disney World, completed it in 2004. Church leaders believe it to be the World's Largest Messiah, though that hasn't been officially confirmed. But if Christ is even half the man he used to be, they'd get the title for sure.

Some folks claim that it's a godsend, in more ways than one, citing a reduction in accidents along the stretch of highway in front of the church, which previously had been considered quite dangerous, with fourteen people killed in 2000 and 2001. However, the Ohio Department of Transportation installed a cable down the median about the same time the Drowning Jesus emerged, and since the majority of fatalities had been determined to be crossover collisions, the intervention was physical, rather than divine.

Of course, others may disagree. And some might even choose to be baptized in front of the Mega-Messiah. Thumbs up or thumbs down, you can't miss him.

Update: On June 14, 2010, God apparently answered. Lightning struck the statue's right hand, setting it and part of the nearby amphitheater on fire, completely destroying the statue. The story immediately went viral on the media and the Internet and theories abounded from God being angry at the church, Christianity and society—not necessarily in that order—to it being a random occurrence and therefore proof that there was no God at all. But the next day, church

★ ★

Hey, Dad! Can you give me a hand down here?

leaders announced plans to rebuild the statue, perhaps even making it bigger and most definitely fireproof, despite the mysterious failure of lightning resisters and grounding rods that contributed to the destruction of what now might be called Extra Crispy Jesus. As of this writing, no date for resurrection has been set.

Is God trying to tell them something? Perhaps. Or maybe He's just laughing at the entire plan.

★ ★

Flee Market
Monroe

Right next door to the Crispy Touchdown Jesus is another bonus-sized offering—Traders World family-friendly flea market (601 Union Rd. 45050, 513-424-5708, www.tradersworldmarket.com). With over eight hundred booths in a dozen enclosed buildings and almost four hundred outside vendors when weather permits, Traders World is two miles of literal shop 'til you drop. And they sell everything—from antiques to zebras. Well, actually the latter are statues just for decoration, but they have been known to peddle live domestic pets, not to mention offering a huge selection of clothing and supplies for same. From laser graphic engraving to mountings for your favorite dead insects to stretch mark cream from Africa to tarot card readings, they have it all. And no Nordstrom or Saks Fifth Avenue, this—it's cheap.

And therein lies the rub. With so much stuff for sale, how do you sort through it to (a) find what you want and (b) make sure it's of decent quality? While there are no easy answers to the second question, the first is easily resolved by asking the first person who looks like they know what they're doing for a map. They'll either direct you to the "office" that is in the middle of all this brouhaha or take pity on you and give you one from their stash.

Or you can do what this author did, and forget about the shopping and soak in the Noah's Ark-esque ambiance. The place is a zoo—both human and animal, with lots of (fake) giraffes, rhinos, elephants, donkeys, and according to one account, anatomically correct horses at all four entrances, although walking a mile or so in ninety-degree weather to verify this can present a challenge. Colorful murals grace many buildings; a shark juts out from an undersea theme, while a "Mail Pouch" barn and tropical beach provide three-dimensional optical illusions. Who needs those expensive 3-D movies when you can have this for (almost) free (the entrance fee is only two bucks per car)? You can have your picture taken in a "Little House on the Prairie" setting and try to count the number of giraffes atop each building (there

"Big" being the operative word here . . .

are twenty-eight). In fact it's hard not to experience sensory overload even if you're sitting down and enjoying a jumbo Diet Coke.

The brainchild of Jay Frick Sr., this family-run business started in 1984, after Jay retired at age sixty-two. According to daughter Chris, who manages food operations among her many other duties, "Dad was one of the first people to drive down I-75 when it opened in the early 1960s. He saw the land and worked out a deal with the farmer."

Son Jay manages the day-to-day operations, including handling police inquiries about counterfeit handbags and NFL jerseys. But we're talking bargains here, so it's wise not to examine such things too closely.

Staying Afloat
New Richmond

Without cardboard boats, New Richmond might be sunk. As home to one of the first, most famous, and largest cardboard boat regattas in the country, it also has the dubious honor of having the world's only Cardboard Boat Museum (311 Front St. 45157, 513-493-1675). Which kind of makes sense, given the town's location on the Ohio River.

The museum is curated by the odd-sounding but nationally recognized Team Lemon, the most prolific builders of these vessels in the country. But the name should hardly strike fear in the one to six person crew: Built with only cardboard, duct tape and paint, a certain percentage of the things are expected to sink and in fact the regatta has a "Titanic" award reserved for the most dramatic such occasion.

Included in the museum's bizarre and numerous displays are a Delta Queen replica, a ten-foot guitar, a school bus, an Easter basket, a coffee cup, and a John Deere tractor (say what?). The museum also offers classes in building and design, student tours, and rental options for reunions, off-site meetings, and parties. Nominal donations are suggested to keep it afloat.

But to get the full effect of this unusual sport, stop by the New Richmond Riverdays (P.O. Box 265, 513-553-4146, www.nrriverdays .com) in August to watch these puppies churn two hundred yards down the Ohio River. It's not every day that you see a six-passenger locomotive, a fifteen-foot dragster, a five-crew seaplane, a Viking longship, Harley Davidson replica motorcycles, and a stealth airplane—all basically made of paper—compete for a trophy and the bragging rights of being the best in show.

★ ★

Variations on a Scream
Oxford

This author went to Miami University for four years and never heard of the Motorcycle Ghost. But it was the late 1960s/early 1970s, and who remembers much of anything back then, anyway?

Nevertheless, this legend, which began in the 1940s, concerns waiting on a dark, winding road just outside of Oxford (Earhart Road 45056; park facing south before the bend on Oxford-Milford Road). There are three different versions, all ending in an eerie white light, or variation thereof:

Version 1: Girl meets boy, they fall in love, her parents don't approve. The kids arrange a signal for secret meetings. She flashes her porch light when she wants him to come pick her up on his motorcycle. On one occasion the boy has had too much wine and when he sees the flashing porch light, he screeches off on his motorcycle and crashes into a barbed-wire fence and is decapitated. N-i-ice.

Version 2: There is an alleged serial rapist running around campus, and the girl is afraid she will be attacked, so she and the boyfriend rig up the same signal. She will flash her porch light if she feels she's in danger, and he will come rescue her on his motorcycle. She thinks she's about to be attacked, flashes the light, and he comes flying to her rescue, but crashes and dies before he can reach her. Hasn't this already been done?

Version 3: A real tearjerker. The boy has gone off to war, comes back to find his girlfriend with another guy, speeds off on his motorcycle in a rage, and crashes into a little boy on a bicycle, killing them both.

If you want to encounter the ghost, simply park near the girl's house, which is now owned by a Mr. Falk, and flash your headlights three times. According to the first two versions, the boyfriend will appear on his motorcycle thinking it's his girlfriend. You will see one single bright light coming toward you, and when it passes, if you look in your rearview mirror, you may even see the ghostly red taillight riding off into the distance before it fades away entirely. In the third version, when you flash your lights, you will see two different lights. The first will be red, allegedly the reflectors from the boy's bike. It will vanish, replaced by the bright white light of the motorcycle crashing into it, which will disappear as well.

If by chance the cycle lights don't disappear, it means that the headless ghost is waiting around the corner for you. Drive off quickly in the opposite direction before it shows up in your backseat!

Captain Underpants
Piqua

In brief, Piqua and underwear go back a long way. During the turn of the last century, it was home to several different underwear companies, most notably Atlas Underwear, which introduced BVDs and popularized the union suit, one-piece flannel long johns, often bright red, that buttoned up in the front and also had a rear "access hatch" that was the butt of many jokes, so to speak. Often men, particularly farmers, wore the same suit all week or even the entire winter, which brings to mind all sorts of nasty hygiene questions we'd rather not think about. Spring was heralded by removing the red long johns, washing them—hopefully not for the first time that season—and putting them away for the warm months.

Piqua had some pretty big panties to fill during its underwear heyday, between the late 1880s and the mid-1980s. Atlas produced long johns for doughboys in World War I and flame-retardant undergarments for astronauts in the 1960s. Johnny Weissmuller, an Olympic Gold Medalist, modeled Piqua Hosiery swimsuits. He was released from his contract with them so he could star in the first Tarzan movie in 1932.

Women often worked in the factories, which makes sense considering how few men hang out in the lingerie department, much less admit to sewing the stuff (the Victoria's Secret catalogue and fashion show are another story entirely). Anyway, the job not only provided the ladies with much-needed income, but offered a way to socialize, perhaps pitting Atlas panties against Allen size-A cups in the local softball league. Good thing they hadn't invented thongs yet.

Other textiles were also made in Piqua, most notably swimsuits, knit items, and turtlenecks. Only one firm, Medalist Apparel (803 North Downing St. 45356, 937-773-3152), remains today, but they are not open, so to speak, to the public.

In the late 1980s the folks in Piqua decided to honor their town, the Underwear Capital of the World, via a festival. Strip away the size-50 boxer shorts, three-mile clothesline with skivvies and bloomers, and autographed unmentionables of celebrities such as Whoopi Goldberg, Ted Turner, Bette Midler, and George Bush the First (it was an election year), and it turned out to be your basic, tame Ohio fair, with hot dogs, local bands, and half the populace running around in their underwear—outside their clothes, of course. The festival was discontinued in the late 1990s due to lack of attendance. By then the Madonna look was pretty much passé, anyway.

But we still have—ta da!—Captain Underpants! The brainchild of popular children's author Dave Pilkey (www.pilkey.com), the tighty-whitey-clad hero hails from none other than Piqua. So although history has pulled a wedgie on the town's underwear production and festival, its heritage lives on.

Shoelace Valhalla
Portsmouth

Shoelaces are like potato chips. You can't just have one; they always come in pairs, thanks to the marketing savvy of Sole Choice (830 Murray St. 45662, 740-354-2813, www.mitchellace.com), formerly Mitchellace, which has been producing them since 1902. And it makes sense, because if you lose or break a shoelace, you want them both to look alike. We're not talking SUVs or flat-screen TVs here.

But even though a shoelace is a small thing, Sole Choice is the largest manufacturer in the United States, shipping more than four million pairs weekly to shoe factories and retailers around the world. And it adds up to something big for Portsmouth: It occupies 360,000 square feet of manufacturing space on a five-acre site, making the nondescript industrial town the Shoelace Capital of the World. Talk about tying one on . . .

Like the shoelace itself, Sole Choice's beginnings were humble. In the 1890s Charles Mitchell developed a machine to dispense the little suckers. It impressed management at the Selby Shoe Company, which was located in Portsmouth, and Mitchell was invited to move there to manufacture his machine. He also perfected a braiding technology, and soon the family-run enterprise became a veritable font of shoelaces. A group of private investors bought out the company in 2009 and renamed it, but the location and basic products remain the same.

Today they make all kinds of other stuff, too: shoe cleaners and polishes, insoles and footcare accessories, and more in blister packs. Hopefully they don't mean that literally.

Up in Smoke

Ripley

In 2006 Ohio voters passed a law prohibiting smoking in public places and private clubs, the first state in the Midwest to do this and the first tobacco-producing state to enforce such a ban. Yet Ripley, located in Brown County, which harvests the most tobacco in the state, continues to organize the annual Ohio Tobacco Festival (P.O. Box 91, 45167, (937-392-1590), as it has every August since 1982. It's held outside, where people can still puff away.

Smoking is right up there with religion and politics as topics for discussions that can flare up more quickly than a lit match. And in Brown County, "Tobacco paid for a lot of mortgages and put a lot of kids through college," local grower Bill Fauth told the *Cincinnati Enquirer.* "It's been vital to our economy and our history." Yet today's farmers are dealing with government-enforced reductions in tobacco-growing quotas and are being given grants to learn other job and agricultural skills.

★ ★

But the festival is so dang wholesome. You have your carnival rides, frog-jumping contest, cornhole tournament, cheerleading competition, and Sunday prayer breakfast. There's even a tobacco queen, a teenage girl who wears a crown and represents the industry at festivals throughout the state, a hard sell that should build her character, considering the controversy surrounding adolescent smoking. OK, so maybe some of the activities are a little bit marginal , like tobacco cutting and (eeew) spitting contests and (cough, cough) cigar- and pipe-smoking competitions.

If you'd rather breathe fresh air and are still interested in the area's heritage, you can visit the Ohio Tobacco Museum (703 South Second St., 937-392-9410). The 1850s two-story Federal/Georgian–style building was home to the family that owned the Espey Heavy Munitions Works in Cincinnati. (Add moonshine, and you've got the ATF trinity of alcohol, tobacco, and firearms.) Along with early farm and Civil War–era production equipment, you'll find information on the origin of White Burley tobacco and Native American tobacco usage. Or perhaps photographs of Civil War soldiers rolling their own cigarettes will light up your day.

Most of the locals really like the Tobacco Festival, even those who don't smoke. "I'm against smoking, but the farmers here should be proud of their heritage and I hope the festival continues. It's the biggest event of the year around here," lifelong resident Judith Gray told the *Enquirer*. Well, there is quite a market for nicotine gum and smoking cessation patches . . .

The Mummy's Non-Return
Sabina

Remember the 2002 film *Bubba Ho-Tep,* in which John F. Kennedy (patched up and turned into a black man) and Elvis are trapped in a nursing home that's being terrorized by an ancient Egyptian mummy? Perhaps not . . .

Or maybe *Weekend at Bernie's* from 1989, wherein two young executives must create the illusion that their murdered boss, Bernie

Lomax, is alive in order to avoid being questioned and drag him from one hilarious situation to another?

Sabina's most famous resident appears to be a combination of the two. According to www.graveaddiction.com, "on June 6, 1929, the body of a fifty-to-sixty-year-old African-American man was found outside the town. . . . The man had no identification on him, just a piece of paper with an address in Cincinnati" that turned out to be a vacant lot. "No one they talked to recognized the man. They decided to call [him] Eugene, named after the person they questioned who lived closest to the vacant lot."

Since Eugene appeared to have died from natural causes, the Littleton Funeral Home (104 North Jackson St. 45169, 937-584-2431, www.littletonfuneralhome.com) went ahead and embalmed the body. They waited for someone to show up and claim him, but that never happened. Then the local gendarmes got the bright idea of propping him up in an outbuilding near the funeral home for all to see. Perhaps someone who knew him would pass by and identify him. They even bought Eugene a new suit for the occasion.

Over the next thirty-some years, Eugene was visited by an estimated 1.3 million folks and became somewhat of a celebrity, adding credence to the philosophy that no one really appreciates you until after you're gone. He also took some road trips a la Bernie:

"High school and college kids would sometimes take him to other towns and put him on park benches," states the site. "One time a fraternity at The Ohio State University 'kidnapped' him and took him back to Columbus!" Like a parent with a misbehaving teenager, "the funeral home would always get a call from the police to come and pick him up."

Eventually, however, the funeral home accepted that Eugene was going nowhere, fast, and they interred him in a simple plot in the Sabina Cemetery (330 North College St.) in 1963. One final indignity: The tombstone lists the burial year as 1964. Still, it could have been worse; he could have been buried in the section for pets.

★ ★

Stoned!
Springfield

Just because you've been out of a job for a while doesn't mean you
can't keep busy. Consider H. G. "Ben" Hartman, who rather than
getting stoned on grass or alcohol, got really hammered, as in building a massive rock garden (Hartman's Rock Garden, 1905 Russell Ave.
45506, www.hartmanrockgarden.org).

OK, so he may have been suffering from a syndrome called demen-
tia concretia, "an excessive compulsion to build, using whatever materials are readily available, usually concrete, bottles, cans, scrap metal
and other industrial and household junk," according to www.eccentric
california.net. And it was during the Great Depression, before drugs to
control compulsive behavior came into general use. "Today," continues the site, "if one of your relatives started building a concrete and
scrap-iron tower in your backyard, you'd have them on Prozac—and in
a Lazy-Boy—in no time, squelching their propensity to turn your home
into a tourist attraction."

So the initial project, a stone and concrete fish pond, grew into a
35-by-140-foot accumulation of statues, castles, moats, churches, and
more, consisting of approximately 250,000 individual pebbles from
various construction sites interspersed with pieces of mirrors and pottery. A huge fortress with a drawbridge and moat is composed of
approximately fourteen thousand stones, while the Tree of Life has
some twenty thousand. Handwritten signs identify each tableau, and
statuary, flowers, figurines, and Chucky-size gnomes spice it up a bit
(in the PG-rated sense of the word, of course).

It kept Hartman busy for seven years, until 1939, and resulted in
models of the White House, Independence Hall, Custer's Last Stand,
Mount Vernon, Noah's Ark, Lincoln's birthplace, and more. Along with
religious and historical subjects, Hartman also included depictions of
topics of the day, such as scenes with boxer Joe Lewis and the popular
Dionne Quintuplets, at the time the only identical quintuplets to have
survived infancy.

Ben died a few years after completing the project, and for a while the Hartman family maintained the property. But like many people these days, they were caught between a guess-what and a hard place when it came to making ends meet'.

In 2008, the Kohler Foundation turned back on the faucet—of money that is—purchased the property, and began a year-long restoration, reopening it in June 2010. The garden can easily be seen on the corner lot and serves as a concrete testament that you can always find something to do.

Two-Timed
Union City

The entire town of Union City (45390, www.unioncityvillage.com) must deal with residing in two states; specifically, Ohio and Indiana. We're talking separate city halls, school systems, and police and fire stations. And for years Union City was in duel, er, dual time zones because Ohio used daylight savings and Indiana didn't, making things an hour earlier on the Indiana side during the six months of spring, summer, and early fall. So if, say, you were planning to attend your kid's soccer game on the Ohio side of town at 6:00 p.m. and you left your home in Indiana at 5:45 to get there a few minutes early, by the time you'd arrive, it might already be over and you'd be screwed. Of course, on the other hand, if you wanted a little extra drinking or shopping time, it would be convenient to buzz across the state line to get that extra hour.

Nevertheless, both places now follow daylight savings time, so it's no longer an issue. Still, how did Union City get from there to two heres? Especially since the Ohio side was platted a good ten years before the Indiana side.

As usual, the answer has to do with economics. In 1848 five separate railroads announced plans to meet at the Ohio-Indiana state line where Union City—originally called Union—is now located. This greatly enhanced the community's importance as an industrial center, adding

★ ★

jobs and fueling the establishment of businesses and commerce, as well as making Union City a trade center. Of course, there were tricky situations, even then; for instance, when you had to change trains at the state line. And thank goodness Indiana didn't side with the Confederacy during the Civil War!

Today, however, it's a lively and diverse community with art galleries, restaurants, and cultural opportunities on both sides of the fence. And going back and forth is easy—unless you're on parole or worried about being extradited across state lines.

Phalanx Fail
Utopia

If you're going to try to create a Utopia, the least you can do is fail spectacularly to assure a place in history. Which is exactly what followers of French philosopher Charles Fourier aimed to do—make history, not screw up—in 1844, when they carved out a thirty-room communal brick house and several private residences in the middle of the Ohio wilderness. Back then the commune-like arrangement was called a "phalanx," with shared activities like eating, working, and cooking, although participants could own private property. A Jersey Shore version, the North American Phalanx (NAP), had been successfully established in Colts Neck Township by Fourier three years earlier, in 1841.

As any former commune member or reality show contestant knows, what sounds like a great idea in theory does not always work in the real world. Especially if you believe that you're about to enter a thirty-five thousand–year period of peace and that the oceans will turn to lemonade as long as everyone else agrees with your beliefs. But for a fee of $25 a year, which included a small parcel of land, a lot of folks might just have been going with the flow.

But—no surprise—they soon ran out of money and didn't get along anyway, so the phalanx disbanded a couple of years later. Another sect, the Spiritualists led by John O. Wattles, purchased the land.

★ ★

Although it might seem hard to believe (we're talking pioneers here!) they had even less common sense, ignoring the warnings of the locals and moving the communal structure brick by brick to the edge of the river, completing it just in time for one of the biggest floods of the century.

In fact, some 156 Spiritualists were partying at the hall on December 13, 1847 when the icy river surged forth, washing out the building, sweeping them away. Most perished, and the spot where they drowned is rumored to be haunted.

However, by 2003, the state of Ohio thought enough of both groups' efforts to erect a historical marker, designating "Utopia" as being located off US 52 between State Routes 133 and 505, some twenty-five miles east from exit 71 off I-275. Along with a creepy underground church where Wattles and his crew practiced their rituals, you can also see the remains of Wattles's stone house, and when the river water is extremely low, might even glimpse the original foundation of the structure destroyed by the flood.

But Utopia? Not so much. It doesn't even have a Starbucks!

Cabbage Patch
Waynesville

Waynesville is known for its seventy-some antiques stores and has nothing to do with cultivating cabbage or fermenting and processing sauerkraut. Which is probably better for the community's image, since sauerkraut is made by a lengthy procedure involving scraping scum and mold off the top of a liquid-filled crock, adding tons of salt, and in some cases, stomping it with your feet.

The festival started in 1970 when the Waynesville Retail Merchants wanted to hold a sidewalk sale and decided to sponsor a sauerkraut dinner as well. "There really is no reason for us to be holding a sauerkraut festival here," festival chairman Ron Kronenberger told the *Cincinnati Enquirer.* "One of our merchants had it for dinner one night

★ ★

and the next day the merchants were trying to think of ways to raise funds. They decided to have a sauerkraut festival on the same week-end as the firefighters did their fish fry weekend, and the sauerkraut festival was born." Well, that certainly clears things up!

Regardless, the two-day festival (Waynesville Area Chamber of Com-merce, P.O. Box 281, 45068, 513-897-8855, www.sauerkrautfestival. com) has been a success ever since, attracting an estimated three hun-dred thousand visitors who browse among the almost five hundred–plus craft booths and sample the offerings from some fifty different food vendors. Along with something called a German sundae—mashed potatoes topped with sauerkraut, bacon, and cheese—many of the latter peddle such questionable delicacies as sauerkraut pizza, fudge, doughnuts, cookies, and pies; egg rolls and cabbage rolls; Polish cab-bage soup; "and of course several pork and sauerkraut combinations," according to the festival website, which also adds, "Many non-kraut items are also available," ostensibly referring to food items and not peo-ple of Germanic heritage. Recipes can be found in the cookbook *One Nation Under Sauerkraut* by local historian Dennis Dalton, which is also for sale at the festival (a suggested subtitle: *Divisible By Gas*). Addition-ally there are contests and prizes for the largest, greenest, most magnifi-cent, and most pathetic cabbages.

For those who have difficulty digesting the various offerings, there's always the fish fry. And you can take comfort in the fact that every-thing comes from the good old U.S. of A. "You won't see anything made in Taiwan here," Kronenberger boasted to the *Enquirer*. But aren't egg rolls of Chinese origin?

Hearse Looking at You!
West Union

Feeling a little stiff? There's nothing like a visit to the Lafferty Memorial Funeral and Carriage Collection (205 South Cherry St. 45693, 937-544-2121) to perk things right up. Because no matter how old you are or tired you feel, it's usually better than the alternative.

★ ★

Laffertys have served the West Union area in a "funereal" capacity for more than a century and a half, starting with William Voris "W. V." Lafferty (1830–1922), who founded the business in 1848 to meet the demand for caskets, which he, as a furniture and cabinet maker, was often asked to build. What a cheerful thought! Anyway, old W. V. taught himself to embalm during the Civil War period, though his son Theodore (1862–1914) and Theodore's son Latour (1889–1933) went to school to learn the undertaker trade.

Meanwhile, the first three generations of Laffertys had accumulated quite a bit of stuff, including horse-drawn hearses and funeral buggies as well as embalming equipment, the use of which we'd rather not think about. Then along came the fourth generation, James William Lafferty (1912–1987), who attended auctions and snapped up additional horse-drawn hearses and motorized coaches. They were stored in various places, and upon his death his wife, Grace, and son John decided to construct a building for their display, which opened in 1994. It's to die for: a total of nine vehicles and other memorabilia, including funeral home ledgers and written instructions from clients as to the disposal of their remains.

Union County is on its sixth generation of Lafferty funeral directors. So there must be a lot of satisfied customers, both aboveground and below.

Split Decision
Wilmington

What a bunch of jerks . . . soda jerks, that is. There seems to be a real food fight between Ohio and Pennsylvania over who invented the first banana split.

Here's the scoop: In 1904 David Strickler of Tassel Pharmacy in Latrobe, Pennsylvania, whipped up a dessert in hopes of capturing the taste buds of students at nearby St. Vincent College. He decided to go one better on the traditional sundae by adding a banana and is also credited with designing the specially shaped dish to serve the concoction.

★ ★

In the opposite corner is restaurant owner Ernest R. Hazard of Wilmington, Ohio. The year was 1907, and he too was interested in attracting students, in this case, from Wilmington College. Since it was winter and there wasn't much to do, Hazard held a contest to see which employee could come up with a new and tasty recipe. According to the website www.bananasplitfestival.com, Ernest "took a long dessert dish, arranged a peeled banana and three scoops of ice cream in it, and added a shot of chocolate syrup, a little strawberry jam, and a few bits of pineapple. On top of this, he sprinkled some ground nuts, and garnished his invention with a mountain of whipped cream and two red cherries on its peak."

Not only did Ernest win the contest (well, duh!), but he invented the name as well, despite his nay-saying cousin Clifton "who didn't think that anyone would ever walk in and ask for something called a banana split."

In honor of the invention, Wilmington holds a Banana Split Festival (45177, 937-382-1965, www.bananasplitfestival.com) each June. They regard the Latrobe folks as Johnny-come-latelies, despite the sticky situation with the timeline. "It's a claim Wilmington refuses to accept," assert the site.

The spirit of competitiveness continues through the festival itself, as participants try to outdo each other with elaborate and gigantic ice-cream creations. With poodle skirts, classic cars, and 1950s and 1960s music, the festival focuses on the real influence of the banana split: the baby boom generation that romanticized such soda fountain fare before they had to worry about blood sugar and clogged arteries. A highlight—no surprise here—is a "build your own" banana split booth.

No matter who invented the thing, it's not likely to lose its ap-peel. Dairy Queen alone sells twenty-five million a year. And let's face it—it's all good.

★ ★

A Pheasant Experience . . .

Wilmington

Unless of course, you happen to be one and then you're toast or maybe
under glass (either way, it's curtains). But the victims, er pheasants, and
in fact all the other critters at Cherrybend Pheasant Farm (2326 Cherrybend Rd. 45177, 937-584-4269, www.cherrybendhunting.com) are
treated well until they reach, um, their final destination.

But that's beside the point if you're a hunter or other sporting type.
Billed as Ohio's premier pheasant hunting reserve, this family-owned

Giving you the bird at Cherrybend Pheasant Farm

370-acre working farm has it all: birds, dogs, corn, soybean, wheat stubble, and plots of sunflower, millet, and sorghum as well as an airfield that you can fly into if you're so inclined (of course you'll need a plane with either a pilot or a license). They offer courses, seminars on building a better relationship with your hunting dawg, special events and (really!) early bird discounts which provide additional "bird credit" (their words). What more could you possibly ask for?

Well, how about lunch or dinner? The Hunter's Room serves up meals in a rustic lodge atmosphere on weekends during peak season or for special parties. There's also a formal dining room which seats up to twenty-eight and where you can enjoy your catch on fine china. Or you could go for the European/Continental option which also includes bird cleaning and talking about the hunt around the campfire. Yum! Let's eat!

Stormy Weather
Xenia

It's nowhere near the scope of Hurricane Katrina, but on April 3, 1974, Ohio had its very own full-scale disaster when an F5-force tornado struck Xenia (45385), ripping though thirty-two miles of homes, schools, businesses, and farmland, killing thirty-three and injuring another 1,150. It destroyed almost half of the city's buildings and made ten thousand in a town of almost twenty-seven thousand homeless. A train passing through Xenia was struck and blew seven of its forty-seven cars onto Main Street, effectively blocking access.

The Xenia twister was the diva of what became known as the "Super Outbreak," 148 tornados within a twenty-four-hour period, the largest of its kind in recorded history. According to www.xenia tornado.com, during the height of activity, fifteen tornadoes were on the ground simultaneously, with a total of 315 persons killed and another 5,484 injured within thirteen states and Canada. All told, they covered a mind-blowing 2,598 miles.

A tornado can happen to anyone—at least anyone who lives in Ohio, as this author found out a few months ago, when an F3 wreaked destruction about a half-mile from her condo. (Meanwhile said author, who was visiting her son and his wife at the time, was, along with her son, skeptical when her daughter-in-law insisted they retreat to the basement during the warning sirens.) Sometimes having your homeowner's insurance automatically deducted from your checking account can be a good thing.

However, Xenia has had a lion's share of stormy weather. The Shawnee Indians referred to the area as "the place of the devil wind" or "the land of the crazy winds," depending upon the translation. Either way, it might have behooved the Great White Fathers to pay attention to that when they decided to build the town. But nooo, they went ahead anyway, and records of storms, which go back to the early 1800s, show twenty tornadoes in the area since 1884.

After the 1974 twister, convoys of generators, floodlights, bulldozers, and dump trucks arrived overnight from nearby Wright-Patterson Air Force Base to help clear the debris. And its residents worked hard to rebuild the city and surrounding community, only to have it hit again by another, albeit smaller, tornado on September 20, 2000. One person was killed, and a hundred injured.

The second tornado followed a path roughly parallel to the 1974 one. Coincidence or bad luck? No one seems to know, but folks in Xenia might want to make sure their home homeowner's or renter's insurance policies are up to date. More than most, they probably understand what the victims of Katrina and other natural disasters have gone through.

Alternative Universe

Yellow Springs

Yellow Springs (www.yso.com) is far out—in more ways than one. Located a few miles north of Xenia on Route 68, the small community, home to Antioch College (One Morgan Place 45387, 937-767-7331, www.antiochcollege.org), is an alternative oasis, surrounded by traditional farms and verdant countryside as well as strip malls, golf courses, and other pursuits popular with mainstream America.

Yet it's a universe of its own: Just ask the people who live there and the tourists from Dayton, Columbus, Cincinnati, and elsewhere who come to bask in its overall weirdness and pick up a few souvenir bongs and original art, along with pottery, knit goods, and silver made in Third World countries, only to return to their nice, safe suburban homes. Doesn't it just make you feel good all over?

But the place always marched to the beat of a different drum, even when the Shawnees roamed the area. They bathed in the water of the "yellow spring," which was known for its restorative powers. Of course, it didn't take long for paleface to scope it out, and in 1804 Lewis Davis built the first cab in the area and established a boarding house and tavern within a few feet of the spring, resulting in its eventual popularity as a health resort.

Even back then the village attracted divergent forces: fashionable parties who arrived via stagecoach to partake of the spring, and an experimental community known as the Owenites, who were looking to create a utopia. This being 1825, these were followers of Robert Owen, rather than actor Owen Wilson, who was born nearly 150 years later. However, Yellow Springs has had its share of famous residents, such as reclusive comedian Dave Chappelle, who spent part of his childhood there and lives on a farm nearby. But we digress, which happens a lot in this place.

The building of the town itself is attributed to Judge William Mills, son of one of the first settlers, lawyer Elisha Mills. Along with helping to attract Antioch College to the location, he convinced the railroad to swing by, establishing Yellow Springs in the firmament of viable industry. Founded in 1852, Antioch College built its reputation in liberal arts and was ahead of its time in terms of cultural diversity. An early bastion of student activism and freethinkers, it produced such grads as Rod Serling (1950) of *Twilight Zone* fame and Coretta Scott King (1951).

Worlds and mindsets collide and coexist in Yellow Springs.

During the 1960s both town and gown reached their hippie heyday, serving as a flash point for civil rights activists, antiwar protesters, New Leftists, women's libbers, and other controversial folks. In subsequent years, however, they began to fade—not unlike an aging hippie relative who's somewhat of an embarrassment that no one quite knows what to do with. The college hit a low point in 1993 with a sexual offense policy that required that not only students be sober when they have sex, but ask permission to kiss. Now that's taking things a little too far in the other direction. In 2007, Antioch College suspended operations due to dropping enrollment and financial issues.

State Roundup: Homes of Excess

Several of these have been discussed, but below are some where you can actually stay and one that you can only dream about unless you donate to a charitable cause—and even then you may only get as far as the Party Barn. But hey, it's all an adventure, whether you're looking out the bedroom window of your elegant suite onto the manicured grounds or politely being turned away by the security guard at the gate.

Great Stone Castle 429 North Ohio Ave., Sidney 45365, 937-498-4728, www.greatstonecastle.com). About a half-hour drive from Dayton, this immense 1890s limestone mansion features a wraparound porch and overlooks expansive lawns and the quaint town of Sidney. And it's four stories and three turrets of the real McCoy, with hand-carved staircases, wood appointments, tall ceilings, and stained-glass windows as well as genu-u-ine Victorian furnishings. Not only do you get a continental pastry and fruit breakfast in the airy, cheerful conservatory, but you can also partake of various spa services, including seaweed facials, eyebrow tints, and a cinnamon sugar body polish. Yum!

Landoll's Mohican Castle (561 Township Rd. 3352, Loudonville 44842, 800-291-5001, www.landollsmohicancastle.com). Approximately an hour and a half northeast of Columbus, this 1,100-acre estate offers some of the best nature Ohio has to offer, including one hundred thousand–plus daffodils in spring and wildly colorful fall foliage. Hike and explore the seventeen bridges, clear brooks, and wooded valleys, along with some thirty miles of trails. Or do the indoor luxury thing with the enclosed pool with a waterfall and cave; a hot tub surrounded by flora and fauna; and well-appointed, luxe suites for the king and queen in all of us. Or go the full monty and get a secluded cottage, which offers even more privacy and solitude, amid the best accoutrements, of course. Hey, even the Italian-tile floors in the bathroom are heated, something the digs of Marie Antoinette probably lacked.

Ravenwood Castle (65666 Bethel Rd., New Plymouth 45654, 800-477-1541, www.ravenwoodcastle.com). Located about sixty-five miles southeast of Columbus, it could be borderline chintzy, except for its terrific location—Hocking Hills—and its skilled management, veteran bed-and-breakfast hosts Sue and Jim Maxwell. The rooms have themes—the "Sherwood Forest" boasts "trees," a "dungeon," and a chain-link lighting fixture, and there are motif cottages as well, such as "Jolly Old England" or brightly colored Gypsy wagons. Communal dining is available at the Gothic Great Hall, with its heavy carved tables and giant fireplace. But be forewarned: This is an "authentic" experience: no in-room TVs, phones, or microwaves!

Wexner Estate (New Albany 43054, just outside of Columbus, east on SR 161, turn south to Kitzmiller). If you ever happen to spend time at this forty-five-thousand-square-foot, $45 million Georgian estate built by Limited billionaire Les Wexner, and decide to gossip about your experience, they might have to kill you. While the object of speculation and perhaps exaggerated accounts, the Wexner camp keeps a tight lid on exactly what is in the house, which supposedly has a gallery featuring Les's priceless art collection; a formal dining room with a table that elevates so staff can prepare meals on the lower level; and an "orangery," a Renaissance-inspired greenhouse traditionally used by aristocrats to grow citrus. Well, la te da. . . . And to think he was the child of immigrant parents, and had to borrow $5,000 to open his first store in 1963. But if you donate big bucks to one of Les and Abigail Wexner's favorite causes or attend the Annual New Albany Classic equestrian event to raise funds for the Columbus Coalition Against Family Violence held on the grounds near the Wexner Party Barn, you might catch a glimpse. Hooray for capitalism!

Since then, alumni and other donated several million dollars with the hopes of re-opening the College in fall of 2011. We're waiting. . . .

But although Yellow Springs and the college were down, they certainly were not out, obtaining funds for renovation of both and reinventing the area as a trendy, arty destination. So if you visit, keep an open mind. Homeless people and radicals rub shoulders with famous authors and the wealthy. You might pick up some silver earrings for a few bucks or spend thousands on home furnishings and stained glass. And good luck trying to figure out who the Antioch students are— with Antioch College being temporarily closed and Antioch University being a separate entity, with campuses in five cities, including Yellow Springs—sometimes they're not even sure themselves.

A Moo-ving Experience
Yellow Springs

Looking for an "udderly" delicious milk shake? Arguably the best in the state can be found at Young's Dairy Farm (6880 Springfield-Xenia Rd. 45387, 937-325-0629, www.youngsdairy.com). Since 1958 they've been selling fresh products from their Jersey cows, milking them for all they're worth. We're talking dozens of flavors of homemade ice cream, a month of sundaes, and even gelato! That's in addition to having several full-service restaurants, a petting zoo, miniature golf, batting cages, and a "cow-lander" of seasonal events, including a tractor show, pumpkin festival, hay wagon rides, fall corn maze, and cut-your-own Christmas trees. Young's also caters to your very own herd, be it a family or class reunion, company or small group picnic, wedding, or bar mitzvah.

Actually, Young's is pretty old, beginning in 1869 when relatives of founder Hap Young built the landmark red barn, which is still in use today. After World War II ended, Hap purchased the property, and along with sons Carl, Bob, and Bill, "farmed the 60 acres, plus up to 500 additional rented acres . . . grew grain, raised hogs, and milked cows," according to their website. Today it's run by "Chief Ice Cream Dipper and CEO" Dan Young with the help of his wife, Cathy. Several other members of the Young family are employed there as well.

They started small—in a ten-by-ten-foot sales room—but soon were selling milk by the gallon, expanding to cheese and ice cream. They kept adding stuff—a bakery here, a restaurant there, a parking lot everywhere—and before you knew it, were attracting something like 1.4 million visitors a year.

Many of these are local folks, though others come from the "big cities" of Columbus and Cincinnati for the whole farm experience. That is, everything but cow tipping, although the servers, many of whom are in high school or college, would sure appreciate the extra money.

index

index

★ ★

index

index

index

★ ★

Sandra Gurvis (www.sgurvis.com) is the author of fifteen books and hundreds of magazine articles. Her titles include *Day Trips from Columbus* (Globe Pequot Press); *Careers for Nonconformists* (Marlowe), which was a selection of the Quality Paperback Book Club; *America's Strangest Museums* (Carol/Citadel); and more. Her books have been featured on *Good Morning America*, CBS *Up to the Minute*, ABC *World News Tonight*, in *USA Today*, excerpted in various magazines, and featured in other newspapers and on television and radio stations across the country. Her newest titles are *Paris Hilton: A Biography* (Greenwood), and *Managing the Telecommuting Employee* with Michael Amigoni (Adams, 2009). Her novel, *Country Club Wives*, a satire about women, money, and homeless animals, is also now available on Kindle.

A major aspect of her work has been on the Vietnam protests and their aftereffects and particularly relevant to today's political situation is her recent nonfiction title, *Where Have All the Flower Children Gone?* (University Press of Mississippi). The book, which took five years to write, covers all facets of the Vietnam era, from tracking the student protests and conservative movements to comparing the controversy surrounding Vietnam to the Middle East. Her novel, *The Pipe Dreamers* (Olmstead) is a fictional exploration of the late '60s/early '70s, mostly set in the small college town of Hampton, Ohio. She has also written on this topic for the *VVA Veteran*, *Ohio State Alumni Magazine*, *People*, and many other publications. More information can be found at www.booksaboutthe 60s.com.

Other bylines and credits include *People, YM, Entertainment Weekly, Fiction Writer, Woman's World, Parenting, The World and I, Coast to Coast, USA Weekend, Chicago Tribune*, and numerous trade and corporate publications. She has had short stories and essays published in *Country Living, Columbus Monthly, Mature American, Guide to Literary Agents, Times Outlook, I Love Cats, Ohio Jewish Chronicle*, and *Cat's Meow* (anthology) and has created travel promotional materials and

PHOTO COURTESY OF CAROL WELSHEIMER

advertorials as well as articles on various destinations. A former teacher of adult nonfiction at Long Ridge Writers' Group/Institute for Children's Literature, she lectures frequently on writing, the '60s, and her books.

Along with being selected for residencies and fellowships at the Mary Anderson Center in Mt. St. Francis, Indiana; the Vermont Writers Studio in Johnston; and receiving a grant from the LBJ Library in Austin, Texas, she is a member of the American Society of Journalists and Authors (ASJA) and the American Medical Writers Association (AMWA), having received certification from the latter in 2004. She lives in Columbus, Ohio.